Millionaire Traders

HOW EVERYDAY PEOPLE ARE BEATING WALL STREET AT ITS OWN GAME

KATHY LIEN
BORIS SCHLOSSBERG

John Wiley & Sons, Inc.

Copyright © 2007 by Kathy Lien and Boris Schlossberg. All rights reserved

Published by John Wiley & Sons, Inc., Hoboken, New Jersey.
Published simultaneously in Canada.

Wiley Bicentennial Logo: Richard J. Pacifico

No part of this publication may be reproduced, stored in a retrieval system, or transmitted in any form or by any means, electronic, mechanical, photocopying, recording, scanning, or otherwise, except as permitted under Section 107 or 108 of the 1976 United States Copyright Act, without either the prior written permission of the Publisher, or authorization through payment of the appropriate per-copy fee to the Copyright Clearance Center, Inc., 222 Rosewood Drive, Danvers, MA 01923, (978) 750-8400, fax (978) 646-8600, or on the Web at www.copyright.com. Requests to the Publisher for permission should be addressed to the Permissions Department, John Wiley & Sons, Inc., 111 River Street, Hoboken, NJ 07030, (201) 748-6011, fax (201) 748-6008, or online at http://www.wiley.com/go/permissions.

Limit of Liability/Disclaimer of Warranty: While the publisher and author have used their best efforts in preparing this book, they make no representations or warranties with respect to the accuracy or completeness of the contents of this book and specifically disclaim any implied warranties of merchantability or fitness for a particular purpose. No warranty may be created or extended by sales representatives or written sales materials. The advice and strategies contained herein may not be suitable for your situation. You should consult with a professional where appropriate. Neither the publisher nor author shall be liable for any loss of profit or any other commercial damages, including but not limited to special, incidental, consequential, or other damages.

For general information on our other products and services or for technical support, please contact our Customer Care Department within the United States at (800) 762-2974, outside the United States at (317) 572-3993 or fax (317) 572-4002.

Wiley also publishes its books in a variety of electronic formats. Some content that appears in print may not be available in electronic formats. For more information about Wiley products, visit our Web site at www.wiley.com.

Library of Congress Cataloging-in-Publication Data:

Lien, Kathy, 1980–
    Millionaire traders : how everyday people are beating Wall Street at its own
game / Kathy Lien, Boris Schlossberg.
        p.   cm.
    Includes index.
    ISBN 978-0-470-04947-1 (cloth)
    1. Investment analysis.   2. Portfolio management.   3. Electronic trading of
securities.   4. Speculation.   I. Schlossberg, Boris.   II. Title.
    HG4529.L546 2007
    332.64–dc22   2007008852

Printed in the United States of America

10 9 8 7 6 5 4 3 2 1

CONTENTS

CONTENTS

PREFACE

How many times have you heard the often-quoted statistic that 90 percent of all traders fail? Yet everyday, millions of ordinary people around the world wake up, turn on their computer, and try to make a living by trading the financial markets electronically. As in every profession, there are successes and failures. The same statistic of failure exists in the restaurant business, especially in our hometown, New York City. New restaurants spring up on a near daily basis, some are successful, most fail, but the possibility of hitting it big never deters people from trying.

We have found 12 people who have hit it big trading for themselves. These are not hedge fund managers or employees of big money center banks, but regular people who started with as little as $1,000 and turned their small initial stakes into a six- to seven-figure fortunes. These people come from all walks of life, live all over the world and trade a variety of electronic markets. Some of the traders focus on equities, others on futures or foreign exchange. Each has a very different style of trading, some that are even in direct conflict with each other, highlighting the fact that there are many paths to success in the financial markets. However,

PREFACE

all of these traders practice discipline, stick with their strategy, and always cut their losses. None of our interviewees were successful from the start. Several have blown up at least one trading account. But instead of walking away from the markets, they learned from their early failures and used that experience to improve and ultimately succeed. We convinced them to share their stories and tell us how they got started, their best and worst trades, their number one rule of trading, and the many lessons that they have learned through their experience. We hope these stories inspire you to believe that success is possible and that everyday people can beat Wall Street at its own game.

Kathy and Boris
New York
September 2007

ACKNOWLEDGMENTS

We want to thank everyone who has participated in our book as well as the following people who have helped with the transcription and translations:

Sally Ann Barnes
David Rodriguez
Benjamin Chun Lap Chang

CHAPTER 1

THE ART OF TRADING

It ain't about how hard you hit, it's about how hard you can get hit and keep moving forward. That's how winning is done!

—Rocky Balboa

Trading is a battle between you and the market. The traders we interviewed for this book have offered a wealth of insight into the art of trading. We have distilled their most important ideas into this short summary highlighting one unique idea from each trader that can help you succeed in your battle with the markets.

1. IF THE NEWS IS GOOD BUT THE STOCK PLUMMETS, BUY THE CRASH

Buying crashes is not for the faint of heart. For many traders, the experience is akin to jumping out of a plane without a parachute. Yet Dana Allen has made his living doing just that. How does he profit from other trader's losses? By looking for tell-tale signs of divergence. Technical divergence setups where price makes a new high but momentum indicators do not is one of the bread-and-butter routines of many successful traders. However, Dana Allen takes the idea one step further by trading fundamental divergence. He likes to buy stocks that sell off on good news speculating that the initial reaction is often simply due to short-term profit taking. Once the sellers are done, Dana likes to scoop in and buy value at a cheap price and then quickly resell it higher once demand reappears. By making sure that he only buys quality companies with good news, Dana has the fundamental support for his trades and more often than not is able to bank gains in the process.

2. KNOW YOURSELF, KNOW YOUR TRADE

In trading, knowing yourself is more important than any particular trading strategy that you may choose. Your personality needs to be in sync with your methodology, otherwise you will not be able to follow the rules of the setup. Knowing your strengths as well as your limitations is rule one of becoming a successful trader. As Rob Booker points out in his interview:

> I am a 50- to 100-pip-a-week trader. Meaning I have pretty much decided that that's about the limits of my human capacity and over 50 to 100, I start getting a little bit crazy. I become a little bit less disciplined and a little bit more euphoric to put it mildly. So, I have not generally done a lot to increase that pip target over time, even though systems that I build might produce bigger gains.

If you have a short attention span and seek instant gratification, long-term swing trading strategies will not work well for you, no matter how robust they may be because you will not have the patience to successfully see them through. Conversely, forcing oneself to become a scalper is sheer suicide for a trader who may be much more analytically, rather than instinctually, inclined. Therefore, it is imperative that you know what type of trader you are and trade within your comfort zone. There are many ways to succeed in trading but they must be aligned with your personality.

3. REVENGE IS NEVER SWEET

The most dangerous time for any trader occurs right after a major loss. The instinct for *revenge trading* (the desire to get it all back at once) can be far more damaging than the initial loss, leading many traders to make impulsive, irrational decisions that often lead to complete destruction of the account. Therefore, traders would do well to heed Chuck Hays' advice, which could save them from needless ruin:

> Revenge trades are the most costly trades. If you have a bad trade and you try to make it all back at one time, you're going to lose more money. I think I learned from experience that the best thing to do is to try and get back and get even a little bit at a time. It's a whole lot easier to make a half point on a 100 contracts than it is to make 10 points on 10 contracts. I just try to focus on making good trades, do the same thing over and over again . . . and string together some singles.

By chipping away at his losses, Chuck focuses on reestablishing control over his trading by assuming less and less risk until he has slowly recovered his losses. This strategy stands in sharp contrast to what many novice traders do, which is to create even more risk by trying to hit homeruns after a large loss, and shows why Chuck is one of the premier traders in the game.

4. TRIPLE YOUR DEMO TWICE BEFORE TRADING FOR REAL

This insight from Hoosain Harneker is perhaps the most practical piece of advice from any of our super star traders. Nobody can master a professional skill right away. Doctors practice on cadavers, lawyers spend countless hours in moot court, and mechanics toil for months in classroom garages. Practice does not guarantee success but lack of practice almost always ensures failure. In foreign exchange, which is Hoosain's market of choice, every dealer offers a practice platform allowing traders to experiment with virtual money rather than real capital. In other financial markets plenty of software tools exist to allow the trader to "paper" trade in realistic market environments. For example, our other interviewee, Paul

Willette, who was already a successful equity trader, spent three months paper trading his account when he decided to make a switch to electronic stock index futures.

What makes Hoosain's advice even more valuable—albeit much harder to follow—is that one has to achieve substantial success on the demo before moving to a live account. By mandating that you triple the demo, Hoosain requires that your trading methodology has a discernable edge that should serve you well in the real market. While his rules of trade are difficult, they are well worth following because they instill the discipline necessary to succeed in the real market.

5. DON'T LOSE YOUR COOL—ALWAYS USE A STOP

Although this rule is practiced by every professional trader to control risk, Franki Law, the Forex (FX) trader from Hong Kong, offers additional insight into why it is so valuable. In his interview, he states:

> There are many people who will go long a currency pair and keep injecting money into their accounts if they get margin calls to buy at even lower prices in hopes that a rally will help them to recover their entire account. For example, if you are long 10 lots, and the price falls, you add 20, if it falls again, you add 30 etc. Although the ability to recover quickly may seem extremely attractive, it is very dangerous and it is something I will rarely use. The reason is because I feel that if I keep on posting money into my account to meet a margin call and adding into a losing position, I am essentially at the whim of the market. I can only hope that the trade moves in my desired direction, but I am essentially stripped of my decision making power. Perhaps the price movement would have called for a short, but since I am buried so deep in the long position, I can only let the market take me where it wants to. So what would I do if I got a margin call? I would close my position and wait for the next clear opportunity or setup to get into the market because it avoids letting the market dictate my profits and losses and allows me to be the decision maker once again—I get to choose when to get into the market, what product, and what size and this control is very important to me.

If you do not use a stop, you are at the mercy of the market and lose all control over your trade. Since trading at its core is ultimately an exercise in control over the chaotic and often unpredictable markets, a stop is a must for any long-term trading success

6. PROTECT YOUR CAPITAL—PROTECT YOURSELF

This is perhaps the most basic but often the most overlooked aspect of trading. According to Indi Jones:

> Clint Eastwood would be a great commodity trader because he told the Million Dollar Baby that rule number one in boxing is to protect yourself. And I think the same is true in trading. If you want to trade, your capital is everything. So, if you want to be a great trader, you have got to protect that capital. No capital, no trading, no life and its the same whether you want to be a Million Dollar Baby in boxing or a Million Dollar Baby in commodity trading, I think it's the same thing—protect your capital.

The market will forgive many things including bad, even stupid trades, but it will not forgive the loss of capital. Once all of your capital is gone there is no opportunity to recover. That's why capital preservation is always the foremost concern of every trader we interview.

7. AVERAGING DOWN IS FOR LOSERS, BUT AVERAGING IN CAN BE THE DIFFERENCE BETWEEN SUCCESS AND FAILURE

Most traders will tell you that averaging down into a trade is a mug's game. However averaging in is a strategy employed by a number of our interview subjects to a great success. What's the difference? Intent. Traders who average into the positions expect to be initially wrong on price and size their trades accordingly. Roland Campbell is one such trader:

> That to me is absolutely the key to my success. I average in on every trade I make and I average out whenever I exit. I have a tendency where, as soon as I buy a currency, it will dip 10 pips.

Before I would get upset, but now I love it because I feel like I can get in at a better price, so I hope it dips another 10 pips. I know the price I want, so I will average into that price.

Roland allows himself about four average ins before he calls it quits. "If it goes much further than four average downs, I have to start considering whether this is the right trade to be in," he notes, "but nine times out of ten that strategy works for me." Roland always knows his "uncle point" and unlike novice traders who are never willing to pull the plug on a bad idea, Roland will always stop himself out when a trade goes bad. However, in the majority of the cases, he will succeed in turning a profit on most of his scale in strategies, showing once again that all rules of trading can be broken as long as they are done so for a good reason.

8. TOPS OR BOTTOMS ARE ONLY EVIDENT IN HINDSIGHT

There is an old trading adage that goes like this, "They don't ring a bell at the top." While tops and bottoms may seem obvious in retrospect, in the heat of the battle they are rarely clear. That is why Tyrone Ball's point is so valuable. He said, "I came to understand that you can't pick the top and the bottoms of your trades, you just got to be willing to take money while it's still in your favor and cut your losers small. I mean it sounds too simple, but most can't do that." Market profits can be very elusive. Like ice cubes in your hand. Therefore, banking at least some profits when you get them is a cornerstone to most of our traders' success.

9. TURN HAPPENS ONLY ONCE BUT TREND IS CONTINUOUS

For anyone who is a fade trader trying constantly to pick tops or bottoms, Ashkan Balour's deceptively simple observation should provide a moment of pause. He states, "Basically I am continuation trader. When the trend is going in that direction, I don't see any point in trying to find the turn. It will tell you when it's reversed. If you look at any chart pattern where the market's reversed, you'll see a daily reversal. Reversal only happens once, but the continuations happen all the time until the moment the reversal is hit." In a sense, Ashkan argues rather persuasively that the higher probability trades occur with the trend since, like in physics, price will stay in motion until it is counteracted by a stronger opposing force. Until such time comes, Ashkan believes, it is much more productive to trade in the direction of the major trend.

10. THE LAST 25 PERCENT OF THE POSITION CAN MAKE A DISPROPORTIONATE CONTRIBUTION TO YOUR OVERALL PROFIT

Everyone wants to be able to let their profits run, but in real life financial instruments rarely follow a smooth straight path to riches. Instead prices often retrace the majority and sometimes all of their gains leaving many inexperienced traders empty handed. Paul Willette, however, has come up with a method to harvest some profits right away while ensuring that he can still benefit from an occasional extension run in his favor. What's noteworthy about his insight is that even leaving a small proportion of his original position on could contribute significant profits to his overall account.

How does this work? Let's assume that we trade like Paul does with a position of 20 contracts. The stop on the position is 1.00 ER (a mini-Russell 2000 stock index future) point. At +1.00 points in his favor, Paul would sell five contracts and move the stop to breakeven. At +2.00 points he would sell another five contracts. At +3.00 points he may sell an additional 5 contracts. At +5.00 he may sell two more contracts and at +7.00 he may finally sell the last three remaining contracts. In total the trade would have netted +61 points, but note that fully 31 of those points—or more than 50 percent—came from the last five contracts or just 25 percent of the original amount of the trade.

Paul teaches us that we do not need to make money on more than a small portion of our position in order for the whole trade to be substantially profitable.

7

11. MAKE YOUR MONEY WORK FOR YOU

In a rush for capital appreciation, many traders often overlook the immense power of compound interest. Marcelino Livian is not such a man. Instead, much like the largest money center banks and the savviest hedge funds in the world, Marcelino always looks to get paid while holding a position. This is the reason he trades FX exclusively on the side of the carry, letting the positive interest rate differential between the currencies work to improve his average entry price while he waits for his trades to become profitable. While his method may be far less glamorous than the swashbuckling style of the scalpers it is no less profitable and should be taken just as seriously.

12. BEAT COMPUTERS AT THEIR OWN GAME BY USING PROBATIVE ORDERS

Almost 70 percent of trading on Nasdaq is now done through automated order-entry programs. Many traders have bemoaned the onset of computerized trading robots as the end of face-to-face markets, but Steve Ickow has not only adjusted but prospered under the new regime by probing out the logic behind the software algorithms. Steve says, "A high percentage of Nasdaq volume is now composed of black box trading. So a lot of times I will test price just to see where the market is. Let's say I am long and I start bidding up and bids come with me then I know I am good. Let's say I offer and now no one joins me, no one is an aggressive seller. That's how I get information on the stock by constantly bidding and offering." Whether you are a machine or a human being, when it comes to financial markets ultimately you are either a buyer or a seller. By constantly probing the logic of the machines, Steve Ickow is able to figure out their true intentions and turn that information into profitable trades.

CHAPTER 2

THE MAN WHO BUYS CRASHES

DANA "DAN" ALLEN

Ever since he was a little boy Dana "Dan" Allen was fascinated with trading. He started reading the *Wall Street Journal* at 9 and opened his own commodity trading account by the time he was 21. Dana's trading career has been characterized by one overarching theme—the uncanny ability to buy a dollar's worth of value for a nickel. Be it commodities, stocks, or options, Dana has succeeded in finding deep value in whatever instrument he traded, often increasing his initial investment tenfold. The man who buys crashes, Dana Allen, thrives on making bids when most other market participants are running for the exits. Although his trading style is not for the faint of heart and can be seemingly chaotic, Dana has managed to face the risks and walk away with returns that most retail traders can only dream about. We had a chance to interview Dana from his home in Nevada.

■ ■ ■

Q : Were you always fascinated with trading? Did you read the *Wall Street Journal* when you were in high school?

A : Oh younger than that, I started reading it when I was eight or nine years old. I'd look at the commodities section and at the charts and I always thought, gee, you know, I can make money in this. Of course, I was too young. But when I was 21, I think right on my birthday, I started trading commodities. So I guess at that point I had to be the youngest commodity trader in the United States at that time.

Q : When you say you started trading commodities, were you trading retail?

A : Yeah, I was. It was back in the very bad commission days. I was still in college and I was trading mostly copper because I was a geology student.

Q : What were the commissions like at that time?

A : Oh outrageous [laughter]. Yeah, it was so bad; I think it was $50 to $100 a side or something like that. It was terrible.

Q : And how much was each point worth?

A : It was $250 per penny.

Q : So copper had to basically move a penny for you to overcome the commission costs, right?

A : That's right, it had to be a fairly big move. Back then my broker had to pay $600 a month for a five-minute delayed quote fee which provided as much information as anyone can get free now. These days, everything is so much better. The information is free, and it's faster. The commissions are 1 percent of what they used to be. I can do options and the commission is a dollar fifty to both buy and sell where it used to be like 50 bucks each. In many ways it's never been better than it is today to trade.

Q : Did anybody in your family trade stocks?

A : Yes, my father did as an investor. But he was a business man, not a trader. I started off doing it myself and then, like most people, I started with the minimum account size of $3,000 [laughter]. And sure enough you always have to blow up when you have such a tiny account.

Q : How long did it take you to blow up?

A : Oh I think six months. That's pretty good when you trade commodities on 3,000 bucks [laughter].

Q : That is pretty good. That's very impressive. You really held out. You treaded water for a long time there. The reason for the question about family was because one of the interesting things that we're finding is that a portion of the traders we're interviewing came from families with strong interest in trading. We were wondering if that had a big impact on you or just a marginal one. Did you and dad talk stocks when you were younger or was this really your own personal pursuit?

A : It was mainly me reading the *Wall Street Journal* and when he would talk to his friends I would pay attention.

Q : So after you blew up the account in college what happened then?

A : Well, for a while I didn't do all that good, I'd refill the account, blow it up again, but later when I started a company in 1988 or

1989, and I played the options on copper, I turned $2,000 into $40,000 in about six months.

Q : How did you find time to trade while you were doing a start up?

A : Long hours [laughter]. Plus I actually used the money to help the company.

Q : So you used your trading profits to help capitalize your startup?

A : That's right.

Q : That's true entrepreneurial spirit. So you ran $2,000 to $40,000. Did you catch a big trend? What happened in the copper market?

A : It went up a lot. It went from about 57 to 85 and of course now, you know copper finally has had its day in the sun. I was very happy with the move because I was buying 70-cent options when copper was at 50 cents and they had a December expiration. I think I bought them in May—it went up a lot. [*Authors' note:* Dana was buying the right to purchase copper at 70 cents a ton when it was only trading at 50 cents/ton. This is a highly speculative strategy that assumes a very large price move over a short period of time]

Q : Was it a one-shot deal where basically you bought options in May and then they just matured into a very fat profit?

A : That's right. I sold some on the way up, but I made a very, very good profit, 2,000 percent or so.

Q : Most people typically get out early, what made you hold on to the trade?

A : Technical analysis. I was following a chart on it and it still looked healthy and so I held on to it until it started losing momentum.

Q : Were you following the daily chart?

A : Yes. Now I use much finer stuff. But back then I think that was the only thing available [laughter].

Q : Was this trade something fundamentally researched or was it frankly just luck that you caught a really nice move and then managed to hold on to it? What made you go long copper at that point?

A : Well, I thought it was undervalued, and then I watched the chart and it dipped down, looked like it washed out, lost its downward momentum, premiums on options became very small, and so I thought quite bit about it and got lucky. I've done that a couple times. I bought Boeing at the market turn in 1982. I bought 25 calls when it was 16 and it went to 28. That was my entire stake in the market [laughter]. I had very little money at that time, but I made another nice killing on that trade. The stock was selling four times the earnings, and it went up to about 28 before the November expiry. Now that I know a lot more about options, I wouldn't have played them that way.

Q : You made a nice punt. Were they trading for teeny (one-sixteenth of a dollar)? They must have been very cheap.

A : I think it was three-eighths or maybe less, maybe an eighth, somewhere in that range definitely under a half. Actually, I think my percentage on the trade was 3,000 percent. But I've also been wrong. One time that I was very wrong on the market was in 1998. I read some articles which made a very good case that S&P was way overvalued, so I started buying S&P 500 put options and I lost a lot of money [laughter]. I quit fighting the tape The next time, actually, I nailed it pretty good, which was in late 1999 The market was just absolutely insane and I was in on the run. At the same point, I was involved with the dotcom startup and we were being offered just outrageous valuations. So, I actually thought it was going to crash in March or April 2000. I felt that way since January, and I wasn't alone. I think in *Forbes* magazine, [Bob] Metcalf of 3Com and [Gordon] Moore of Moore's Law wrote articles about why they thought the dotcom boom was going to crash. If I had it to do over again, I could probably come up with some options techniques, to take advantage of the crash. But back then I didn't feel like shorting stocks because you never know how far it could run. Also, the option premiums were outrageous then. Now I think I would have done *put backspread* and things like that or selling credit spreads, which are good ways to play a runaway market. [*Authors' note: Put backspreads* involve selling put options that are close to being in the money and then using the premium collected to purchase twice or three times as many of far out of the money put options. The strategy works if there is a sharp move down, breaks even if the underlying instrument rallies, and loses money if the instrument declines only slightly.]

Q : At that time you didn't do anything because the premiums were just fat right?

A : I didn't do much in terms of shorting, so that was a missed opportunity. I could have made a lot of money, and I did make some. But in retrospect, I could have a done a lot better because I really felt that what happened was going to happen.

Q : Basically, all the way through 2000 you're very much involved in startups and were just doing recreational trading.

A : Yes, you can say that. It was not full time. In 1998 and 1999, I had two years where I made 50 percent pretty much back to back, and it wasn't actually all that high tech. I was personally in high tech myself. In '98 and '99, valuations were so high. I was buying value stocks and avoiding all the overpriced stuff, and at that point that wasn't the best thing to do.

Q : At what time did you say to yourself I'm going to do this as a full-time trader?

A : 2002 was the time when I really buckled down and saw some very interesting automated trading models and found TradeStation. Actually made a lot of money off their stock too. So it was basically September of 2002 when I really started applying systems and doing it as a full-time job.

Q : Did you develop your own systems or did you buy other systems and modify them?

A : I was trading my own systems, but using TradeStation software to do it because you can actually back test the system.

Q : Why did automated trading attract you? Do you have an engineering mindset?

A : Yes I managed software development. Plus a lot of people say you can never have a completely automated system that will work. But we all know one of the greatest enemies of trading is emotion. People have a tendency to sell at the worst possible moment. I'm no different, but if you back test something, I think it's just natural for you to do a better job.

Q : So currently most of your trading is systems driven?

A : It is, but I don't have it fully automated yet, and I'm working on that now. I can get into positions automatically. I have one system that is very hectic—basically a crash buying system and so you don't know what stock you're going to be in. Using a list of over 200 stocks, it buys the worst crashes. It can go into many different stocks all at the same time on bad market days [laughter]. So I have to manage the positions. The system does work, but you feel like you're losing money until you add it all up at the end day and you end up positive.

Q : Is it kind of like trying to crash land a plane?

A : Yeah, and so I definitely wanted to get that automated.

Q : We're curious about the crash-based system. Clearly the system searches the market using whatever algorithm you have programmed and puts you in a position. We guess that's done automatically. It simply buys at whatever trigger you have. But once you are in position, you are managing the exits manually, is that correct?

A : That is correct, and while you're watching one, another one might be dropping another 2 to 3 percent on you before you look back over on that screen. So I don't enjoy it [laughter]. Clearly it would be better automated. The other thing is you automate the exits—you can back test them. I have basic rules on how to get out, just haven't been able to get them into the computer. I think that with back testing I will find a better way of getting out of position than by watching each stock individually. Wealthlab is what I use now, their back testing is superb.

Q : The system clearly sounds like it buys dips; does it also sell rallies?

A : My back testing indicates that it doesn't work as well on the short side. When they rip up, they continue to go up, so my back testing indicates that it is two or three times better to buy crashes. You're not buying something that's been going down for a week. I'm talking about interday crashes. It's more of an extreme interday crash and then picking up hints that the crash is coming to an end. That's proprietary, of course.

Q : Bottom line: You're primary a long-side trader in stocks because you found that bias to be much more profitable?

A : Yes, you have to know yourself, and I do have a long bias. I tend to buy stocks in oversold conditions, and I am not as good at shorting. That's another reason for automated systems. If I can find something that works very well on back testing on the short side, I'll be very happy to do it, but emotionally in my brain, I have a long bias.

Q : When you are in the midst of holding six, seven, eight positions, do you have either a mental or an automatic hard stop that serves as your risk control? For example, is it a 5 percent move down from your entry price, or is everything discretionary at that point?

A : It tends more toward the discretionary side, but there's also a time stop. I don't want to be in the trade overnight.

Q : So, for example, if at the end of the day you're still negative on the position do you time stop yourself? Will you get out on the close?

A : Yes. I don't want to be in too long. I'll give you a valuable piece of advice: The most dangerous stocks are biotech. So I avoid biotech because they can just go down and down and down.

Q : Because it's very hard to gauge value in those stocks, right? They don't have any assets except whether the drugs either work or don't.

A : Exactly—they are very emotional stocks.

Q : Generally, you're either going to stop yourself out on time or you're going to hopefully have a net positive move before the end the day and take profits?

A : That is correct.

Q : And the system is a day trading system, so you always try to stay flat overnight?

A : Yes, probably 90 percent of the time, but sometimes the crash occurs late in day. Those I hold.

Q : Do you find day trading to be more of a function of your own psychology namely that it helps you sleep at night, or do you believe that there is actually an edge? In other words, according to your back tests is it better to day trade?

A : Yes. I'm just looking for that intraday bounce. I'm not looking to pick up a position.

Q : So it's kind of like a game of hot potato?

A : Yes, you are buying in effect extreme fear and then there's a point where that fear tends to bottom out and then maybe a little optimism comes in and when that happens you get out. When you get the opportunity, there are four or five distinct and different type of behaviors in these crashes. And from experience you can see them on the charts if you're watching a one-minute chart. But I consider myself an omnivore trader. I do use many, many different methods including some long-term trades like in oil/gas stocks. From 2003 and 2004 until now, I've held positions sometimes for nine months. So I do some pure value investing and I throw trading on top of that as I watch the stock a lot and get to know it. I get to see the everyday things. So I might buy in and sell out 5 percent of the position during the day from these intraday patterns that I've noticed.

Q : How much of a bounce back do you look for? Would you unload the position at 2 to 3 percent profit?

A : It if keeps having momentum, I'll hold it and watch it. But it's actually less than that. You can imagine how hard it is to follow four or five stocks in a crash.

Q : Is there a cadre of stocks that you follow whose patterns and fundamentals you know quite well?

A : Yes, there are about five to seven stocks and that will change year to year.

Q : And you'll be in and out of those stocks, if not on a daily basis, then certainly once or twice a week based on this kind of a thing?

A : That is correct. If I really like the stock, I'll hold it. If I just like the technicals, then I'll get in and out. I trade different stocks different ways.

Q : When you buy dips, there's always an enormous danger of a retrace right back to negative territory after the bounce. How do you manage your trades? Do you scale out of half, go to break even? Do you ever allow winners to become losers again?

A : Sometimes. Of course, that's never the plan and it depends how far it goes. So if I'm just up a half percent, something that's almost down to the noise level, I won't necessarily cash in. I am a pattern trader. I'll watch both the 15-minute chart and one-minute chart, and I will also watch level two and start to get a feel for it. It takes a lot of experience to do this, to get a feel for when the stock is running out of momentum. Once they are quieting down and people get a bit nervous, I basically want to get out immediately at that point. But I do use scaling a lot, both in and out.

Q : Do you use any indicators to help you? Or is just pure observation of price action?

A : Both. I do believe in a lot of indicators. If you're in a trading range, the stochastics work great. Also RSI. And I follow the moving averages —the 5, 10, 20, and 100. I use that on a daily chart and also use it on a five-minute chart. To find extreme oversold levels I have found MoneyFlow works the best.

Q : So you use all those diagnostics to help you make your decision?

A : That is correct. But also experience seeing what works and what doesn't work and developing a feel for it. If the position starts to make you feel uncomfortable, then to me that's an indication that your mind is picking up something that's dangerous.

Q : When you are talking about feel, it sounds like your primary diagnostic is the level two. You really watch price, you've obviously watched action over and over, for thousands of hours.

A : That's correct.

Q : The moment you see something in the price action that triggers a concern, you liquidate?

A : That is correct, yeah. And when you mentioned about feel, I can develop a feel for five to seven stocks. But I can't develop a feel for 150 stocks. So that's where you have to have an automated system doing it for you.

Q : When you're doing swing trading, is it also really from pure observation of price flow or do you look at charts? Do you have certain technical setups that are relatively orthodox?

A : Yes, I'd say so. It's double bottoms primarily. I am a little bit of a bottom feeder—but I will get out, I won't stay in if they stay weak. My preference is to have a basket of stocks where the fundamentals are good. There is much less danger for them to continue to crash. One of the things I've found after trading from the long side for any length of time is to avoid stocks that have debt. The worst moves tend to be in stocks that have a lot of debt, with drops of 50 to 75 percent. Another thing I've found is management is absolutely key.

Q : So it sounds like, on your longer term trades, you're much more fundamentally oriented. You really want to know the story behind the stock and you will hold through the day-to-day noise if you believe in the story.

A : That is correct. In fact, I never hold a position for a long time in a company where I don't like the fundamentals. Now on swing or intraday basis trading, that is pure technical. On the crash system that I told you about, I actually don't even know the companies, Sometimes I have to look up to see what the stock is, never seeing the symbol before [laughter]. And I do try to read the press release, see how bad the news is, and so forth, and then manage a trade from there on out.

21

Q : Obviously biotech was one sector that you would just stay away from, but has there been a time when a stock crashed, you've read the news releases as to what caused the crash, and the news made you say, "You know what, I don't want to touch this, this is just too toxic"?

A : Yes. Like if they cooked the books or someone's been arrested. The crashes I like best are when the earnings are good but the stock collapses.

Q : That's a very interesting trade. So you actually like it when you have a positive fundamental surprise, but a negative price movement and there's a disconnect between the fundamentals and what the price is doing?

A : Yes, my favorite. Because people are just selling out of fear, there's no real reason for it. They say, "Gee, it should be going up, it's going down, I'm getting out." You know.

Q : There's one unifying theme that tends to run through all of your trading, be it specs in options or be it swing trading or even intraday trading—you are most comfortable with a value based trade. You like to buy value cheap, whether it be on an intraday basis, swing basis, or even speculative basis and then see it rally.

A : For long term that's 100 percent correct. One such trade I did was in 2003. At that point we'd had a real crash just like with the '29 crash, very similar, and then I remembered an old *Wall Street Week* episode, John Templeton was on and he said when he started out during World War Two, he took all the $1 stocks and bought every $1 stock on the stock exchange. So that triggered a memory as we just had a real similar market crash—worst one since 1929. I decided to modify it a little bit to look for companies with no debt. I had two criteria: One that it really had to be a good growing company, at a good value, or it used to be a decent $20 to $40 stock that crashed to one. One of my biggest wins was TradeStation, which I bought for 1.02 and ended up selling for $12. Another was AES, a big power company that's used to be $60 a share and was down to $1. I got a five bagger out of that. Another one was Dow Corning. It got over 100 and came down to a dollar, got a seven bagger out of that. Now it's over 20.

Q: That's fascinating.

A: Yes. There is nothing better as a trader than to see what you think is going to happen actually happen. The market is humbling to all though. My best results come after rough periods, where I literally pray to God and ask Him for help and tell Him if things go right, it's not me. The worst results follow periods where I decide I am really good at this and have figured out the markets.

Q: What is your best trade?

A: That's easy, it was this year. Saw PTSC on a deep value scan—magicinvestingformula.com—and loved the huge cash position, no debt and high profits, bought some at .08. near New Years 2006. It exploded almost immediately, and by March sold the last of it on the high day at 2.10 for a 26 bagger! I wish I had bought more of it.

Q: Let's change tact. You told us the best trade. Now tell us the most painful trade?

A: [laughter] Yeah there's been several. My worse trade in terms of losing money in a short period time was TMR. I ended up walking away from it with a profit, but this gets back to the issue of company management. It was an oil/gas driller down in Louisiana. They had a tremendous new field find and they hit this well. I think it was 33 million cubic feet a day [laughter]. I already had a position in at a dollar, and I saw the press release come across the screen and I took a look and there are still people offering to sell the thing at 2.10. [laughter] I just bought everything in sight. I ended up at one point with 70,000 shares and it did very well for while. It actually got up to a high of nine.

Q : You were holding the whole position at nine still?

A : Yeah, and I had actually increased along the way and I traded in and out, because I got to know the stock and so forth. And then they started missing wells. They had a shareholder meeting in Texas and there were a lot of enthusiastic investors. Then they went from 90 percent hit rate on wells to a 30 to 40 percent hit rate on wells. The stock was trading in a channel and every time it would hit bottom, I would buy and then sell at the top. But it broke the channel at 7.80, I should have just gotten out right then. But in next three days lost $150,000, so that's the worst loss I've taken. I did get out for a $150,000 profit, but three days before I had a $300,000 profit.

Q : It breaks the channel and obviously you make the classic mistake we've all made where you say no, no it's going back up.

A : Exactly.

Q : But every single day that it going down, were you saying to yourself, "No, no it's going to bounce, it's going bounce?" What was preventing you from pulling the trigger?

A : What was going through my mind was, if I sell it now, it's just going to drive it down lower. I was looking for a way to get out. I made a mistake. I had a friend who actually forgot all about it. She had stops and followed my recommendation to get out at

24

7.78 or something. She lost maybe 10 or 15 cents on the panic spread because it was crashing so hard. She [laughter] did much better than I did. If I am ever in the same situation again, there are two things I would change: One, I was overconcentrated. I should have not had that big of a position. Two, I knew that there was a problem with management. So I'm never taking a large position in a company where I have questions about management. The third thing—I should have sold at least half of it no matter what was happening. I should have sold it right then and there. I made a mistake on how I handled the trade.

Q : The days that it was dropping, did you go to bed and say to yourself, "You know, if it goes below five I'm just blowing out of the position, I don't care what price I get. I'm just not going to take anymore of this pain." Did it ever come to that point?

A : Yes, it was just a classical terrible, emotional trading experience. I'll fill it in with a little human interest story: Sometimes I'd make $40,000 or $50,000 in one week on the stock. So one day I said to a buddy, "I've always wanted a new Corvette." About a week before this happened, I went out and ordered a new Corvette.

Q : So not only the pressure of the trade but you had the burden of the Corvette on your shoulders?

A : That's right. Yeah [laughter].

Q : You spent money that you didn't quite yet have, Fortunately, of course, the story still ends up very positive for you. After that experience did you modify your exit strategies? Are you a lot more cautious these days in terms of getting out?

A : Yes, and became better at not taking concentrated positions.

Q : Let us go back to some general life questions: Are you married? And if you are, how does your spouse react to your trading?

A : I'm not.

Q : So you don't have anybody to answer to, which makes it a lot easier.

A : That is correct and I'm using my own money and I've actually turned down money. I've had people offer me money, several times in the last two years. But the thought of losing someone else's money . . . you know, having started a business where people invested half a million dollars—a lot of it from friends and not being able to return their money for a long time—that was just terrible. So that's why I'm hesitant to take other people's money. I want to be absolutely sure that I can get them a profit. I hate losing my money. But I can handle it. The idea of telling someone else sorry, you know, the account is down 5 percent this month, is an extra burden that I don't want.

Q : Do you have multiple trading accounts or do you concentrate on one?

A : I have five. All for different reasons. Cyber-Trader I like. That's actually what I'm looking at right now on my screen. I have Fidelity, because of Wealth Lab. I like Wealth Lab, wonderful back-testing. And I have Interactive Brokers because you could trade just about anything there is and the commissions are wonderful.

Q : When you decided to start trading full time, you obviously had capital. Did you walk into this venture essentially saying to yourself, "Oh, I can do this for a full year and not have to make a dime"?

A : Well no. And if you lose your money, it is a self-correcting problem. It prevents future losses [laughter].

Q : But were you capitalized enough to basically not have to draw income off your trading for a while?

A : No, not really. I was fortunate enough to do very well. I'll give you the actual figures. I had money tied up in other things, but the starting capital I had in December 31, 2002, was $172,000. And I was very blessed, because of very good appreciation. I was able to pay all my expenses and multiply the stakes.

Q : That's impressive.

A : Thank you. There are a lot of horror stories out there; but I was able to succeed. Like my original traditional IRA. I had a very small one, it was like $18,000 as of October 2002, and since then its grown to $200,000. So I was able to do an 11 bagger on that, and, by having it in an IRA, I don't have to go through the tremendous pain of all the accounting [laughter].

Q : I can imagine the reconciliation of your trades must be tremendous. It's probably 3,000 to 4,000 trades per year, maybe more, right?

A : Yes, actually more. I think I average something like 7,000 to 8,000 trades a year. And now that I'm doing options, it's even more complicated. I might have on one trade with four or five different options on certain stock. So I think my trade numbers are actually going to go up.

Q : When you started trading and you went into trading full time, did you write a business plan for yourself? And then did you set daily, weekly, monthly earning targets, or was it much more fluid than that?

A : I did write a business plan but made several changes. For example, I had an automated system in 2002 to 2003, but the results weren't what I was expecting. Then one day I was, just walking outside taking a hike, it hit me. I had optimized the system to go from 70 percent to 130 percent profit and as result it just ended up breaking even. [*Authors' note:* Dana refers to the constant danger of system based trading, namely the desire to overoptimize your strategy in order to produce more profit. In fact such tactics often lead to sub-par results as all trading systems typically require very large margins of error.] So it's things like that that have happened where I correct my mistakes and write a new business plan. I am a firm believer in doing that. Another thing I've heard some people say is just look at all your trades. Van Tharp pushes that idea. You can't do that all the time, but I will do that occasionally, and I'll pick up some really big revelations such as a certain type trading is not making me any money at all.

Q : How often do you do that kind of analysis? Once every three months?

A : Yeah, if that, maybe three to six months, but I suggest to other people to do it once a month [laughter].

Q : Do as I say, not as I do?

A : That's right. Just did it recently and picked up that something I wanted to do for safe trading was actually working much better than I thought. Some other things were masking the profitability of this low risk system. Just figured that out three days ago through a review of trades.

Q : Is there anything else that you could share with us regarding your analysis or is it proprietary?

A : It was very proprietary. I can tell you that some of the discretionary stuff I was doing was not working very well and it was masking what the safe strategy was doing.

Q : So you are coming to the conclusion that the systematic approach is actually the most efficient approach for your type of trading?

A : I believe that's the case, yes.

Q : Did you have any mentors when you started trading and, at present, do you have a support group or a group of traders you talk to?

A : Yes I do. Starting off I didn't really know any successful full-time retail traders. It is a fairly rare thing, but I strongly suggest to people to to go to Trader's Expo, one is out in Las Vegas, and you get to be around all these other people who are full-time traders and get to talk to a lot of top authors. I found that to be a wonderful experience. In the San Francisco area, where I used to live, I formed a group of about four other traders and we would talk on Yahoo! chat and get together every week and have trading sessions together, which I would suggest.

Q : What would that be like?

A : You have a laptop, someone has an Internet connection, and we all have wireless, and then one person would put up a projector on the wall, and we look at the chart and try to decide on a trade and discuss this particular stock. I find that process very valuable. I think everyone gains from it and on top of that, after the market closes, you share experiences. We watch video tapes together from various authors and so forth.

Q : Can you run us through a typical trading day? Especially now that you're in Nevada. Obviously you start the day quite early?

A : Sure. I try to get up before the market opens, check some things out. I have a lot of software I have to open up. Then I bring up the charts on the positions that I have. I am actually putting in a better multiscreen setup here now.

Q : How many screens do you look at usually?

A : Up to now I've done something people think is pretty wild, I use one screen. [laughter] A 21-inch old CRT, but I'm switching over to three 19-inch flat panels, to use with two computers. That's an unusual thing about me—I often do 50 trades a day and I was doing it across one screen and people say how do you do that? [Laughter.] I do a lot of switching—wouldn't recommend that to anyone—on the stocks I am most interested in, then check for news. I go use the stock boards on Yahoo! There's a lot of knowledgeable people on some stocks like EGY and CWEI.

Q : What kind of a news services do you use?

A : I use Yahoo! It is my main source.

Q : Is most of your trading done in the first two to three hours of the market between 6 and 9 A.M. your time?

A : To an extent. As mentioned to you, I'm doing a lot more option trading where I am looking for specific skews in the market, searching for those all day long, whatever time they happen, I'll try to enter into some very low-risk trades on that.

Q : When you are talking about arbitraging options, are you looking at discrepancies between the underlying and the option? Where you could offset one with the other because there's some skew that you feel you can take advantage of? [*Authors' note:* This is a very sophisticated strategy that tries to exploit momentary mispricing between the option contract and the underlying security. Often options value will be driven unnaturally high or low after a big order sweeps through the market. At that time a trader can sometimes take advantage of the discrepancy by buying the option contract and offsetting the risk by selling the underlying instrument.]

A : Yes and now I can also use single stock futures. I'm looking for those types of things—as low risk as possible. If I can make 2 percent or more per month with no—or very low—risk, then that's a heck of a deal.

Q : Where did your interest and education in options come from?

A : I traded options since I was 21. Then sort of moved away from them, part of it was the bid-ask spreads and the big commissions. But now the commissions are almost nothing. They're wonderful, and the bid-ask spreads have gotten better. Plus sometimes you get fills that are between the spread. Let's say the option is 7.40 to 7.80 bid ask. You put an order at 7.60 and you wait 5 or 10 minutes and very often someone will go out and hit it. I found that if you bid with very small lots, then the market makers see them as irritants and will take your bid just to get you out of the way. You put 10 out there and they won't hit it. But if you put one or two out there, they'll hit it just to get rid of you.

Q : Was there any particular books or seminars that you attended that sharpened your knowledge in options?

A : Yes. I read Larry McMillan's book and met him at Trader's Expo and talked to him. One thing I think is a little bit of a weakness in that book and all option books is they don't really discuss what makes money and what doesn't make money. So I'm doing some software development to prove a strategy—both so I can make money off the software and I'm interested in actually publishing it. Also, I am reading Natenberg now, excellent book. And Thinkorswim free seminars are wonderful, strongly recommend them.

Q : Could you share one or two strategies that you think *do* have a high probability of making money in the options market?

A : Yes. Things related to selling nearbys that are going to decay much faster and then, if you can get a volatility skew on top that in your favor, that helps. Also covered calls on lower-priced stocks with huge volatility. I'm doing that on RMBS now. Diagonal Bull and Bear spreads have a good chance for a profit. [*Authors' note:* These are various option strategies that essentially try to sell one strike price against another in order to take advantage of the volatility differences between a set of similar options with different strike prices.]

Q : Let us wrap this up with a couple of final questions. Where is the drudgery in trading? Do you find anything boring or annoying, or is everything about this discipline really interesting to you?

A : Good question. Well I think the worst thing is—maybe it's not boring—but the worse thing is losing money [laughter]. And having to deal with paperwork and the taxes is very boring.

Q : How do you deal with losing money? Have you gotten to the point where you can shrug it off or does it still simmer and burn and you become very annoyed?

A : I definitely got used to it. I can lose $5,000 or $10,000 in a day and not get affected, but if I lose money 17 out of 20 days, then it still does affect me.

Q : What's been the longest losing streak you can remember? Have you ever had a string of 10 to 12 days where it's just been nothing but bleeding?

A : Pretty much, yeah. I have. That's the very worst. If it's a slow bleed, it does wear you down. Part of it is that you want to be in tune with the market. Sometimes I just get so in tune with the market, know exactly what it is going to do. And then there are other times when I feel out of tune. I'm out of phase. It's not doing what I expect, what's going on here?

Q : When you're out of tune, what do you do to get your mojo back?

A : I try and drop back to 40 percent cash, sometimes even 70 percent cash. I try to figure out what the reason is. I also think there is a humbling factor that does make you better in the long run. I think the greatest deterrence is that most of us don't think high consistent returns are possible. You can't achieve something if you don't think it's possible. All you have to do is make a percent a day, that's 200 percent per year! [Laughter.] There are stocks that move around 3 percent, every day and so it's got to be possible, and because I believe its possible then it helps me to get better results.

Q : Last question of the day, what would you say is your number-one rule for trading?

A : I think my number one trading rule is to not worry about being right, just focus on making money and just deal with being wrong. The purpose of trading is not being right, the purpose is to make money, and I think that's my number-one rule. Don't get hung up on your current positions.

LESSONS FROM DANA ALLEN
Look for 10 Baggers

One of the most impressive aspects of Dana Allen's trading is the amount of trades in his career that have returned him more than 10 times his initial investment or, as he calls them, 10 baggers. Whether in options, stocks, or commodities, Dana has been able to achieve these incredible results by always buying value. Using John Templeton's maxim that investors get the best bargains when the world seems to be coming to an end, Dana has been able to pick up bargains at severely distressed levels more than once during his trading career. In fact, using the same method that Templeton employed half a century before him, Dana bought as many $1 stocks on the NYSE and Nasdaq as he could find, following the 2001 market crash—a strategy that proved to be extremely profitable in the ensuing market recovery. One critical rule that Dana always follows is to only buy securities of companies that have no debt. This is a very wise approach because debt-ridden companies can collapse even if their underlying business remains relatively sound especially if they are forced to divert their cash flow to service debt.

Stocks Have an Upside Bias

Over the past two centuries, stocks in the United States have returned an average of 7 percent. Massive stock corrections notwithstanding, equities are the only financial asset that show an unequivocal uptrend on a longer timeframe. Therefore, selling rallies works less well in the stock market than buying dips. Stocks have a natural upside bias as they to tend appreciate with the expanding economy. Many market analysts refer to this phenomenon as the upward drift. Certainly stocks can fall mercilessly for days, weeks, and even years on end. Over the long term, however, they tend to rise rather than fall. As a wise man once said, the race does not always go to the strongest and the swiftest, but that is the way to bet. And that is the way that Dana Allen generally bets preferring to buy crashes rather than sell manias.

Stops Should Use Time as Well as Price

One very interesting part of Dana's methodology is the use of a time stop as well as price stop. After all, trades travel through both time and price, yet traders only focus on the price part of the risk. Dana uses a simple end-of-the-day stop on his crash-buying system. If the price hasn't reached his objective by end of the day, he terminates the trade even if it remains above his stop. The basic premise of his setup is that prices should quickly bounce off their depressed crash levels as bargain hunters swoop in. If the bounce hasn't materialized, that may mean that the majority of the market does not perceive value at these levels and further declines may be in store. Therefore, a time stop as well as price stop could help traders to minimize risk.

Best Trade Setup Is a Disconnect Between Fundamentals and Price

Divergence is one of the most common setups in trading. Typically, divergence is traded off technical factors when momentum indicators disagree with price action. However, Dana Allen likes to trade divergence based on fundamental reasons. One of his favorite trade setups occurs when a company reports superior earnings but the stock sells off on profit taking. This is a very interesting strategy because once again Allen positions himself on the side of value. Once the wave of initial profit taking crests, and the selling is completed, the same stock can often present a compelling value as long-term investors buoyed by strong fundamentals return to the bid. The one exception to this setup is the biotech sector. Dana feels that financial value of biotech stocks is extremely difficult to gauge, given the fact most of these companies live or die by the actions of the FDA's Center for Drug Evaluation and Research and have no assets aside from their intellectual property.

CHAPTER 3

THE 100-PIP TRADER
ROB BOOKER

Even though Rob Booker is a former lawyer turned full-time trader, if you asked him to describe his job, he would tell you that he is a "back tester" first and a trader second. In less than five years, he has gone from being a $2,500 trader to a client of a major bank who trades a respectable-size account. He practices defensive trading and focuses on preservation of capital. His number one rule of trading is, "If I can't prove that a system works from my testing, then I have no business trading it with real money." A fan of the casual attire lifestyle, his humorous laid-back approach has built him a huge following. He is one of the funniest traders that we know as well as one of the most humble. He has taught over a thousand traders how to trade and all of them call him their friend, as he strives to maintain a lifetime relationship with each one of them.

From his office in Wheeling, West Virginia, Rob took a few hours to talk to us about his approach to the market and to share some of his tricks of the trade.

■ ■ ■

Q : Can you tell us a little bit about your background in the financial markets? Were you exposed to the concept of finance as a kid or was it much later?

A : If I had any experience in anything related to stocks or investments when I was young, it was probably somewhat negative. It's not that I was discouraged from being involved in the markets, but I was always encouraged to think of what I would call more traditional occupations—law or medicine. I don't know enough math to save my life—and I always heard that to work in the markets, I would need to have a strong math background—so Wall Street wouldn't have been much of an option in my mind anyway. Honestly, I was never encouraged to think about working in the markets, so I guess you wouldn't call it discouragement but it never arose as an option, as a career, or even as a hobby, and it wasn't even something I was remotely interested in. The earliest that I can remember being interested in investing at all was when I took a course in high school as a freshman and it was a business course. We were expected to buy stocks at the beginning of the semester with a play account and then track the quotes in the newspaper for the semester and see how it turned out.

Q : Did that whet your appetite in the financial markets enough to keep you interested?

A : No, I think I took the class and forgot about it. But I really enjoyed taking the class. I remember I bought Pioneer stock. It was the company that made electronics and I really wanted a Pioneer stereo with a CD player at the time. So I decided that I would pick a stock based on something that I liked and I am fairly certain I came in last [laughter]. So much for investing in something just because I liked it and not because it had true upside potential. Yet during that semester of high school, I was entranced by the thought that you could actually buy a piece of a company or invest in something and then basically play the game of waiting to see if you had made the right decision. I was seriously interested in it at the time and then I just forgot about it. In fact I completely forgot about it until much later on.

Q : That's very interesting, because not everyone who is successful at trading actually majored in anything remotely related to it in college.

A : Yes, exactly, and I never actually took any economics classes in college at all. The big scary class at BYU [Brigham Young University] when I was an undergraduate was Economics 101 and it seemed so daunting from all the horror stories I heard about it. So, although I was interested in business—and, by that time, I was once again interested in the markets—I was just too fearful at the time to really take the plunge and study economics in college. I missed the opportunity to get a really good foundation, which I think would have assisted me later on in my trading career.

Q : So then you went on to study law?

A : That is correct. As soon as I graduated from BYU with a degree in Italian, my wife and I moved to San Francisco where I started law school.

Q : Was that because of parental pressure?

A : Mostly, yes. I think it's unfair to blame the decision on my parents, but in my mind, I really did enroll in law school because I believed, from my upbringing, that it was the "safe" route. That's exactly the reason why I went. I think I was strongly encouraged by my parents to pursue a traditional occupation that would allow or enable me to support my family. And any pressure I felt from my parents was positive—they were excited for me to go to law school and told me that they believed I would do very well. They were probably more excited than I was about law school. It was never forced on me, and I sort of followed that path because I had come to the conclusion that that's what I wanted to do and I had a vision of a legal career that was quite different than what's practically possible as an attorney. It did not take long for me in law school to realize that I would have no interest in practicing law.

Q : What kind of law were you studying?

A : Well, in law school it's just so general that at the beginning you don't get a lot of chances to specialize in anything. So I took courses ranging from criminal to constitutional to business law. When I was in law school, I took a summer job at an investment bank in San Francisco and my wife worked for a hedge fund. The exposure to these jobs started me thinking again about a career in the markets. So I started picking courses in transactional law or corporate law and found that I was once again fascinated by the idea of trading and realized that I had caught the bug a long time ago and I just couldn't shake it and I kept coming back to the same thing. One day while working at the investment bank, I met a trader. Later on that same day, someone told me that the trader I'd met made $600,000 the year before. That seemed to me to be way more money than I could make practicing law. Then I was told that this trader would probably make over $1 million in the current year. I started wondering what the heck I was doing in law school.

Q : That's really interesting that you took an internship at an investment bank because people who study law usually take internships in some of the big law firms. What made you take it?

A : That's a good question. It's very kind of you to even ask that question, that you would assume that a big law firm would have had any interest in me, which they did not. I made the decision to work at an investment bank mainly because I didn't have an alternative available to me. Although I was fortunate to get into a good law school, my grades were absolutely terrible. I was uninterested in a legal career from nearly the very beginning and my grades seriously reflected that lack of interest. So I took a job where I could get one, and the place I could get a job was as a lowly staff-assistant-type position at Montgomery Securities in San Francisco and I absolutely loved the environment. I was actually working at Montgomery Securities on the day they helped take Netscape public. Everybody in the office, especially in the operations department, was fascinated by the idea that this company with no revenues could be taken public. I remember people telling me that this new company was doomed to failure and there was no way it could ever survive. Well, we know now that the founders of the company were made very rich and that the company was sold to AOL in 1998 for $4 billion. The day Netscape went public, we watched as the stock kept going up and everybody made predictions as to how far back down it would go. But it really never did go down for as long as I was there. And I think that was one of my formative experiences, where I realized that the markets were an amazing vehicle for wealth creation and they made people wealthy very quickly. Maybe that's not a great lesson, but it certainly was one of the things that attracted me to the markets once again. And I never lost interest for longer than a day after that.

Q : Did you ever finish your law degree or did you switch careers before that?

A : I did finish law school. I could honestly say that there are very few regrets in my life, but one of those would be that I did not take a job as a trading assistant at Montgomery Securities but rather continued my legal studies and went all the way through and finished law school.

Q : When did you decide to switch careers?

A : Once again my not-so-fantastic grades in law school threw me an opportunity to look elsewhere. I had job offers after law school to work in law firms, and what I realized at that point was that it just simply wasn't going to work for me. So I attempted to enroll in a Ph.D. program on the East Coast. My wife and I moved to the East Coast and when I decided that the Ph.D. program wasn't for me, I actually worked at several jobs, whatever I could do to earn money and support my family. Anything to avoid law. I was happier making one-third the amount of money in other jobs. Once again the markets came back up and within just a couple of years I had been introduced to a private currency trader in southern California. That's when I really sort of realized that I didn't need to work in an investment bank to be involved in the markets. I didn't need to have a business degree. I didn't need to have a lot of special connections. What I really needed was a good Internet connection and some information on how to get started and the perseverance to make it through the bad times, the hard lessons that we all seem to go through. So that was the beginning of my currency trading career.

Q : It seems like your wife at the time was extremely supportive or at least very flexible to be moving around with you?

A : Well, she's never been the type of person who would encourage me to do something that wouldn't make me happy and money was never our first concern as a married couple. The first concern was quality of life and whether we are doing things with our time on earth that allows us to spend time together and allows us to feel comfortable and good about what we're doing. As long as I was moving forward in those plans, money wasn't going to be a problem. Because of this, I'm very familiar with the dilemma that a new trader has in attempting to work a full-time job and try to trade at the same time. We were deeply in debt after law school. I defaulted on student loans to pursue currency trading as a career. We experienced enormous financial pressures, including the inability to pay our rent or make our car payment or really have enough money for basic essentials. But we decided that was the direction that we were going to go and once I made that decision I wasn't going to give up. I didn't have any special training or a trading account funded by parents. This was something that we had to do from scratch.

Q : So you started immediately in FX, in Forex, or did you first dabble in futures or stocks or something else?

A : I've never made an equity trade in my life, except in ninth grade when I bought Pioneer stock and it went down at least 10 points by the end of the semester.

Q : Tell us about this trader from southern California? How did he get you involved in the markets?

A : I was introduced to the trader in southern California through a friend of mine who had been very successful in business. My friend said, "You know, if you're interested in trading, you should talk to this guy who's trading my money." At the time, my friend said that he loaned this currency trader in southern California approximately a million dollars, and this currency trader was paying my friend between 6 and 8 percent per month in interest. I thought, well here's something: this trader is amazing! He must be throwing off enough gains to produce that 6 percent in interest monthly and still have enough profit left over. In fact, my friend at the time had received back the entire amount of his principal over the course of about 12 months and now was receiving basically interest payments. So I thought, if somebody is so successful at currency trading that they can do that type of thing, that they can borrow money at ridiculous interest rates, then that's something I want to learn about. One thing led to another, and this currency trader introduced me to his methodologies, which seemed too good to be true. And you know what they say about that. We discovered later on was that he was raising money and making payments to the people who had given him money in the first place by raising more money on the side. Eventually that game caught up with him. By the time I found out that he wasn't for real, I had already sort of lost my first account and had decided that I could figure it out myself if I spent the time necessary to do so.

Q : It must have been pretty scary to be in such a financial strain and then not to trade well when you first started. How did you find the confidence to keep on doing it?

A : I wasn't very good at practicing law when I first started, or doing much of anything else that I first started in life, and I always approached things from that perspective. I mean on the first day that I drove a car when I was 15 years old, I wasn't very good at driving, but over the course of time I became comfortable and successful at driving and that didn't happen overnight. I understood that there were going to be some losses, and so the financial pressure came for the reasons that you feel financial pressure. Meaning if you get an eviction notice or if you can't make your car payment you naturally feel pressure. But I don't think I felt pressure to figure out trading immediately. I think I'd met enough traders in San Francisco and spoken to enough people who helped me realize that this was not going to be any different than playing sports or having a first job or learning to drive. There was going to be learning period during which I felt uncomfortable, made a lot of mistakes, and had to learn for myself some of the things that you simply can't learn by reading a book or listening to someone else as much as they try to help you.

Q : Did you make a lot of mistakes in the beginning?

A : Oh, certainly, yes! Do you have a page limit for the book? I made every mistake that you can possibly think of. Here's the basic list:

1. I made too many trades.
2. I traded with lot sizes that were way to big—I was risking 5 to 10 percent of my account on each trade when I should have been risking less than 1 percent.

3. I traded multiple systems at the same time.
4. I traded any currency pair that I liked.
5. I traded at all times of the day.
6. I traded long-term and short-term.
7. I read way too many books about systems and far too few books about discipline.

Q : Did you take any classes?

A : No. I did read a lot of books, but I never took any classes. I think the best book I read at the early stages was *Reminiscences of a Stock Operator*, which most people know to be the not-so-secret biography of Jesse Livermore. I also found a lot of wisdom in biographies of successful people, including John Rockefeller, Gandhi, George Washington and other Founding Fathers. In many cases, I found more trading wisdom in the biographies than in the trading books.

Q : How long did it take you to get it right?

A : Eleven months. During that time I tested my brains out. I built my own trading systems and tested them endlessly. I tested for hours and hours every day. I traded with a demo account and a small live account.

Q : Did you at any point feel like giving up?

A : Probably every day [laughter]. I probably felt that way on a regular basis at the beginning and some of it was because I was also working at the time. I would develop Web sites. I took a job selling T1 lines or Internet service at the very infancy of the Internet. I took a job as financial recruiter, a headhunter. The one thing that I would not consider doing was taking a job working in a law firm and that was simply because I didn't want to get sucked into the lifestyle and go down a path that I felt really uncomfortable with for the long-term. So I did a lot of things on the side and as much as I could just to make sure we could stay afloat during the time that I tried to learn how to trade.

Q : So you worked full time while you were trading? Or was it more like part time?

A : I'm absolutely positive that I worked full-time hours, and some of those hours were the 9-to-5 type while some were side projects where I did consulting work like write a contract or help with a web site. I looked for whatever work I could find that I would be able to do in the middle of the night ideally.

Q : So how did you manage to trade while working full time?

A : I just didn't get a lot of sleep. The only answer I can come up with, looking back on it now, is that I woke up at 2 or 3 o'clock in the morning and I would watch the London or European sessions. The reason I did that was because I had been first introduced to currency trading from someone who was taking trades in the middle of the night and trading during those sessions, so that's the session that I was drawn to. And so I would get up really early and then by the morning I would be ready to work or do whatever else it was that I was doing to earn actual money and then I would come home and I would try to sleep and spend time with my wife and get up early again. So I literally made it work by just getting very little sleep.

Q : Do you think that was the key that you felt like you had to make this work?

A : Yes, I made a decision one time, like I do with most things. I made a decision that I was going to make it work. It was clear to me that other people could trade for a living, and if it was possible for other people to do it, then I could persevere long enough to figure it out. I knew it might take me longer than someone else, but I wasn't in competition with someone to do it faster. I knew that I wouldn't have a large account like someone else might have, but I wasn't in competition to have a certain size account. I was just trying to figure it out so I could be consistently profitable. I also had a very good friend who was a financial planner, who told me that the secret was to grind out regular profits on a regular basis. The goal wasn't to hit the jackpot or pull the slot machine or win the lottery, the goal was to consistently grind out profits week after week, and if I could be profitable each week, the amounts that I made wouldn't matter as it would prove that I was able to keep what I had earned. And I think I just decided that was the main focus—if it was just $50 week or it was even just $25 week—at the beginning the amounts were irrelevant and really figuring it out was more relevant. Then, later on, I figured I could find more money to trade with if I had to. I can't emphasize this enough. The big lesson for me here was that I didn't have to make $1,000 per day or even per month. I just needed to make something and not give it back. I learned that if I took care of my trading capital, the rest would take care of itself.

Q : How much did you start trading with?

A : $2,500. It was partially mine and partially an investment that a good friend made in me. In the first few days of trading, I made 10 percent in the account. I should have closed the trading software down and not opened it up again for a month.

Q : What happened?

A : I almost remember it exactly; the account went from $2,500 to about $2,752 and some change and I had a 10 percent gain in the account and I should have shut it off and walked away for at least a week. I was positively euphoric. I was the Warren Buffett of currency trading. I remember, I had heard these stories about guys, returning 6 to 8 percent a month or more, and I figured I could just continue to do something like that. But I didn't stop. Two weeks later I took a trade, placed no stop-loss, and 72 hours later I had lost 90 percent of my capital. I remember drawing it down to the point where it was at $2,500 and saying to myself, "Maybe I can get out at breakeven and it will be like the bad trade never happened. Then it was down $2,000 and then it was $1,500 and by the time it got down to that level, I just thought it can't get any worse so I just might as well just leave it open. And of course it would get worse.

Q : So what do you do differently now?

A : I try my hardest to not lose money. That's my first concern. I know this sounds heretical, but making the money isn't the hard part. When I first started trading, I was in a very bad spot financially. A close friend who had been very successful in business took me aside, looked me in the eye, and said, "Rob, you've convinced yourself that making money is difficult." Then he said, "Making money is easy. Keeping it is difficult." He wasn't speaking about trading, but he could have been and he was right.

I have found that it's not terribly difficult to develop a profitable trading system. What requires real grit is the ability to hold onto the profits, to not overtrade, or increase the size of the trades beyond what is an acceptable risk. So the name of the game for me has been to not lose money first, and then just grind out profits week after week as a second goal.

Q : How long did it take you to figure out that you needed to trade defensively?

A : It was 11 months into my trading that I really started practicing this. After losing that $2,500, I spent 11 months testing and experimenting and reading not just about trading systems or methodologies. I tried to learn and adopt the principles that would guide me from a mental standpoint from then on. I was determined to never fall into a trance on a losing trade, what I call *possum trading*, where you sort of fall asleep and act like if you don't watch it, it will all get better. I promised that I would never let that happen again. That was the big goal, and it took 11 months not just to figure out entries and exits, but really get to the point where I could trade on a practice account consistently enough that I wasn't gambling with the account any longer. And so the central goal became to never lose the starting capital. If I could keep my capital, I could stay in the game. Trading is a game of survivability.

Q : What was the process like in terms of teaching yourself? Did you teach yourself basic chart reading, or did you learn about fundamentals first?

A : I exclusively started with technical analysis. Economics intimidated me, so I at first avoided fundamental analysis. Instead of reading about economics, I took a copy of Alexander Elder's *Trading for a Living*, and I read about moving averages. During that 11-month stretch of time, I literally sat at the charts and back tested and experimented exclusively with moving averages. At the end of 11 months, I actually remember somebody asking me if had chosen one of my moving averages as the 62-moving average because it was "Fib" ratio and I asked them, I didn't understand what the word "Fib" meant. I hadn't actually done much other analysis except for my own testing and experimentation with moving averages. I would plot moving averages on the charts. I would move forward one candle at a time. I would experiment with different timeframes, different currency pairs, until I had accumulated just an enormous amount of research of my own in how price interacted with those moving averages and what I could expect from a given type of trade. I wanted to be able to open a trade and answer the questions: What could I expect to lose? What could I expect to win? And when those win/loss ratios became acceptable and I could trade the strategy consistently week after week after week—profitably—then I knew I was defending my account.

I knew that I was consistently grinding out some profits week after week and trading with a system that might not have been perfect, but certainly produced gains on a regular basis.

Q: So the way you essentially back tested is to go back into the price charts and look for examples of what you thought was going to happen, right?

A: Yes.

Q: You didn't use some sort of programming language to mechanically back test?

A: Right. That's the other part about it. At a number of levels I was really too uneducated or stupid to know at the time that you could even program anything like that. I wasn't even aware that there was some type of programming language or charting platform that would allow me to back test that stuff automatically or mechanically. And now I'm happy I didn't have any of those tools because I gained a lot by watching the charts and not doing it in such a mechanical way. I became familiar with the way that price moved on the chart for the British pound/U.S. dollar. I got familiar with the U.S. dollar/Japanese yen. I became accustomed to looking at the price move up and down in regular, repeatable patterns. I seared into my memory the trends, the ranges, and just a few currency pairs became familiar like friends.

Q: Do you think that's still the way you primarily back test at the moment, because we're sure there are a lot of new traders who find things like Easy Language very, very daunting in the beginning.

A: I say this to everyone now and I've been saying it most recently in the following terms. I have a career as a back tester. Then, on the side, I have a part-time job and that's being a trader [laughter]. So yeah, I still engage in that process of testing every day. In fact, before we had the phone call today, I've been working with another set of moving averages on another timeframe chart together with people who have come out to my office to have a *back testing fiesta*, as I like to call it. My entire office is organized so that groups of people can enthusiastically engage in the process of testing together.

Q : So no one in the office knows Easy Language or any other programming language?

A : I actually now know Easy Language well enough to program most of what I do, and additionally I work with at least two different programmers if I needed to help optimize mechanical systems if I chose to do so. But it's very seldom that I'll optimize something or program it until I actually have already proven that it works just the way it is. So I might program it or optimize it in order to facilitate the process of sounding off alarms or alerting me to the opportunities, but I still don't engage in any type of mechanical trading whatsoever, meaning I never let the computer make the entries and the exits.

Q : So you back test more for reference and to create a foundation?

A : Yes, absolutely. It's a scientific process: hypothesis (the ideas for a trading system), then experimentation, then results, and so forth. If I can't verify it, I won't trade it. If you and I plotted a random indicator on price charts, on any timeframe, on any currency pair, with at least 5,000 to 10,000 bars of data, and locked ourselves in a room for six months, we could build a system from that one indicator. It's all about verification and experimentation for me. I have no actual preference for one type of methodology, whether it be fundamental analysis, price action analysis, order flow analysis, support and resistance trading, or astrology [laughter]. As long as it can be verified, historically, I'll take that preponderance of evidence and say at least it shows a statistical advantage, historically. And although past results are not indicative of future performance exactly, they certainly provide a lot of evidence to support some methodology that I'm considering. And if we don't have any statistical basis for what we're trading? Then we're just taking the random walk down Wall Street, as they say, and what good is random trading?

Q : How far back do you usually test?

A : Well, when I did short-term trading, which is any timeframe below one hour, I generally don't go back any further than the advent of the euro, meaning I'm trying to take advantage of a current market. I want to actually experiment with the market in a similar way back then as it is to now. So I do not want to experiment with the 15-minute charts in a time where the Deutsche mark and the Italian lira and the Spanish pesetas were all basically floating and affecting volume. I won't do anything short term any further back than 2000–2001. If I'm experimenting with the daily charts or something longer term, I'm more willing to go back into the mid to late 1990s. But if I go back too far, I'm going to go back to a time when currency trading was all done with the good old boys club and they were all using rotary phones. It feels uncomfortable to me to go back any further than that.

Q : Yes, the market was traded very differently back then.

A : Exactly. Traders were writing down their orders and the British pound/U.S. dollar currency pair would have one-hour candles that were 100 pips large each time. It doesn't make as much sense to me to expect the market to be similar then as it is now.

Q : In the beginning we talked about how you focus primarily on technical analysis. However, over the past few years have you incorporated any aspect of news in your trading?

A : On a weekly basis I actually draft what I call "crib sheets" or "cheat sheets" about economic fundamentals and I'll take an 8.5 by 11 sheet of paper and I'll write out major economics statistics from around the world. I accumulate that information using free resources on the Internet or paid resources like Bloomberg, and I keep a regular accounting of statistics from all over the world.

Then I laminate those cheat sheets and I actually take them in with me into the shower in the morning and I'll just put them against the wall and, because they're laminated, they stick against the wall and I just memorize and track economic statistics from around the world. So that when I'm taking longer-term trades, for instance, trades that are going to last from a day to as much as one, two, or three weeks, I understand the underlying economic fundamentals. For instance, I might understand that inflation and wage increases are still really strong in Australia, which might lead the Australian central bank to either increase or keep their high base interest rate. I might understand that, at the same time, Japan has an economy that is finally coming out of a deflationary period, and that interest rates are possibly going to rise over the next 18 months. I might understand simultaneously that economic data coming out from the U.S. shows that the Federal Reserve is likely to pause on interest rates and then go into a cycle of loosening monetary policy. If I understand those background economic fundamentals, it gives me a little bit more information on why I'm taking the longer-term trades that I'm picking. I generally never take a longer-term trade or a shorter-term trade solely based on any type of economic fundamentals, meaning it won't be the reason I picked the trade. But it could factor into how long I stay in the trade. It could factor into whether I feel more confident or less confident in a trade. Oil is a perfect example, I track oil and I watch the Canadian dollar and its response to oil prices. So I may use fundamental analysis as part of the picture. But I never exclusively use fundamental analysis to make a decision about a trade.

Q : Now would you ever use fundamental analysis as a reason to *not* get into the trade?

A : I'd use it to some degree. For example, I might not short the British pound against the Japanese yen for any extended length of time knowing that an interest rate differential is going to create some sort of significant transaction cost to hold a short British pound/Japanese yen trade for anything longer than a few days. So I might be more reluctant to hold something longer, and I might be reluctant to even initiate that type of a position in the first place knowing those type of things about fundamentals. Although I have in the past made short-term trades immediately following major economic events such as the nonfarm payrolls report, it has been quite some time now since I have done it. I think that it is absolutely far more dangerous than it ever used to be. Far easier to lose a significant amount of money and it has become, on the retail investing side something of a scheme or a trick that people want to teach other people to try and do that becomes a really, really quick way to lose a lot of money. It's sort of a get-rich-quick-lottery/slot-machine-type mentality. So I will rarely participate in any short-term moves around economic events. I'll usually let the market settle down, and I'll just buy or sell depending upon how it fits into the bigger picture.

Q : It's interesting that you talk about interest rates or carry. Do you ever factor it into your shorter-term trades, or just longer-term ones?

A : Into my longer-term traders, absolutely. My good friend and trading partner, Maxwell Fox, and I did a long-term interest rate study that tracked the interest rates, the monthly average or the monthly base rate for the Bank of England, the Bank of Canada, the New Zealand Reserve Bank, the Bank of Japan, the U.S. Federal Reserve, and the Swiss Central Bank and we plotted rate differentials from the early '70s, I can't remember the exact year, but it was 1974 or 1976, all the way through to the present, and then we tracked the average monthly spot price for each of the currency pairs that would be affected individually. What we generally found was that spot prices lag interest rate movements quite a bit. For example, in August 1990, differential between the pound and the yen interest rate peaked at about 10.5 percent—meaning that the Bank the England has an astoundingly higher interest rate than the Bank of Japan. I believe the Bank of England had a base rate at 15 percent and the Bank of Japan had a base rate of something like 4 percent, and what we found was even after that differential started to come down to 10 percent, the spot price continued to rise afterwards, meaning it took a while for those carry trades to actually unwind. There wasn't as quick of a process of unwinding. It didn't turn on dime. Actually, spot prices took a while to catch up.

So, returning to your question, in my longer-term trading analysis, I might take into account the fact that although interest differentials are converging or diverging, it takes the spot price a while to catch up with some of that interest rate movement. But it does, in fact, historically tend to catch up with the interest rate differential. So if there's any primary long-term fundamental tool that I use in forecasting currency movements, it's definitely interest rate differentials from nation to nation.

Q: How many hours a day do you spend trading?

A: Three to six hours per day, which includes the planning of trades and analysis, and so forth. The rest of the time I write, answer e-mail, and spend time with my family or my other community responsibilities.

Q: What is your typical day like?

A: If you look at my day from a 24-hour perspective, it goes something like this:

I go into the office at about 7:00 A.M. Eastern time, and I trade the short-term New York session if a setup comes along, and if I haven't already reached my profit goal for the week. I answer e-mails and keep an eye on long-term charts at the same time. I also chat on instant messaging with some of the best traders that I know. By 12 noon, I'm done with the short-term trading, and I move on to producing content for my Web site, and planning long-term trades. In the afternoon I try as often as possible to also go back home and spend time with my family, wrestle with my son, or play with my baby daughter, and help out around the house. In the evenings I do more long-term analysis, read with my wife and kids, help put the kids to bed, and then do more long-term analysis.

I don't often get up in the middle of the night any longer, but when I do, that is a perfect time to check on some of the longer-term trading.

Q: What is your goal for the week?

A: I have a point target in my trading account, a goal for a number of points of profit, or pips, that I want to make per week. But I don't have a dollar-based earnings target. I find that thinking too much about a certain dollar amount, or an item that I want to buy, takes my focus off what the market is able to give me, and puts the emphasis dangerously upon what I want the market to give me. I've pretty much consistently decided that Rob Booker is a 50- to 100-pip a week trader, meaning I understand the limits of my trading capacity—and over 50 to 100 points of profit, I start getting a little bit crazy. I become a little bit less disciplined and a little bit more euphoric to put it mildly. So I have not generally done a lot to increase that pip target over time even though systems that I build might produce bigger gains.

This is actually something that I strongly believe in. There are two things that I haven't mentioned so far that I feel are really important, and one of them is that there is a misconception that, in order to be considered successful as a trader, one has to earn a certain dollar amount per week, or per month, or per day. One thing that I've tried to communicate to beginning traders is to never be concerned with comparing your own pip results or percentage results or dollar results to anyone else except for yourself. I'm not in competition to make more money than Joe Trader. I'm in competition to make sure that I make enough money to support my family. So I've been to expos and conferences and I've spoken around the world and traders who are new to trading will say, "Well, Rob, how many pips did you make last year, or this month?" and I'll discuss it with them and they'll say, "Well that is far less than Joe Trader, or so and so making."

And I will tell them all the time, well I wasn't aware that Joe Trader was trying to pay my bills. I wasn't aware that I was under some demand to compete with anyone else. That's really important for me and has been a real benefit to me in the long run. Just to remember that I'm not in competition with anybody else for a certain type of gain. So, no, the answer is I have not generally increased that goal and when I have increased that pip goal, I found that I become somewhat overconfident after a series of wins or too despondent after a series of losses. What I do when I trade for 50 to 100 pips a week is if I have a good week, then the next week after, I start it all over again. I reset the clock. I reset the pip count to zero and if I have a bad week the next week when I start back up it's a blank slate. It's a 50- to 100-pip week. I don't have to make back what I lost the week before. I just have to produce what I know statistically I can produce. Not what I have to produce in order to make up for a previous loss, or prove that I'm better than someone else. I just have to take advantage of what ever comes my way during the week to reach that goal.

Q : That's a good point. So you don't increase your positions the next week to cover losses that you may have made the prior week?

A : [Laughter.] No and that's always been troublesome for me and when I have done that, its certainly where I've gotten into the deepest pit, which is when I've had a really good week and I've thought the market's just going to shower me with sweet profit forevermore and I will never see another losing week. Well, usually that's right after the market's ranging in exactly the way I like and then it's going to break out into a trend the week after and just savagely beat me to a pulp. So I try to say never trade the last trade, only trade the opportunity that is in front of me. Once I reach my weekly goal, I either stop trading or reduce the size of the trades so far that I can't possibly do any damage to my account. The overarching goal for me is to protect the account, then all I have to do after that is make money every week and build the account bit by bit. The most amazing financial discovery in the history of humankind is the principle of compounded gains. I tell this to every new trader: If you can build your account, bit by bit, you will realize spectacular profits over the long run, even if it doesn't look like much in the short term. I might be overemphasizing this point. But it has been important for me to remember that making money as a trader means that I grind out regular profits, over and over again, and focus on consistency, not on the big score or a huge lottery-type payoff.

Q: Let's talk a little bit about your trading tactics. Do you typically make your first trade more of a probative trade or do you go all into the position?

A: It depends on which trading system I'm going to be employing. If I'm taking a short-term trade based on the 15-minute chart in the New York session, which I call a *New York–session box trade*, I'm all in on the first trade and all out at the exit point, meaning that it's a point-A to point-B trade. It's not based on a news event. It's not based on a spike that's created by any fundamental analysis necessarily. But it's basically a support-and-resistance system that triggers an entry and triggers an exit that is very well defined and I'm all in from the start. On my long-term trading I am much more likely to initiate a position with between 30 percent and 50 percent of my total available position size for that trade and then add to the position as it goes in my favor and is proving to be the right decision. I prefer not to add to losing positions or cost-average. That has never worked for me personally.

Q : What timeframe charts do you look at?

A : My favorite timeframe chart is the one-hour chart. That's where it all happens for me. In the past I've extensively used the 15-minute chart and others, but right now my main focus is on the one-hour.

I often take positions on the one-hour chart and hold them for a day or longer. I regularly hold these positions overnight, and because I've got a defined risk and a specific profit target, I can just let the trade go without my attention. Like most traders, I check on my trades regularly (and somewhat compulsively), but I generally try my best to let them run their course.

Q : So you basically range trade more in the short-term and trend trade more in the long term then?

A : [Laughter.] Well it is exactly the opposite. Historically, I look for breakouts into trends on the short-term charts and in the long-term, I have been far more successful trading the corrective patterns in ranging markets.

Q : So how many positions do you generally have at the same time?

A : When I first started trading, I would have a whole basket of positions open at the same time. I might have six or seven positions based on a similar system on a similar timeframe chart across a variety of currency pairs. So I might take a position on the British pound/U.S. dollar and then simultaneously take a position, for instance, in the euro/Canadian dollar. Although I wouldn't necessarily be trading the same currency pair and they wouldn't be very correlated, the same fundamental principals would be used to initiate the trade, affording only a minor bit of currency pair diversification. But as I became more familiar with the currency pairs, I preferred one over the other. It is far more likely that I would actually trade one currency pair that I felt most comfortable with and maybe on occasion initiate a total of two or three separate positions at any given time.

Q : So basically a total of maybe three positions, no more than that at any time?

A : Right.

Q : Do you ever average down?

A : I am not a proponent of adding to a losing position, and recently I took a 6 percent loss on one account I manage, because I averaged down against my own rules and then could not—per my money management guidelines—add enough later on. So I exited the position at the maximum loss I allow myself to take, and boom! The trade turned just a bit later on. Whenever I break my rules, I get burned.

I prefer instead to add to winning positions, and those have been my big winners. When I'm on the way to a profit target that I have tested to be better than 80 percent accurate, there are stages along the way where it makes sense for me to capitalize on the good decision. It's not enough for me to always just let it run the course to profit—I want to maximize to the full extent the possible profit because my equity is growing as the trade is profitable, I can add positions and still keep my risk low.

I like to use the analogy of a relationship. If you are in a terrible relationship, and you can see that it's not working out the way that you wanted to, you should end the relationship. We've all been in relationships we should have ended more quickly. Trading is the same—if I'm in a position that is not doing what I expected it to do, I don't need to last it out or put more time and effort into it. I get out and move on. Conversely, if I am in a good relationship, I want to nurture it and let it grow. That's like a winning trade. You want to watch it grow, not cut it off. People who take half their profit off from a winning position are doing, in my opinion, the same thing as walking out on a perfectly good relationship.

Q : Are there any currency pairs that you avoid trading and any currency pairs that you love to trade?

A : One of my favorite currency pairs to trade in the short term, meaning the New York session in particular, during hours that I'm actually awake when the market is moving is the euro to the Canadian dollar (EUR/CAD). That's one of my all time favorite currency pairs in the short term. I also have a huge preference in the short term for the British pound/U.S. dollar just because it's what I've traded the longest and traded the most. I strongly dislike, and that's putting it mildly, the euro/U.S. dollar in the short term. I find that it's heavily traded, and there's a zillion levels of support and resistance. That means it has far less likelihood to break out of a range and travel very far or even stay within a range and travel far, and so in the short term, it does not provide the kind of opportunities that I'm interested in at all. In the longer term, the British pound/U.S. dollar is still my all-star favorite, all-time greatest currency pair ever. I love it the most. I don't trade the euro/Canadian dollar ever in the longer term, it's really a shorter-term type of currency pair.

Q : What is it about the euro/Canadian dollar that makes it such an interesting pair for you, because we are sure many traders have never even looked at that currency pair?

A : Well, in the shorter term, it's one of my favorites because if it tends to breakout, there's very often nobody on the other side to catch it, meaning there's not another set of orders on the other side waiting for it to get to some level based on an option or large stop-loss orders. I mean when the euro/Canadian dollar starts to move, it is because there is actual real momentum behind it and therefore it is not advisable to get in the way of that in a short-term. However, in the longer term, it doesn't tend to trend for long periods of time very much and isn't susceptible to the type of analysis that I do on the longer term for other currency pairs and it therefore simply does not test well for me in the longer term. So, if it breaks out of a recent level of support or resistance that's been intact for a couple of days, it's far less likely to stop very quickly like the euro/U.S. dollar or even the British pound/U.S. dollar to a certain extent. I attribute that to the fact that its not as heavily traded, there's not as many people waiting for it to get to certain level and so it is sort of off the radar or not really paid attention to.

Q : You've talked a lot about these systems that you're trading. Do you typically have your favorite system for the week that you're trading or are there a some systems that only give a few signals every so often, and that's why you're okay with trading multiple systems at one time? How do you manage that, because there are so many different indicators out there and there's so many different ways that people could trade, potentially creating a lot of counteracting signals?

A : I'll only really focus on two different strategies at the same time. That is, I'll have two strategies that I'm willing to trade and one strategy at least that's sort of in the laboratory being ready to replace a strategy that I'm no longer comfortable with for a variety of reasons. I might be bored with it. My schedule might not be able to accommodate that strategy any longer. Or, quite frankly, it might not be profitable any longer. It might have gone outside of the statistical deviation of where it's supposed to be producing results.

My short-term system on any given currency pair like the euro/Canadian dollar will produce anywhere between 5 and 10 trades per week that last anywhere from 15 minutes to 12 to 18 hours at the very most on the far outside of the bell curve.

Then on the longer term I'll really only be opening trades two or three times a week at the very most. Those are generally going to be on the British pound/U.S. dollar or the U.S. dollar/Swiss franc or maybe even the Canadian dollar/Japanese yen currency pairs. So I'll be somewhat diversified and I'll be waiting on one timeframe chart for the longer-term system to play out, and on the short-term charts, I'll have some activity that I can take advantage of and everything else just gets blocked out. Like I said, I'm a back tester as a career, so the majority of the time is spent verifying that what I'm doing is falling within the statistical norm of what I should be expecting.

I also experiment with new versions of the systems, all the time, to make sure I'm getting the most out of each of them. And very little time is actually spent in scanning the charts and hoping that I see something that I like. I've always found it to be far more detrimental to my trading to open up the charts in the morning and just look around for some action than it is to say here's the timeframe I watch, here's the system I use, and that's it, that's all I am going to focus on. There could be a thousand pips out there on every other timeframe chart, but I don't care about it. When I hear people say that they missed a trade on the U.S. dollar/South African rand because they weren't looking at that chart, and they've got 25 currency pairs on their screen and they're missing trades all the time, I always tell them that I missed on dating Julia Roberts in college, but then I never even met her. I never had a chance anyway. We're sometimes expecting to be able to take advantage of opportunities that our schedule really doesn't allow for, our mental capacity really doesn't allow for, and our trading capital really doesn't allow for. But we still get involved in it because we want to have a piece of the action. This fear of "missing out" on market action is what gets traders into trouble because we start to make trades out of a desire to make money, instead of reasonable analysis.

If you think of other professions, you can realize where specialization and focus come into play. The best lawyers are specialists in one type of law. The same for doctors and accountants. Successful traders are the same, so why should it be any different for a retail Forex trader if I specialize in the British pound/U.S. dollar in the long term and the euro/Canadian dollar in the short term? If it does well and pays the bills then there shouldn't really be a whole lot of temptation to experiment with real money on any other timeframe or currency pair.

Q : So you like to only trade the New York session, which is 7 A.M. to 12 P.M. EST. Do you ever place a trade afterwards?

A : I'm willing to place trades afterwards, based on the tested results of the system that I use, but it is very rare that the euro/Canadian dollar, for example, will create a New York session box trade after 12 noon. So I'll either miss that trade or take it later in the very rare circumstances that it occurs outside of the 12 noon time, which is usually between one and two times a month at the most, and that's my main short-term trading time. I'm generally always available during that time to take trades. In the longer term I'm opening trades anytime day or night because my setup only happens two to three times a week at the very most and I can see them setting up from a mile away. I publish the idea, I actually plan ahead for it. I know that it's coming. I set alarms and I've got a PDA that can tell me when the price is getting close to the entry and I make myself available. I make the sacrifice and I make sure that two or three times a week. I'm available and it's usually not that inconvenient for me to be up an hour early, or wake up in the middle of the night for a few moments to make sure that the entry has triggered, and it's what I expected it to look like. Then I just let it sit and I don't worry about it after that.

Q : On your shorter-term trades, do you ever use longer timeframes for verification? Do you care about what's happening on the daily charts at all, or do you just focus primarily on your own short-term signals?

A : I have a reputation for saying that confirmation is for Catholics that are 12 years old. In seminars I like to ask why people look at other indicators and they always say confirmation, cause that's the "c" word. I generally say that the difficulty in actually agreeing to place a trade increases proportionally to the number of timeframes that a trader will look at. Meaning the more timeframes and currency pairs that a trader looks at in order to actually justify taking the trade, the more confused that trader generally becomes because there could be conflicting signals. There would be a completely justifiable short-term buy trade on the British pound that would conflict completely with what someone might see on the 240-minute chart. What that does in my estimation is create a little bit of a conflict but if through testing and statistical evidence I can prove that incorporating a longer timeframe chart into my shorter timeframe trading makes it more profitable, then I'm perfectly willing to do it. Like I said before, I think nothing is really valid or invalid in trading, only testing makes it so. That's one of my favorite quotes that I made up. You have people walking around all the time saying never do this and never do that, well testing is really what makes the difference in whether something works or not. So I am willing to do that. I've on occasion actually traded short-term from the long-term charts. Meaning instead of looking at the long-term trend and then picking an entry on the short-term charts, I've actually looked at the long-term charts and basically just traded for the very short-term when it hits a major level of support and resistance. So it was actually sort of the opposite of looking for confirmation.

Q : So do you have any alarms or any beepers by your bed to tell you if things are happening over night?

A : I've tried the whole gamut. I've tried the baby monitor thing. I've tried the making my computer make some horrendous loud noise in the middle of the night, and what I do now is I essentially set the computer to send an e-mail to my PDA and it just buzzes or vibrates and I'm sent a text message to the PDA.

Q : What kind of equipment do you use?

A : I do 99 percent of my work on a Dell laptop. No extra monitors or anything. I do have a desktop that I can hook four monitors up to, but I usually have it running a music service or cable TV. At the office, I also have a few televisions and lots of food and music and other traders around me. It's a great environment for testing and trading.

Q : What was your best trade ever?

A : On December 4, 2003, I bought the euro/U.S. dollar at 1.2150, and I held on for 300 points. Every 25 or 50 pips, I added to the position. The euro was a rocket ship at that time, and I held on for dear life because I kept adding to the trade, and it moved so fast, I didn't have to hold it for long. This was one of the big lessons for me to realize that if I got the trade idea right, I needed to capitalize on it and instead of taking money off the table during the trade, I needed to move my stops up with the move, and then add more to the position. The key was to be aggressive when I was right. In this particular trade, I was very fortunate to seize the moment and pounce on the trade because we don't get long trends every day or every week in Forex—but when we do get a trend, it's really important that we get the most out of it.

I should have held that trade a lot longer if you look at it from a historical perspective, but there were not a lot of us back then that thought 1.3000 itself was a reachable goal.

Q : What was your worst trade ever?

A : My first account, it was that first trade that lost 90 percent in 72 hours. I had bought the euro, and I was enjoying a 10 or 20 pip gain on the trade, when I read some commentary online from some guy that said that euro was going to fall. I trusted someone else's convictions without testing anything for myself. Trusting in the analysis of a person I'd never met, I shorted the ever-loving heck out of the euro/U.S. dollar, and I held on because I was sure that he would never be handing out advice that was not top-notch. He would surely never be wrong and he positively knew what he was talking about.

Of course, his idea was garbage and I had done no testing to prove that he knew what he was doing. Of course, I took double the size of my regular trade. Of course, as the trade went against me I added more. Of course, as it really started to go against me, I sunk away and acted like it wasn't happening. It was a demoralizing experience to say the least. My friend who invested in the account with me was very supportive and basically said, "Never do that again." We remained friends.

Q : What is your favorite part of trading?

A : I think it's solving the pieces of the puzzle. It's approaching a problem and each trading system that I build or each trade that I take is really the foundation of having taken a complex set of information or data and coming up with a solution and then getting some what immediate feedback. So I like that process of the immediate feedback loop and putting together the pieces of a puzzle.

Q : Do you think it is more about entries or exits?

A : It's about both. It's about money management, and entries, and exits, and being disciplined. It's a complete package. I hear nonsense all the time about, "It's not where you enter, it's where you exit." And I have been guilty of saying those types of things myself and I was wrong if I ever did say it. Trading successfully is more like surgery or flying a plane. You've got to get all of it right. You can't say as a surgeon, it's not about the incision, it's about the stitches later on—that would mean it's ok to cut a leg off to do a skin graft. As a pilot, it's about the takeoff *and* the landing. You've got to get both right.

And how do you get them right? You test. You never trade anything before you test it.

Q : Lets talk a bit about the business of trading. How often do you pay yourself or extract your trading profits?

A : Every two weeks. I actually am set up as a business, and I am an employee of the company. I get paid and taxes are withheld automatically. This makes it a lot easier at the end of the year. We are paying taxes along the way. I've been told a thousand times that this is not the most economical way to do it, but I live well, I don't ever have to worry about it, and I am very happy.

Q : What do you do about medical bills? Insurance? Basic life expenses?

A : We run the medical insurance through the company. And I have very few basic life expenses. My wife and I try to be very frugal. We try not to spend a lot of money, and a lot of rooms in our house don't have furniture. To put it succinctly, we've tried to live below our means.

To put it less succinctly, a wise trader told me that when I was learning to trade that I should not attempt to live like a successful trader. I see a lot of successful traders who have doors on sawhorses for desks, or work on an old computer, or who still drive a used car. I also see a lot of unsuccessful traders who are driving new cars, have lots of credit cards, have brand new computers, and who spend a lot of money as if they've already started to make a lot of money. It's a matter of personal preference, of course, but I prefer not to spend money.

Q : Right now you do some coaching and mentoring, correct? How many people have you coached and mentored?

A : 1,057.

Q : How many of those are profitable?

A : At any given time, I'm in close touch with or I'm tracking the performance and communicating with any where between 550 to 600 of those traders. This means I'm not receiving an e-mail from them every day, but they're updating their performance on my Web site or I'm in touch with them often enough to understand how they're doing. So I can't speak necessarily for all 1,057 of them in every moment of the day, especially the ones that I worked with in 2002 or 2003 that are long gone and just basically moved on, whether they're either doing well or not, but in that 550 to 600 persons, you've got a group that's about 50 percent strong. That is they are actually profitable week in and week out or at least at the end of the month. Meaning they're able to produce a consistent amount of profits on a regular basis, not 1,000 pips a week but something reasonable. For example, there's one individual who does between 400 and 600 pips a week. There's another individual who I worked with in New York, she recently discovered that she was really a 20 pip a week trader and consistently since early summer this year, every single week, week in and week out, counting the losses and wins every week, she comes out net 20. She's absolutely positively consistent with that and has been able to increase the size of her trades to make 20 pips worth more money. Then there's a group of people in the 30 percent range that are still struggling at breakeven or up slightly better or slightly worse. These are individuals who work full time, who have external pressures, who are new to the training, and who don't have a background in trading at all and are having a seriously difficult time working with the terminology or just the fundamentals. Finally, there's the remaining group that for a variety of reasons, because my training isn't adequate for them or because they simply weren't as serious about it as they thought they were or because they're impulsive or because of whatever other reasons, they're still losing money, or because I am not helping them in the way that they will respond to. I'm making some changes to the way that I train people to do a better job of conquering some of the deepest trading problems that some of this group have. I have flown unsuccessful students out to my office and put them up so that I can work with them personally. I haven't been able to make every single trader a hedge fund manager, but I have done a good job of laying the groundwork for a lot of people.

Q : Is there any strong characteristic of a person that gives you a sense that they're not going to make it? Or is not cut out for trading?

A : I don't know the right way to put this, and I guess I can be as immodest about this as I need to be to explain it, and I don't mean it to be that way. But I can generally tell from the beginning if someone's goals are somewhat outlandish, meaning if someone on day one of the training writes to me and tells me their goals for the training are to make between 1,000 and 2,000 pips per month or to take a 10,000 account and double that account before the end of the month, I can then really tell from some of those types of catch phases that I'm working with an individual who needs some deprogramming. So I invite them to consider some alternative perspectives so that they can approach trading from a different mind set. Those people don't always listen, though, because they're under some type of external pressure. When you're trading to pay your bills, it's significantly more difficult to stop when you're ahead by $20, especially when your gas bill in the winter is $250. They've got pressures on them that are more than just what an average impulsive individual would have. The second type of individual who's a little bit behind on the curve is going to be somebody who's just naturally impulsive. Someone who naturally makes decisions that are significant, really quickly, doesn't put a lot of thought into it, talks a lot about how their gut reaction to something is, XYZ, and they have a feeling that it's going to go up or down. Those types of individuals I invite as well to consider a different mindset and perspective. The people whom I can recognize are more successful at times are the people who seem to be very laid back about the training, meaning they're not as severe or have a type-A personality about the training or trading in general, but who are the type of people who enjoy testing and enjoy experimentation and are interested in validating or verifying the success of a system before they actually implement it with real money.

Q : You mentioned earlier that you have a network of traders that you trade with or communicate with. Are these all former students or external colleagues?

A : Ninety percent of them are former students. The rest of them would be professionals in the industry whom I trust, whom I might write and say, you know, I'm in the middle of this trade right now, and it's just awful, or it's going well, etc. Basically people who have different experience and can offer me a little bit of perspective. So there are people outside that range, but I feel really comfortable working with people who are former students. I am in the office right now in West Virginia, and here with me there's an individual from London, there are two people from Florida, two people from Arizona, and they're all former students and they just come out to hang out and test and trade. They're at varying levels of success, but that's really actually irrelevant. It's really about having a group of people to interact with, collaborate with; we sit down in front of the white board and we project the charts onto the white board where we can write on it. We actually back test together on a regular basis and make it a part of our daily routine. These types of people, they come and go as they please in the office, which is perfect since the office was open for that type of thing to take place.

Q : That's great. Does your wife trade at all?

A : No.

Q : She has no interest?

A : No interest whatsoever. She attended the French Culinary Institute in Manhattan and she's a pastry chef, so she has interests that lie in different areas.

Q : Wasn't she working at a hedge fund before, when did she become a chef?

A : Kind of off topic, but not so far off the topic. She worked two and half to three jobs the entire time that I was in law school to pay the bills, and she got up at four o'clock in the morning to go downtown to San Francisco to reconcile trades for a hedge fund, and this hedge fund manager lost between $70 and $80 million in one day on OEX options. My wife was reconciling the trades the day after all these option trades blew up and that represented at least 35 or 40 percent of the total assets in the fund at that time. So she worked all kinds of jobs and worked just a ton of hours to help us get by.

Q : Why did you decide to settle in West Virginia?

A : I'm in Wheeling, which is outside of Pittsburgh, Pennsylvania, and this is a long version of the story, but I sold a business to a group of people in Charleston, West Virginia. I traveled to West Virginia, loved the state, loved the pace of life. I'd lived in big cities my whole life, so my wife and I visited here and settled down to live in a place that was safe, quiet, close enough to a big city that we could get everything we wanted.

Q : Do you think that having children has changed your trading style at all or at least the times that you can trade?

A : Significantly. In some respects it's like anything else that would take your focus away, but in another respect I want my to spend time with them instead of doing other things, so it's not like having a regular job where you don't want to be there and you're thinking about trading. With having kids, I could care less about the charts and I just want to focus on them. Before I was much more used to getting up earlier and taking far more short-term trades. But as soon we adopted our first son, I became much more focused on developing systems and trading from the longer term charts.

Q : Did you ever play any sports?

A : I was a wrestler, but I was 0 and 1 and the only reason I scored any points was because the guy kept throwing me outside that circle and every time he threw me outside that circle they gave me two points. Which I guess was the penalty for throwing the guy outside the circle. So, actually, at one point in that match I was ahead of him, because he'd throw me outside the circle so many times and then he pinned me and it was over.

Q : So do you think this ultimately sums up the whole fact that you don't have to feel competitive with other people?

A : I'm not sure that this one experience did anything except hurt my pride for a few years. But now I'm very competitive with myself and I hope that I could be described as the type of person who is not very competitive with other people. I do believe that. I don't really care if somebody does better than I do [laughter]. It doesn't matter, I'm happy for them. Trading is never about the money, it is about the quality of life and whether I can continue to solve the puzzle, so to speak. I am not one to hang myself over losses. One trade is one in a thousand that I took before and a thousand that will come after. It is a lifestyle. For example, I managed some accounts for a while and they didn't go as well as I would have liked, and I let that go. I found that I dwelt on the losses more when it was other people's money, and I was far more emotionally stable when I traded my own funds. Trading my own account is a career choice I made. The losses and ups and downs come as part of the experience. I'm a better trader than I was last year, and the year before, and so on. And I'm going to be a better trader next year and the year afterward. It's a process. You don't just walk into a law firm one day and decide that you're going to be the managing partner. You gotta work your way up. Through it all, I've never really honestly considered giving it up just because I wasn't doing as well as somebody else.

Q : Any parting words?

A : Yes, one thing. I seriously dislike it when I hear people say that they've been taught they should trade only with money that they can afford to lose. I might be the only guy saying this out there, but I seriously believe that that phrase is enormously damaging because it teaches people that the money they're using to trade is not significant enough to be protected. The first and last and most important thing is that I'm a defensive trader. So I feel that there is no excuse for losing the entire amount of trading capital, meaning if that's money that people can afford to lose, then I'd rather have them give it to me and I can take them to the movies and we can take a long walk on the beach, hang out together, and we still have something to show for it later. But it is not money that people can afford to lose. It represents somebody's financial future. We would never move into a house that we could afford to have burn down. We would never buy a car and only buy it if we could afford to have it smashed into a semi-truck. But we regularly open our trading accounts with money that we say we can afford to lose, and so it's as if we're from the beginning saying: "Well, this money wasn't very important to me." I think to certain degree that the money that we're entrusted with to trade is sacred money that not only represents the amount that's in the account today, it represents what it could be later on in life—the quality of life that it could provide for someone. So it's much more important than just money that someone can afford to lose.

LESSONS FROM ROB BOOKER
Fit Trading to Your Personality

In this interview, Rob Booker has shared with us some of his favorite trading techniques. However, we feel that the key lesson to learn from this interview is that knowing yourself is more important than any particular trading strategy that you may choose. You need to make sure that your style of trading is in sync with your personality. If you are a short-term trader, you should focus on short-term profits. If you are long-term trader, you should focus on longer term or bigger profits. Furthermore, you should never trade a strategy with a significant amount of capital without back testing and forward testing it first.

Test Everything

Before Rob Booker implements any strategy, he will spend hours and hours studying the mechanics of the strategy to understand when it works and when it doesn't. He feels that his job is to be a back tester first and a trader second. Therefore, his cardinal rule is to never trade a strategy unless he can first prove that it has been profitable in the past. For new traders, back testing may sound daunting. However, it does not need to be as complicated as it seems. There are a lot of different ways to back test. The fancy way is go out and learn a programming language to generate results systematically. However even though Rob Booker knows how to code now, at the beginning he back tested everything manually. One easy way for new traders to start is to simply review the charts going back in time to look for instances when your setup triggered a buy or sell signal and to record the actual performance of the trade At bare minimum, we encourage traders to first look for at least 20 to 50—this depends on the timeframe you are trading—samples of the pattern and only after that do we recommend traders move into forward or live-testing phase. This means that the strategy is actually traded in current market conditions using either a demo or mini-account. The reason why this is important is because the psychological element of trading can always alter results by revealing the difficulty of reacting to live market conditions. Along the same lines, a minimum of 20 to 30 winning trades needs to be made before the strategy is ready for prime time.

Don't Fall Victim to "Possum Trading"

Rob Booker believes that you should never let yourself fall victim to what he calls "possum trading." When a trade is going bad, it may be very tempting to shut off the computer and hope that it will all get better if you stop watching the market. However, this almost never happens. Instead, more often than not, the losses will only become greater. Therefore, it is important that we all focus on trading *defensively*. Trading is a game of survival. If you can protect your capital, you can always live to trade another day. This is why Rob Booker's first goal is to not lose money and his second goal is to find a way to grind out profits consistently. He feels that one of the biggest mistakes is to trade only with money that you can afford to lose. Of course, he is not suggesting that everyone should mortgage their houses and trade with money that they cannot afford to lose, but what he is telling us is that every dollar, yen, pound or euro is hard earned. If you are trading with money that you can afford to lose, then it means that you are trading with money that you feel is not important enough to be protected. The money you trade should be viewed as potential wealth later on in life. Therefore, before risking it in the market, you need to make sure that you are risking it in a smart way. You only want to apply it to strategies that have already been battletested rather than just jumping into the markets on a whim.

CHAPTER 4

THE COOLEST GUY IN THE ROOM

CHUCK HAYS

Of all the traders we've interviewed, Chuck Hays is one of the coolest guys around both in temperament and in style. He makes his living in the highly chaotic world of e-mini stock index futures where the difference between fortune and failure can be measured in seconds. Yet Chuck rarely loses control and he often wins by violating some of the most sacrosanct rules of trading. Brutally honest, Chuck believes traders should first understand their individual strengths and limitations and trade accordingly. A very generous trader, Chuck has counseled and coached scores of futures traders in his own free time. Due to his natural Midwestern modesty and nonchalance, Chuck tends to downplay his accomplishments. He is, however, one of the best risk takers in the retail trading game. We had the pleasure to interview Chuck from his home office in Minnesota.

■ ■ ■

Q: Were you exposed to the markets in your childhood?

A: Oh, much later in life. I didn't do any trading until 1999.

Q: What about investing prior to that? Did you have any experience with stocks at all?

A: No. None.

Q: What did you do prior to that?

A: I used to take some distressed businesses, some of them were convenience stores and a nightclub, and I would try to fix them up and resell them. Then I worked as a product manager for companies designing automotive test products.

Q: So what made you switch to trading? Did you just like that industry?

A: You know I went to a seminar where they were talking about trading options on stocks, and I actually did that a little bit while I was still employed, but it wasn't very long after that where I figured out that the options markets was really not the way go. It was too expensive. They didn't trade nearly enough, there were a lot of disadvantages, so I decided to stop working and go strictly to day trading.

Q: The seminar you went to, that was your first exposure to finance, what really tickled your fancy? Why did you get so interested in that subject?

A: I think it's the same reason that people would love to do what I do, which is the lure of short days, high profits, high risk. Unfortunately, that's not really the reason people should go into what I do, but that is what the allure is.

Q : How long did you trade options on the side before you came to the conclusion that this was a pretty losing proposition for a retail trader?

A : About a year.

Q : How was that process? Did you break even? Did you lose some money? What was the end result?

A : You know, I think that, looking back, I probably did all right for a while. But like a lot of beginning traders, I ended up losing all of my profits on one or two trades by getting stubborn.

Q : Were you trading news events? Would you buy options in anticipation of some positive news?

A : I was probably more of a technical trader. I never considered myself very good at interpreting news, even today.

Q : How did technical trading come into your skill set? How did you gravitate to that right away?

A : Oh, that is a great question. Well, let me add to that a little bit. I think that almost every trader whom I mentored as far as stocks or futures go wants to make it a science. They want to be able to look at a chart, study, work hard, find some magic indicator of solving the market. In the end, I don't think that's how successful traders trade. But in the beginning, it seems that everyone goes through that process.

Q : They try to engineer a profit, right?

A : Absolutely, and I see it all time with new traders. And no matter what you tell them, you can tell them up front that this is not a science. It's very beneficial to be a good chartist. But that's not what will make you money in the long run. Coming from my technical background, I wanted to make it a science protocol, and I think that probably for the better part of my first two years of trading NASDAQ stocks I still tried to make it a science. I was very fortunate the first couple of years because I traded after the tech bubble burst of early 2000. We had some great down markets and I was a much better short trader than I was a long trader. It was really later on when I decided that the reason there are so many technical indicators out there is because none of them work very well.

Q : How did you even find out about technical analysis, and what did you do to teach yourself the basics of chart reading?

A : I read the book *Trading for a Living* by Elder.

Q : That was the foundation, and then obviously you looked at thousands and thousands of charts?

A : Yes. I was fortunate in the beginning to realize that you couldn't go out and trade a lot of different instruments and be good at them. In the beginning, I only traded three or four stocks, and I didn't deviate from that.

Q : What stocks did you trade in the beginning?

A : In the beginning we had Rambus and CMGI and Yahoo! and QCOM. All those stocks that were skyrocketing $10 to $20 a day. We don't have great stocks like that today.

Q : You entered the day trading business around 1999?

A : July of 1999.

Q : Tell us a little bit about that, what did you do? Did you join a firm, and what was that like? What was your experience just walking in that first day?

A : We were real fortunate here in Minneapolis to have a firm called NBX Trading, and they catered to and specialized in day traders. So we used the firm's hardware and traded strictly for commissions.

Q : What were the commissions like for you in stocks?

A : They were three cents—per side.

Q : So it cost you more than a nickel to just get in and out of a stock?

A : Yes.

Q : This was before decimalization, so you were still trading in sixteenths and eighths and quarters, right?

A : Yes. It was interesting. I was looking forward to decimalization, but it really ruined the markets for day trading stock.

Q : Because it narrowed the bid-ask spread and made the markets very, very thick? [*Authors' note:* Decimalization greatly reduced the difference between bid and ask by reducing the spread to sometimes just a penny. Therefore, a trader who bought on the bid and sold on the ask saw his profit margins squeezed by more than 90%, from 12.5 cents (1/8th of a dollar) to just 1 cent.]

A : Exactly.

Q : 1999. This was the go-go years of the Internet phase, stocks moving $10 to $20 a day. You say that you're a better short, trader than you are long trader. But this was still the last of the long run. How did you manage to succeed in that environment?

A : I think it was really tough for the first six months. I was fortunate that in 2000 the market started to go down. But that time I had been at it for seven or eight months and I had a pretty good idea what I was good at, and then for the next couple of years we had wonderful, down markets. And it was easy to make money, it really was. But I have found out from being around successful traders that almost all of those successful traders are better one way or the other. They're either better long or better short, and they know that.

Q : When you first started out, what was you initial capitalization?

A : I started with $150,000.

Q : So you were pretty well capitalized, and then did you give yourself capital aside from this to live on? So this wasn't a situation where you had to make money right away?

A : Exactly. I think it's a real handicap for people if they are in a situation with the high cost of living and a lot of payments. It is very, very difficult to make money. As a matter of fact, I found with traders who are struggling that if they absolutely have to make money on some particular day, they will lose money.

Q : How much time did you give yourself internally? Did you say I'm going to give myself six months or a year before I succeed?

A : You know, I don't really remember. I do remember in the first year that I lost $50,000, and that was pretty good actually.

Q : So you were realistic enough to understand that this was going to be difficult and you had to just stay in the game?

A : Today I tell brand new traders that you are not going to make money in first year. I've only seen one trader do that who traded futures. But he had a huge amount of experience trading markets prior to moving to futures.

Q : When you first started trading, what was your basic strategy?

A : The same thing as today, although I would love to be a better swing trader I know now and—it took me a couple years to figure this out—that I was a great scalper. I like to play a lot of contracts, sell a lot of shares, for very small profits over and over again.

Q : You would basically fade extremes right from the beginning?

A : Yes, and if you had first seen me trade, I was no different then than I am now.

Q : So you've really stayed very consistent right from the get go. You remained in sync with your core personality?

A : Yes.

Q : The first year you lost $50,000, why do you think that was? Was it a matter of just learning how to have better timing? Better risk control? What were you doing wrong then that you've improved since?

A : I think it's a matter of seeing an entire year's worth of markets where you to go through earnings season. You need to go through slow times. You need to see a holiday season. You need to see all those kinds of markets. At the beginning, you make too many mistakes. I think the first goal for all traders is to learn how to stop losing money. For me that means not trading in the middle of the day and realizing that the very last hours of the day trade differently than the first hour of the day. It's a process where you learn to stop making so many mistakes.

Q: Can you give a more detailed idea of how the first hour of the day sets up and then the last hour of day? What are the differences between the two and what are the unique characteristics of each one of those particular parts of the day?

A: I think the first hour is when we see a lot of retail customers and volume. We also have a lot of news early in the day that gives us kneejerk reactions to play. When you get in the middle day, where the volume drops off, there are different forces at work. I'm not great at sensing those. Fade trades do not work nearly as well in the middle of the day. When you get into the last part of the day, when you have funds balancing their positions it is much more difficult to fade the market within the last half hour, and that's what I'm best at. After doing this for seven years now, I know that. I understand that about myself, and I try to be more careful of the trade at the end of the day. I also trade much smaller sizes at the end of the day.

Q: So your most confident trades are at the beginning of the day?

A: Absolutely.

Q: If we were going to distill it to one simple sentence, and obviously it's much more complex than that, but the overarching philosophy is this. You tend to have lots of news flow at the beginning of the day. Lots of excited retail order flow, lots of what we in the business call *dumb money*, which is just sort of money chasing news. Your basic modus operandi is that once it reaches an extreme you begin to fade it because then you're going to get some retracement and rebalancing, which provide you with profit opportunities.

A : Yes, absolutely. That's what I have made my money doing.

Q : Of course, that sounds a lot simpler than it is because finding the top or the bottom during those times is much more difficult in real life. Timing is everything.

A : Timing is everything and I also understand that I am unlikely to get the best entry when I first take the position. I almost always expect to add to the position when I take it.

Q : So you are always a scale-up, scale-down trader. Your first trade is almost always probative, right?

A : Yes, I firmly expect to add to it anyway. It increases your chance of success a great deal when you understand that because trying to make perfect entries and book them—if that's what it takes for you to make money—then the market's going to take your money and you're going to lose.

Q : On a day-to-day basis that's a great strategy. However, we all know that it comes at a very, substantial cost because in a one-way market that kind of a scale-up strategy can just decimate your profits. You can lose sometimes a week's worth of profits in one trade, right?

A : Yes, that's true. But I wouldn't say it takes a week's worth of profits. It certainly can be hard on you for one day. We've experienced some of those markets right now, where the Dow wants to go up to all-time highs and the rest of the market kind of creeps up with it. If it trends, it's very difficult to make money. However, we are not in that sort of trending market very often.

Q : Do you have a mental limit to how many times you will add into a trade? When you just say, "That's it. It's a one-way market, I'm getting out. I have to cut my losses."

A : You know, a lot of people ask me that, a lot of traders around here ask me that. I don't look at it that way. If we have an average of an 11-point swing in the ER [a daily move from low to high in the Russell 2000 of 110 ticks], everyday you know you might be able to take a point and a half or two and be fine. But if we have a 20-point normal range, you might get three point shake outs and you need to trade accordingly. If you simply trade by hard and fast scientific-type rules, eventually the market will take your money.

Q : Could you explain that a little more? Let's say the average trading range in the Russell 500 is 10 points, just using 10 as an equal number. If you're using stop losses of a point and half that are within the noise level, you'll just get stopped out continuously. Is that what you're saying?

A : What I'm saying is if a spread goes against me a point, or point and quarter, I may add to it there, and do very well on the trade. What I'm saying is there are some markets where we had an average range of about 18 or 19 points a day like this summer, in which case, a point and a quarter or point and a half stop probably won't work.

Q : So when you have this massive range expansion, and obviously you never know that it's going to occur, you never know you're in the midst of hurricane until everything swirls around you. What kind of risk control do you apply to yourself? Do you have a hard-and-fast rule? Or is it always matter of feel?

A : I think it's always a matter of feel for me.

Q: Is there a monetary limit where you'll say, "You know, I just dropped $50,000, that's it. I'm not staying in this trade anymore"? Is there an absolute uncle point for you? Or are you always assessing the dynamic of the market?

A: Yes. Days I quit trading are the days where I just don't have a good feel for what's going on. It's like a pitcher having a bad day. You have to walk away and come back the next day with a zero on my P&L and start over.

Q: When you first started doing that, obviously you would have many, many successful days and then you would have some very bad, big hits to your equity. How did you deal with that psychologically?

A: I think that's the key to being a survivor in this business versus some people who are still sitting on the sidelines now. Oftentimes people ask how did you do today after the markets closed, and I usually know. Every once in a while I can't remember. It's just a game, and I get to start over again tomorrow and do the best I can. I don't have to worry about yesterday.

Q: You basically come in everyday with a clean slate?

A: Absolutely.

Q: It's like having no memory, and that helps you to have no emotion because you're not carrying all those scars around with you?

A: Absolutely. And if people looked at me without looking at my P&L they could not tell from my actions, activity, or emotions whether I'm up or down.

Q : Do you look at the P&L during the day and let it guide you? Or have you now learned to just look at the numbers, whether you're down 20,000 or up 50,000 and not really get too emotional?

A : I don't care—no. My goal is to make another good trade based on what's going on in the market. It doesn't have anything to do with last trade or the trade before or my P&L.

Q : Obviously that's great principle to aspire to. But in real life, what's the maximum amount of bad trades during the day that you've run into? Did you ever make four or five consecutive bad trades where you would either short, short, short, long, long, long and it would go completely against you?

A : You know, I can tell from experience that if I make four or five bad trades in row what the day is like. It's a day where it's creeping up all the day long. It always looks toppy to me, and after making four or five bad trades, I'll just come back the next day.

I've never found a good trader or a great trader who was good at every kind of market, and I know what my weaknesses are and I'm going have those days once in a while. In the long run we are going to have creeper days two or three days a month. I am going to have another opportunity tomorrow or the next day. A lot of new traders and a lot of people who are not trading anymore, they just know they're right and know they've got to make one more trade and then know they're going to have to win. Well, it doesn't work that way.

Q : Let's go back to the start of the career. You are trading for about a year, day trading stocks, starting to hit the big NASDAQ bear market. Your second year in the business what happens? What happens with your stock trading?

A : I'd go in every morning and I'd try to be done by 9:30 A.M. my time which is 10:30 A.M. market time, and I'd typically leave the office. I learned early on that I was a first-hour trader, so I practiced going in for an hour and half, trading and leaving.

Q : You were trading for an hour and half and then just leaving?

A : Yes, because I was very, very good at the first half of the day. It was a discipline that I learned that worked for me.

Q : What would you do the rest of the day?

A : Sometimes that was a challenge. I did find that once I left the office, and I couldn't trade, I wasn't tempted to go back and make one more good gambling trade. I love to win. I learned to accept that after the first hour, it wasn't going to happen. $500 or $5 or $5,000, walk away and string together those winners day after day after day.

Q : At that time did you create any kind of a monetary target for yourself every day?

A : No. I still don't do that.

Q : Do you think that is a dangerous game to play for traders?

A : Yes, and, as a matter a fact, I think it's a huge mistake for people to set monetary goals.

Q : Because it forces unnatural trades to reach those goals, right?

A : That's true and there are some days where there's a lot more opportunity. You can set a $500 goal, and you quit at $500, maybe the day offered $5,000. It's about going in and taking what the market offers you. Making good trades.

Q : So you basically learned to win. The second year you obviously started to have better profits, what happened next? You now have two years under your belt as a day trader and obviously reached a certain level of success. How do you discover stock index futures?

A : I was in a chat room, and one of the guys in there is always commenting about trading futures. So I asked him in private if I could call him and ask him why he did that, and I did. He said the bottom line was if you go trade futures and you are successful at it, you will never look back.

Q : Many of the equity day traders whom we've interviewed tell us that stock index futures are where equity day traders go to die. It's the single most difficult market in the world to trade.

A : I think that it is by far the most difficult in the world to trade, but somebody makes money at it.

Q : So he said once you get into futures, you'll never go back. So what happened then?

A : I started dabbling in both. I was trading two stocks and I traded the S&P 500 and the Nasdaq 100 futures. What was interesting is that I was good at trading the S&P 500, and I typically would lose a little money trading on the Nasdaq, so I stopped trading in Nasdaq and started trading strictly the S&P 500. About three summers ago, the volume in the ES (e-mini S&P 500) increased to such a level that it didn't want to move, which kind of lost its profitability. So I started looking for something a little more volatile and the ER [*Authors' note:* ER is the futures instrument for the Russell 2000—an index of smaller capitalization companies that tends to be much volatile than the S&P 500 or the Dow Jones index.] moves about twice as much per day as the S&P 500. Which means you either make money twice as fast or lose money twice as fast, right?

It is the hardest game in the world, but it's also the best game in the world.

Q : What makes stock trading and futures trading so different?

A : Volatility. Think about this: The Russell 2000 is trading at around 730 and it represents $70,300 worth of stocks, but you're only going to need a couple thousand dollars to buy the contract. So for $2,000, you can buy $70,000 worth of stock. It's very highly leveraged. It is traded by the best of the best, and their objective is to take your money, and they're very good at it. I tell new traders it's like deciding you're going to play football and lining up against a professional team your very first day. They're going to kill you.

Q : What about the physical differences between the two markets? The fact that stocks have a Level 2 with various market makers displaying a variety of bids and asks, whereas futures are traded through a central anonymous book?

A : It's been a while since I traded stocks and looked at Level 2. There are probably fewer games played with futures. However, that doesn't mean that there aren't plenty of games played.

Q : The anonymity of the book makes it advantageous to trade, because it hides your own order flow. But it also makes it extraordinarily difficult to read the true directionality of the instrument, wouldn't you say?

A : I think that's true. The other thing is, I hate for people to try to read too much into what we're seeing in the book. If I were a couple hundred contracts into a trade, and I wanted to sell them, I certainly wouldn't put them out for sale and show them. I would try and hide what I'm doing, and I think that's true of all the really big traders and the really great traders. So I tell people, if it is not on the inside of the bid and the offer it doesn't mean a whole lot.

Q : So what's the basic protocol for you to try and read the price action in futures?

A : Prior to being in a trade, I'm pretty much watching the chart. I'm not watching order flow very much. Once I'm in a trade, I watch the order flow a little better. I will watch for who's refreshing on the bid and the offer. But prior to that time, I'm pretty much a chart trader.

Q : So you'll enter on a chart signal, but manage the trade, by watching the book itself, the order flow?

A : Yes. Yes. I don't know if that's good or not, it's just that I have a difficult time watching the order flow if I don't have anything at risk.

Q : What about the order flow catches your eye and makes you say this is interesting, this is something I need to react to?

A : I think all traders probably follow order flow a whole lot more when they're on the wrong side of the trade [laughter]. It's true, I really pay a lot more attention when I'm out of the money. Every once in while you'll notice that someone continues to sell or continues to buy at a certain level, and that's a lot more obvious if you are a few ticks out of the money. If I'm in the money, I don't pay much attention to it because I like to try and stay in the trade longer.

Q : Are you going back and forth between the book and the chart? Is the book itself overlaid on the chart so you can see both the price action and the chart action at the same time?

A : No. These are two different programs on different PCs.

THE COOLEST GUY IN THE ROOM

Q: Do you physically look at both screens, or do you really almost forget the chart action once you're in trade and you just look strictly at the price action?

A: Oh no, I watch the chart. But I guess the point is, prior to being in a trade, I don't pay a whole a lot of attention to the book action.

Q: Do you use activity in one index as clue to a potential movement in the other index?

A: Yes.

Q: So if you see one index beginning to move, let's say you see the ES starting to move but the ER is stationary, is that enough information for you to try a long trade?

A: Definitely.

Q: Do you always add to positions, or are there some probative trades where maybe it doesn't go your way, you don't have that much confidence in your position, and you just simply say hey I'm wrong and I'm going to get out?

A: Lots of times.

Q: So it's not an ironclad rule that you're going to add to a position continuously. A lot of times you'll just come in and out, and take small hits if you're not really feeling it?

A: Sometimes I make a small trade just to get a better feeling for the market.

Q: When you make that kind of a small trade, and you say you want to get a better feel for the market, what makes you feel the market better by making that small trade?

A: Forces me to pay attention.

Q: Forces you to focus. So the biggest benefit is that now you have money on the line and you want to pay a lot more attention to price action?

A: Yes.

Q: Could you give us an idea of your basic day? How do you start it? What do you do?

A: One of the worst things for me is to go sit at my computer, too soon. If I get up early and I go sit at my computer, by the time 8:30 or 9:30 market time I am so ready to trade that it's bad for my trading style. I'm a whole lot better off to come in 15 minutes before the market opens, look at the major headlines, look at the chart structure. I don't really pay attention to what happened over night and make trades. The riskiest trade in the day is the first one, in the first five minutes.

Q: Why is that the riskiest trade of the day?

A: You begin to see who the dominant forces are, whether they are going to try to move the market up or down, and you want to work hard in that first 45 minutes because that's when the best opportunities exist.

Q: What kind of clues do you see in price action that would make you think—oh, they're going to start moving the market up today?

A: Actually this morning was a great example. The market gapped down, they managed to push ER down a couple of points and it was real obvious when you watched the book to see the buyers move in, and they were willing to buy everything that was for sale over and over again. So this morning was a pretty good example of when we had the opportunity for the market to go down, the bulls moved in and bought it up.

Q: So seeing that made you join the bid and come in with the buyers, right?

A: Yes.

Q: So you try to come in maybe 15 minutes before the open, clearly focus on the first 45 to 90 minutes of trade, what happens then?

A: Then I really want to get away from it for a while. The middle of the day is not what I'm good at. I think most day traders would tell you that is certainly not where they make most of their money. I like to leave my house and go do something else for a while.

Q: Can you give us an idea of your office setup?

A: I use one PC for nothing but charting and it has four monitors on it.

Q: What kind of timeframes do you look at?

A: [Laughter.] It changes all the time. However, I will tell you that I always have a 15-minute chart of ES and the ER. I have a five-minute chart up of both and then I have another chart that I continually play with. I am just like every other trader—I'm always looking at different indicators. I'll play around with them for a while see if there's anything to them. Most often there is not, and I'll clean the chart off and I'll start over.

Q : Are there any indicators that are sentimental favorites or at this point you almost look at a clean chart? You don't even really have indicators on it?

A : I really am in favor of moving averages. What I use is something called *MoveTrend*, which is very similar to a moving average. I will always have those on my charts. Everything else is optional. [*Authors' note:* MoveTrend is a proprietary indicator that tries to create a more timely moving average.]

Q : Do you use that because it removes the noise and gives you a cleaner view of the directionality of the move?

A : Exactly, and that's why it's also important to have a 15-minute chart up looking back several days and see what the trend is. It's very easy to get focused in on a three-minute chart or a one-minute chart or a five-minute chart and miss the big picture. The bigger size is trading longer timeframe charts. You don't want to fight those guys.

Q : To take that to the next step, if you're starting to see selling action on the short-term chart, but on the longer-timeframe chart it looks like it's really an area of support, then it's probably a good, high probability trade to be a buyer at that point?

A : Yes, and I think that right now that is never more evident than looking at a daily chart on the S&P 500, we've been in a long uptrend. But we'll have two or three days in a row where it looks like a bear market, and then the big boys move in and then it will build up some more.

Q : One computer with nothing but charts on it, what else is in the trading room?

A : Well I guess that one trading PC has four monitors and I play around with different charts. But I stick to the most basic 5- and

15-minute charts and they're always up there. On my other PC, I have two monitors. One runs the execution platform through the brokerage firm. I will keep a Web browser up so I can look at the headlines on a couple of news sites. I'm not real big on news sites. I look at Dow Jones, and I'll look at CBS Market Watch headlines. I don't dig much beyond that because I don't care what's happening with individual stocks, I only really care about the direction the market is moving. Then, as you well know, I run my own chatroom.

Q : So, overall this is enough to give you the flexibility you need?

A : It gives me everything I need.

Q : Do you come back to the screen at around 3 P.M. East Coast time?

A : In the last hour and half. I like the first 30 minutes to see what the market is doing. The last hour of day is when the volume picks up a little bit and, although I'm not nearly as good as an end-of-the-day trader, I will come in and try and make a couple of good trades.

Q : Would you say that, on balance, by the end of the day you're going to try to maybe join the trend more than fade it? Of course, every day being different—but if you see strength, do you usually want to go with that strength?

A : Yes.

Q : And will you follow the same methodology if you see strength, but there's a little bit of retracement initially, you may add to the position a couple of times just to stay true to that bias?

A : Yeah, I think that's true. I guess the modification that I make at the end of the day is that I am a lot less likely to fade the market.

Q: But you'll still use those multiple-entry techniques to position yourself?

A: Yes. I think you increase your chances of success several-fold if you are willing to scale in and scale out.

Q: Clearly, every trade is very different, but what would you say is the average time span of your trades?

A: Less than 10 minutes. I have a lot of trades that last less than two minutes.

Q: Is that difficult for you emotionally or mentally, since futures markets can be extraordinarily fast? I mean, prices can literally go up and down one or two points in a matter of 20 seconds. Do you like that? Or do you find that discombobulating?

A: No that's what I like. Give me the volatility, give me short timeframe trades, that's what I like.

Q: The longer you're in a trade, the more antsy you get?

A: Well, if I am in it for 30 minutes, I'm probably on the wrong side of it. If I was on right side of it, I would have taken the money and moved on to the next trade.

Q: Do you find that it's the skill of your trade management that really turns potentially bad trades into good trades?

A: I wish I could say I'm always on the right side and they always go my way, but typically I'm early in my entries. So I expect them to go against me a little bit. It would be nice to always go with the momentum and have it always work out, but that's not typically the way it goes.

Q : Would you say that you're even sometimes surprised if your first entry tends to be the turn trade?

A : I don't know if I'm surprised, but I'm certainly happy about it.

Q : In futures you have a centralized book, first-come, first-serve market. There is no discrimination between large and small players. Is that a great attraction of the market for you?

A : Yes. It is very, very simple, very straightforward. It's a very difficult game, but very simple and I do not think that it helps us to try to make it more complicated.

Q : Is that because basic price action is highly repetitive day in and day out?

A : Yes. However, I think it's important, even though we see the same things over and over and over again, that most great traders are going to find they are good at one or two things, and they practice those same things over and over again. Although we see the same patterns, you're not going to be good at trading all patterns in all market situations.

Q : What kind of patterns do you feel you're best at trading?

A : I'm best in a choppy, scalper's market. I am worst in a trending, creeping market. I could be better and take the middle out of the momentum move or swing move. But it's just not what I'm good at. I'm much better at sensing the tops and bottoms and trading those.

Q : We talked a bit about the fact that the futures market is the most leveraged financial market outside of foreign exchange. [*Authors' note:* Leverage in futures can reach 50:1.] That could be very advantageous, but also it can be very dangerous. Personally, how much leverage do you think a trader should use trading futures?

A : I tell new traders two things: Number one, they should have at least $10,000 in their account for every single contract they trade, even though their broker will allow them to have far less. I tell them if they want to be here next month, next year, then they better have that much money to trade. You're going to have days you lose money and you're going to make mistakes. I also tell traders that if they do not start out with a $100,000, their chances of making it in this business are very, very slim because they're going to run out of money. Their not going to make money for the first year, and they're going to pay some tuition to learn to do this. So, if they come into the market with $20,000 or $30,000 and a mortgage payment, a car payment, and a kid in college, they might as well just give me their money because they'll lose it.

Q : Just to delve into that a little bit deeper, one of things that most novice traders don't quite appreciate about futures is the commission cost that comes with the market. Even though commissions on a relative basis are extraordinarily cheap, the amount of trading you do during the day can really add up. Can you give us an idea of how many round turns you typically do during a day?

A : Well that's a tough question, because it depends on your style. If you're going to be a momentum trader and trade three or four contracts, you may only make three trades a day. If you are like me, where I'm willing to take the money and trade size, it's not unusual for me to trade 20 times a day. Or even 25 or 30 times in the first hour. However, on one move, I may make five or six trades because I'm making multiple entries and multiple exits.

Q : But all together let's just say we take 20 round turns per contract. That works out to basically be about $100 at retail prices, perhaps a little bit less, maybe $70 on a deep discount basis per day. That's per one contract. So, if you're trading, let's just say five contracts, that's $500 in commissions that you must overcome every day aside from all the P&L issues? [*Authors' note:* A typical commission from a deep discount futures broker would cost $5 per contract per round turn. So trading 5 contracts 20 times per day would cost the trader $500 in commissions expenses alone.]

A : Yes.

Q : Which means that in 10 days, that's $5,000 and in a hundred days, that's $50,000 worth of commissions. So you are already in the hole, even if you stay completely even on your P&L.

A : Exactly. If you take a person who comes to the market with $250,000, the chances of them being there a year from now is very high. If a trader starts with $30,000, the chances are very, very low. It doesn't have anything to do with their ability or their discipline. It just has to do with what's going to happen as they learn to trade. Let me add one more thing. We were talking about the decimalization of stocks, and I don't know what stocks trade for now—what? A tenth of a cent commission or something like that?

Q : It's about a half a penny.

A : Well, the nice thing about these futures is we have decimalization—the SP 500 trades in quarters and Russell trades in dimes. One tick will cover the commission. If you made one tick [*Authors' note:* A tick—the smallest incremental value that a futures contract would move—is worth $25 in the mini S&P contract and $10 in the Russell 2000 contract. With commissions set about $5 per contract, if the trader was able to net out just 1 tick at the end of the day he would be profitable in those instruments] all day long on any of those instruments, you will make money.

Q : Futures traders quite often don't even think about points. They talk about how many ticks did I make today. Do you do that kind of internal accounting with yourself? Do you say I picked up 20 ticks, 10 ticks?

A : I don't think about that at all. Instead, did I trade well today? Did I do what I'm good at? Did I trade my plan? Did I take what the market offered me? I don't think in terms of ticks or points.

Q : You said you've mentored some students. How many have you mentored?

A : 30.

Q : Out of those 30, how many have become profitable?

A : Four.

Q : So basically 10 percent?

A : Yes.

Q : The odds never change, right?

A : The odds do not change, and what's interesting is in the first 90 days you can tell whether or not a person is going to make it.

Q : What are some very strong clues that a person is not going to make it? What are the key characteristics that just make a person not cut out for trading?

A : They try to make it a science. They're stubborn and losing trades bother them too much. They're afraid to push the keys on the keyboard.

Q : When you look at somebody who has promise, what would be the primary characteristics of that trader?

A : If you give me someone who wants to be the best at what ever they do, and I don't care if it's ditch digging, building houses, or whatever they will do, whatever is necessary to learn to win or succeed, I can make a trader out of that person.

Q : So it's really the inherent desire to be a winner in whatever activity you're involved in?

A : That's true. If you took guys like Michael Jordan or a successful businessman, they will learn to be the best at whatever they do or the best they can be, and they'll do whatever they have to do to achieve those goals.

Q : Do you like athletics, do you follow sports?
A : Yes.

Q : Do you find that the prototype of a successful trader or successful day trader in futures tends to be someone who is highly competitive and has some kind of athletic background in their history?

A : Yes. I know most about golf because I play a pretty good game of golf. I think that I could take almost any person whom I have played golf with, who is exceptionally good at it. I can probably teach them to trade because, by definition, if they are a good golfer, they are very disciplined. They're adaptive and they make the best of it. They don't take excessive risk. They're always calculating that best way to win.

Q : This is a question we've asked many day traders: Are you competitive against yourself or against everybody else?

A : Myself.

Q : For you it's a matter of self-discovery and self-improvement. You don't care about anybody else and what the market is doing and the fact that some other guy is making 10 million or losing 10 million today?

A : No, that doesn't even enter my mind.

Q : Were you always interested in sports and had a competitive nature?

A : Yes, and what I find interesting is I don't enjoy playing racquet-ball or basketball or golf just for the hell of it. I like the competitive side of it, like a lot of men do.

Q : So it's not the art of the game that interests you, it's the practical results?

A : Yes.

Q : Very interesting. These are questions we ask everybody for the book and we'll just ask them of you. So answer them with first thing that comes to your mind.

A : Okay.

Q : What is your number one rule for trading?

A : Don't be stubborn.

Q : What was your best trade ever?

A : You know, it's odd because it happened this summer. We had particularly volatile markets in June and July. We had a market that was just screaming "Up" on news. I couldn't even tell you what it was, and I faded that market, and it took a little while but I made $69,000 on that trade.

Q : Because the market retraced the whole up move?

A : The whole up move, yes.

Q : So that was sweet. The converse of that—what was the worst trade that you can remember?

A : It was this summer when Bernanke opened his mouth and started talking about the easing of interest rate rises and the market started creeping up, and then it jumped. I was already in a trade, and I got stubborn when, in reality, I should have just taken the hit at the first time. But that stubbornness made me have a bad, bad trade.

Q : Did you average into the position before you threw in the towel?

A : Unfortunately, in that case, I was already in the position when he said it. I was short 200 contracts for the ER, and as soon as he said it, you know it automatically just spiked up four points, and that's pretty costly. Typically, when you get a spike like that, you hope it will retrace 50 percent and you're going to get out. In this case it just continued to go up. And all you have to do is shake those off and come in the next day and make good trades. I just don't want it to turn into a life-changing situation. I bailed. I walked away from the market that day and came back the next day.

Q : You take that big hit then you close the screen and you walk away?

A : Two things: Sometimes there's nothing you could do about it. Sometimes you have situations in the ER where somebody wanted 200 and they entered 2,000, and it will crush the market. There is nothing you can do other than walk away and make good trades. And most traders really struggle with that. You watched me trade enough to know that my strength is coming back from a bad trade because I just try to make more good trades, do the same thing over and over again. Physically, if I'm struggling, what I like to do is trade size for a very small profit. I'll maybe trade 50 or 100 lots for a half point and do the same thing over and over again.

Q : Just to get the rhythm back and to regain some loses?

A : That's right. String together some winners, some singles.

Q : So clearly the one thing you never do is you don't try to get everything back at once. Let's say for argument sake you dropped five points on a trade and then your methodology is I'm going to take half a point, three-quarter of a point to constantly chip away at that loss?

A : Over and over again.

Q : How did you come across that kind of a methodology? Was it natural? Or is this something you really consciously realized was the right thing to do?

A : You know, I think I learned the hard way. Revenge trades are the most costly trades. If you have a bad trade and you try and make it all back in one time, you're going to lose more money. I think I learned from experience that the best thing to do is to try and get back to even over a little bit at time. It's a whole easier to make a half point on 100 contracts than it is to make 10 points on 10 contracts.

Q : What was the most interesting part of this job?

A : You know, people would think that the answer would be making a lot of money or the short work day. But that's not it at all. Winning the game is really important to me. Working with some good traders is important to me. The rest of the things take care of themselves. If people get into business because they think it's easy, they're kidding themselves. It's the toughest game in the world. And trading for an hour and half or two hours a day is probably far more work than the average person puts in their eight hour office job. It is very, very tough. It's tough emotionally. But I liked to try and teach people to succeed and learn to do this, knowing very well that only 1 in 10 are going to make it.

Q : What about drudgery? Is there anything unpleasant about his job?

A : No. I look forward to it everyday.

Q : The wide array of trading that you've done over the last six or seven years, what would you say was the most humbling trading experience for you? The one that really taught you the most?

A : [Laughter.] I don't know. I think I probably learned far more from trying to teach new traders to trade than anything that I did myself. One of the things that I'm sure you know—I've realized that all new traders are going to go through some experiences that are similar. They will have some dumb luck. They will triumph and then they'll have some failure. They'll modify their plans. They'll get punished a couple of times by the market. They'll get tentative. Everyone I've ever taught went through the same progression. It's the people who know how they react to that adversity that tells you whether or not they're going to make it. Have you ever seen anyone who just made it from day one?

Q : Never for long. We've seen people literally take $10,000 and run it to a quarter of a million. But we've never seen anybody hang on to it unless they were able to master the skills. Usually the same attributes that were responsible for that massive gain – greed and fearless risk taking, also become the reasons for their downfall when markets turned against them.

A : Exactly.

LESSONS FROM CHUCK HAYS

Know If You Are Better at Being a Short or Long Trader

Just as few people are ambidextrous, very few traders can trade equally from both sides of the market. Typically, some traders are much more comfortable being long while others have a much stronger preference for being short. There is no right choice in this matter. The distinction is really a function of your individual personality and taste. However, as Chuck Hays points out, knowing your strengths can often be the difference between success and failure. Just as throwing left handed for a righty can be an extremely uncomfortable experience, trading long for a short biased trader can be highly unpleasant—even if the trade is ultimately a good one. Being a short-biased traders ourselves, during the peak of internet bubble we remember making four profitable short trades in Inktomi (INKT) in one day as the stock climbed 16 points from open to close. The issue wasn't whether the stock was going up or down, but how we handled each trade. Because we were much more comfortable on the short side, we executed with confidence and precision and walked out a net winner at the end of that day, proving Chuck's point.

Traders Who Absolutely Have to Make Money Never Do

This is perhaps one of the wisest pieces of advice in our book. Many retail traders get into the business expecting to make money right away. The irony of this profession is that the more you need to make money to pay your bills, the less likely you can do that. The main reason that trading is difficult to master is that it is the only profession in the world that actually punishes you for non-performance. Most workers who work on a salary have the peace of mind knowing that they will be paid their weekly paycheck whether they accomplish their tasks or not. Even salespeople who work strictly on commission, risk only the loss of their time, not their money, if their deals go bust. Trading is the only profession in the world where a wrong decision will result in an instant loss of your money. Few people truly appreciate the negative pressure of this dynamic. Chuck Hays, lost $50,000 in his first year on the job. Therefore, if you are going to trade full time, it is absolutely critical to understand that success takes both time and money.

Focus on the Next Good Trade

As human beings we are all highly influenced by our surroundings. As traders we are especially vulnerable to big emotional swings, cycling from depression to euphoria depending on the outcome of our last trade. Yet real pros never look back. What happened on the last trade has absolutely no impact on what happens on the next one. The markets do not care if you just lost or made a million dollars. They only focus on the future. That's why good traders are able to totally divorce themselves from their emotions. As Chuck says, he only wants to concentrate on making the next good trade, ignoring the good or the bad that preceded it.

It Takes Time to See Different Type of Markets

One of the reasons why trading takes a long time to master is that market environments are not static. Markets do not simply go up or down, but rather cycle between trending and ranging phases. It takes a very long time to learn to understand the nuances of each regime and to make proper adjustments to your trading style. In fact, the markets are littered with stories of traders who made a fortune right out of the gate because they caught a very strong trend only to give it all back when the market started ranging. That is why in trading there is just no substitute for experience.

Timing Is Everything, But You Will Rarely Be Right on the First Try

At its core trading is nothing more than timing. However, timing the entry is an extremely difficult skill to master and few short-term traders ever get it right on the first try. That is why Chuck Hays will often add to his positions. He even coined new terms for his style of trading: *SHADD* for short add and *LADD* for long add. This practice is a very controversial because it flies in the face of the long-accepted market wisdom that traders should never add to their losing position. However, like all trading rules, this one is meant to be broken when properly executed. The key is not to allocate all of your risk capital to the trade at once, but rather to distribute it properly so that you achieve a good blended price on the trade. As Chuck says, "I firmly expect to add to [the trade] anyway. You increase your chance of success a great deal when you understand that trying to make perfect entries and book them . . ." more often means that the markets are going to ". . . take your money and you're going to lose."

CHAPTER 5

RAGS TO RICHES

HOOSAIN HARNEKER

Imagine losing your life savings in a partnership gone wrong and having to pick yourself up from such a calamity. Hoosain Harneker took seven months to save up $1000—an amount that most college students can easily earn working for a few weeks at local restaurant—and started to trade foreign exchange. Hoosain is as conservative as it gets. He refuses to trade a strategy until he has tripled his demo account three times in a row. He goes for 10-pip trades once a day, which may seem miniscule to most, but in the last three years he has turned that approach into an average profit of $500 a day. With his systems engineering background, he has been able to design his own automated trading system, which makes sure that he never turns a winner into a loser. His cardinal rule is to never trade his system during news. Having been broke before, making money on a consistent basis is far more important to him than becoming rich overnight so he locks in profits as often as he can.

From his office in South Africa, Hoosain sat with us to share his story of how he managed to go from rags to riches.

■ ■ ■

Q : How did you get started in the financial markets?

A : As a South African, back in the 1980s our education system did not include any subjects related to finance or investing. We had a subject called *accountancy*, which is basically like bookkeeping. But we did not cover anything to do with investments. The curriculum of those previously disadvantaged did not include these subjects at all. So, with little or no experience, these opportunities were virtually nonexistent to disadvantaged communities and people in those communities, including myself.

Q : Do you live in South Africa right now?

A : Yes. I'm currently an information technology (IT) systems engineer. I originally studied mechanical engineering and then switched to IT. I was quite successful as an IT engineer and I have worked for two companies. Both of them were liquidated, and after the last liquidation, I decided that was it, I've had enough. I'll start a company on my own, and I went into a partnership with five other guys. After a year or so that partnership went horribly wrong, and I ended up losing significantly both financially and in terms of self-esteem. At that point of my life, I was at an absolute low. I don't think I've ever sunk any lower than that. I was truly down and out. I was obviously unemployed. I remained unemployed for almost a year and honestly, having been brought up to believe that a man is the only breadwinner in the family, one of the most humiliating things was lying in bed sleeping while my wife had to get up and go to work. Looking back now, I learned some very valuable lessons during that period, which has still stood with me for the past few years.

Q : Like what?

A : Lessons about planning, being careful, about managing money, about trust, and having trust in other people. Documenting things, signing them, making sure you have witnesses to absolutely everything that you do when it comes to business. I think those are some very, very valuable lessons that I learned that have stood with me since then. It also taught me about compassion, basically feeling for other people as well because up until that point I was, I would say, fairly successful. Being in that situation, you never really think too much about other people and what their situation is until you end up in it yourself. After the partnership blew up, I had huge debts to pay, and I was not getting anywhere close to settling them. At the time, I had a friend in the United States, whom I had met a while back, who used to trade currencies. For no apparent reason one afternoon, he suddenly just popped into my head, and I thought of contacting him to see if he can assist me in anyway. So I got a hold of him. He asked me for $1,000, which he said he would invest for me to help me improve my financial situation. The only problem was that I did not have $1,000. I wrote back to him and I told him, "Listen Steven, let me save up for it, and once I've got a thousand, I'll give it to you and then you can trade it." He actually wrote back to me and he said, "I will loan you the money and I'll help you out." I told him that I was in so much debt already that I would not take another loan from anybody—I had reached the bottom line. I said give me a chance, let me save up for it, and it eventually took me I think seven or eight months to save up $1,000. When I finally did, I e-mailed him again and told him that I had the money. He then turned around and told me, "Listen, instead of me trading for you, I would rather teach you how to trade." This was something that, I must say, I truly appreciated because it gave me a skill that I would have for the rest of my life, and one that I would be able to share as well. So that is basically how I started trading currencies.

Q : It must have been frightening for you in the beginning because you had spent so much time saving up that money. How were you able to trust this friend given all that you had gone through in the past? Did he show you a track record?

A : Yes, he did show me what he what he was doing. He basically sent me the printouts of his trading records and his account statements, etc. As far as I was concerned, this guy was making huge money.

Q : Was he doing it for other people as well?

A : No way, strictly for himself. Generally, he would not touch other people's money, I suppose in my case he was going to make the exception to the rule. But then, on second thought, he decided to teach me his skills instead. Effectively, it was technical analysis with an emphasis on moving averages. At the beginning, I first demo traded it. I did very well on the demo, then went live, and that was when the rude awakening came.

Q : How did you learn from him when he was in the United States and you were in South Africa?

A : He used to take print screens of charts and put them into PowerPoint. He would then illustrate the images and write on top of them and basically give me slides of the graphics. When I received them, I would replicate what he told me on the demo account. For example, I would plot a moving average of 5 and a moving average of 13 to look for a moving average cross. I was such a novice that I had no idea what this guy was talking about at the time.

Q : I'm sure there was a very steep learning curve. Did he explain to you what moving averages were or did he just say okay these are moving averages and I recommend that you use them?

A : He basically advised me on what they were. I would then figure out for myself how to apply them. If you're basically looking at crossovers, then you want the faster line to cross the slower line from the bottom up, creating a buy opportunity. If it crossed from the top down, that's a sell. I actually battled with it in the beginning, but I somehow slowly but surely and through perseverance managed to get the hang of it.

Q : Did you read any books about technical analysis to get a better grasp?

A : At that point, nothing at all. I became quite successful at demo trading and that was when I went live, which was when I got the shock of my life. The first day, I'll never forget it, it was a Friday. I placed my first trade on a mini-account, and it was a nerve-wracking experience, but I walked away with six dollars on my first trade. On my second one, I made five, and at the end of the day, I had made 18 dollars in total.

Q : So your friend was basically a mentor to you. How often then would you talk to him in the beginning?

A : Yes, that's right. In the beginning, I spoke to him about once or twice over the telephone and then the rest of our communication was all done via e-mail.

Q : Would you correspond over e-mail every single day or every few days?

A : Initially almost on a daily basis. I estimate that it lasted for just over a month or so.

Q : So it sounds like you traded exclusively on technicals in the beginning. Did you ever incorporate fundamentals into your trading?

A : It was probably five to six months down the line before I discovered the importance of fundamentals. Although Steve was very good at teaching me technical analysis, he did not explain the importance of news. I only learned this by knocking my head several times. To give you a simple example, if I was in a buy trade, which I'd opened at 9 A.M. and suddenly, at 10:30 A.M., my time, that trade would turn against me horribly, and I could never figure out why this was happening. At one point I actually stopped trading because I had lost three times in a row and that petrified me. I became so scared that I could not trade anymore and I would only look at charts on a daily basis. Every single day in the afternoon, I would call up charts, and I would study them. That was when I realized that roughly 10:30 A.M. and 2:30 P.M. something would happen in the market. I didn't know what, but I would suddenly see a big spike either going upwards or another spike going downwards, etc. I asked the question on one the forums about why it was happening and I never got an answer until about two weeks later, when somebody mentioned one word: "News." That's all they said and I thought to myself how on earth can it be news. When I saw the word "news," I was thinking about a bomb explosion somewhere or a terrorist attack, which obviously is not what this person meant. It was only through further research did I discover the actual news release indicators and learned that they came out on a daily basis. I went out and tried to find as much information about them as I could, such as GDP, NFP and so on, and what I would then do is avoid trading during those times. Even if my signals came up and if I saw that it was close to let's say 10:30 A.M. or 2:30 P.M., I would not enter the trade. I would normally wait about an hour or half an hour after that period and only then I would enter my trades. After doing that, I found slowly but surely, my trading started to improve again.

Q: How long did you demo trade for before you actually went live?

A: About four months.

Q: What gave you the confidence to go live, was it a series of winners?

A: No. I first asked myself the question when I go live, how much money would I start with? The answer was only, $1,000 because at that point, that was all that I have saved up and all that I could afford. I even told myself mentally that if I'm going to start with $1,000, I need to be able to turn $1,000 into $2,000. Irrespective of how long it's going to take me, whether it's going to take one month or two months, or three months, that is what I needed to do. My line of thinking was that if I could make $2,000, I would withdraw $1,000, and at that point, I have recouped my entire capital. Whatever I lose afterwards is not as important because I've got my capital back. So my goal was to double my capital three times in a row back to back in my demo account. Eventually I actually managed to do it and, in fact I, doubled it four times in row.

Q : In four months?

A : No, no, not in four months. It was six or seven months and that was where I got the confidence to go live, but the transition from going from demo to live was not something that I had prepared for. Psychologically, there was a massive difference between trading demo and trading live. The reality is that when it's your own money on the line, it has a huge effect on you psychologically whether you are aware of it or not. I became hesitant. I would see the signals but I would be too scared to enter the trade, and only later did I find out that if I entered I would have made a large amount of profit. When I did get into a trade, I was completely spaced out. I would be so scared of things going against me. One of the main things is that my wife was very anxious about taking risks. She is not a risk taker, not even a calculated one. I never realized just how much of a role she actually played in my life when I first started trading.

Q : Did she support or encourage you in the beginning?

A : I wouldn't say she encouraged me because, in the beginning, she felt it was money that would go down the drain and that I was basically wasting it. I had to work with her and work with her until one day she said to me, "Fine, if that's what you want to do, go ahead and do it." My reasoning to her was, "Look, just give me a chance. If I blow the $1,000 that's it. I'll turn around and I'll walk away and I'll never mention trading ever again."

Q : Did you show her your results on your demo?

A : Yes, and I think that is where she probably got the motivation and started to think that if he's doing that successful in the demo trading, maybe he can do the same with live. So, eventually, she said, "Listen, if that's what you want to do go for it." But my agreement with her was that if I lost the $1,000 that would be it. I would turn around, walk away, and never look back. My belief was that I wouldn't want to turn around in, let's say, a couple years and ask myself what if I had tried it? I am the type of person who would rather give it shot, win or fail.

Q : So did your wife keep a tight noose on you after you started trading?

A : No, the first couple were small successful trades. But there was one day that I had entered into a trade at work and, when I came home, I logged on to my trading station and I was $187 in the profit and my wife was ecstatic. Honestly, I can tell you. she was jumping up and down. Now $187 to an American citizen might be peanuts, but to me, as a South African, that was a small, fortune that I had just earned. She was ecstatic and from there on, I grew stronger and more confident in my trading. Her excitement made me more determined to trade successfully. I mean we've had our ups and downs, but she's always stood with me. In fact she's thinking of becoming a trader herself. The key to my trading strategy is small but consistent daily wins.

Q : Lets talk about your trading. First of all, what hours do you typically trade?

A : In GMT, from about 7 A.M. until, I would say, roughly about 6 P.M.

Q : What is your typical holding period? Are you conservative, aggressive?

A : I'm fairly short term.

Q : Did you have some sort of daily, weekly, or monthly pip target or dollar target?

A : Yes, originally when I started out, my target was simply 10 pips a day. If I achieved that, I would not trade again.

Q : So you would be disciplined enough to close your position?

A : Yes, I would take the 10 pips and stop. If I made it at 10 A.M. in morning or whenever, that would be it, I would be finished trading for the day and I'll wait for next day. The reason I'm mentioning this is because I reached a point, early on in my trading career, where I was starting to overtrade.

Q : That's a problem a lot of people face.

A : Yes, I would make the 10 pips and the trade was over, but then later on I would see another signal and I end up getting into a new trade that would become a loser. This went on until I realized that I was really just a 10-pip trader, so I would take that profit, stop and wait to trade again the following day.

Q : How long did it take you to discover that?

A : It was probably another two months or so into my trading before I discovered it. I was not looking at the dollar amount, I was only looking at the pips because I told myself that I needed to become consistent and focus on the pips because I could obviously increase my lot size and make the dollar amount something I would be satisfied with. Now believe it or not, it's been three and half years since I started trading and my pip target is still the same.

Q : So you aim to make 10 pips a day, but what you would do if you had a losing trade? Would you try to make 20 pips over that 10 or stick to the 10-per-day goal.

A : No, I would still just go with my 10. The aim is that your total number of wins exceeds the occasional loss. I would always have a fixed stop-loss. I used to trade with a stop-loss of 20 pips. If I lost that 20, then I would stop trading, wait for the next day, and would follow exactly the same plan that I had before, which is to only go for 10 pips a day. I wouldn't try to trade two or three or four times a day just to make up that money. What I realized nowadays is that the anger seems to drive you to trade again. You become so angry with yourself about losing the 20 that all you want to do is get it all back and you think that you're going to teach the market a lesson and unfortunately it doesn't work out that way. It's more likely that the market is going to give you a beating instead [laughter].

Q : Do you like to focus on one currency pair at a time or will you trade multiple currency pairs?

A : No. Only one.

Q : So then what are your favorite currency pairs to trade?

A : Euro/U.S. dollar and British pound/U.S. dollar.

Q : Which ones would you avoid?

A : Probably U.S. dollar/Japanese yen.

Q : Is there a reason for that?

A : Yes, I've burnt my hands on it a couple times. I think it is because the price action can be a bit too wild for me on occasion.

Q : Do you ever trade the crosses?

A : No, not at all. About a month ago, I created a system for trading the British pound/U.S. dollar currency pair and that system is working phenomenally well for me. So I'm actually at the moment only trading the pound. I also have a system that trades silver as well. So I focus on those two exclusively right now.

Q : Can you describe how you start your typical day? Do you just survey charts or do you check the calendar first?

A : At around 7 A.M., the first thing I will do is look at the news to see if there are any major releases to be careful of that day. If it's a very quiet day, the first signal normally appears within the first two hours. I'm trading on a system or model, so I've got a little alert that notifies me when the trade sets up. As soon as the alert rings, I enter the trade, I set my profit and I set a stop-loss, and after that, I just forget about it.

Q : So you actually set your target for 10 pips.

A : That's right, yes. Since I have a system to see how my trades are progressing. If I am up six or seven pips, then I'll look at the indicators again. Should I feel that this trade is going to turn against me, for whatever reason, then I would close it out for the profit. Once I've reached 10 pips profit, I also close the trade even if the indicators are indicating that the price may still go in my favor.

Q : What kind of equipment do you use for trading?

A : I use a Compaq P3 laptop connected to my cell phone for Internet access.

Q : Does your trading platform come with charts?

A : Yes. You can actually trade off of the charts. It was a program developed by a Russian company. It uses very, very little bandwidth, which is one of the reasons why I like so much. Also, besides currencies, they've offer trading in the metals, gold and silver. If I ever trade from home, I use a laptop, which I then connect to my mobile phone to access the Internet.

Q : Do you end up trading at work or at home more often?

A : Work. Definitely.

Q : And your company's perfectly fine with that?

A : They are perfectly fine with it, yes [laughter]. In fact, a lot of them want me to teach them how to do it.

Q : In the beginning you told us that during specific hours, news flow would affect your trading, and you would avoid it because of that. So how often would you check the calendar for news flow then? Every single morning or once a week to figure out the times of day that you may not want to trade?

A : The habit is every single morning. In fact, sometimes I will look at those calendars even two or three times a day to see if I have forgotten anything that may be coming up in the afternoon. I actually did try to trade the news in the past with a beautiful subtle sort of strategy for news, but what I found was a bunch of blocks. For example, the platform would freeze only during news times and that actually made it completely impossible to trade efficiently. The specific news release that I use to trade was nonfarm payrolls. I had so many problems technologically that I just told myself it wasn't worth it to trade the news anymore.

Q : A lot of people don't trade news because of the same problems, and they realize that if they have a solid strategy, money can be made in any sort of timeframe.

A : Yes, that is right.

Q : So, basically, would you say that most of the resources that you use are free?

A : That's right, yes. The trading platform and live charts are free.

Q : Do you feel that it is necessary for someone new to invest in something that's expensive? Like one of the premium charting packages?

A : No, don't invest in expensive charting packages. Live charts are available at no cost with equivalent information. I love reading and I love learning. I think that's part of the challenge of working in FX. I spent like $90 here, $150 there, etc. But what I found was a lot of the books that I purchased were quite honestly not worth the paper they were written on. They taught the standard issue such as the moving average crossover or stochastic. I don't even think these guys took the effort to actually thoroughly test the strategies that they were teaching. Admittedly, the strategies would work once or twice. But more times than not, they would not work.

This actually leads me to my next point, which is that just over a year ago, I backed off trading for a while and turned to my current software provider because they gave me the ability to program my own indicators. I had met a Russian guy on one of the forums. The two of us started chatting, and he's the one that actually made me aware of the platform. I started learning as much as I could about indicators and robotic or fully automated trading. I was fascinated by it and actually got to the point where I can now develop my own indicators and I have my own robot, which, basically, does the trading for me. I've got one robot which is quite successful as long as it is shut off during key news releases. It requires a little management, but nonetheless works well if I turn it on and off because news can kill the robots. You need to keep him out of the news, which is something that I learned in forward testing. I've actually got it honed down now. I know exactly when to switch him on and when to switch him off. I started giving classes in South Africa where I teach people how to trade using the robot. In the beginning I had about 4 guys and I've now probably have about 16 live traders.

Q : Do you think systematic trading is really necessary, because you were doing pretty well in terms of a 10-pip target on a discretionary basis. Now that you've created a robot, what difference has it made?

A : A huge difference. When I was trading manually, I would set my target at 10 pips, my stop-loss at 20, and then I would walk away from my computer. When I would come back, I would on occasion find that the trade had become a loser, not because I was wrong about price action, but because I let the price go as high as 8 or 9 pips in my favor. But then I let it reverse and turn what could have been potentially an $80 or $90 gain into a $200 loss. So where the robots come in very, very handy is that I've inserted a function into robot such that it will protect my profit. Effectively, if I set my pip profit at 10, I could leave in a 3-pip profit protection. This means that if the price goes up by 7 pips, then retraces to 3 pips, the robot would close the trade. So I have created a virtual trailing stop that would allow me to walk away with $30 in profit instead of $200 in losses.

Q : So you feel like the robot basically helps you manage the trade better?

A : Absolutely.

Q : Do you have any sort of alert system that you've created to tell you when a trade has been placed?

A : Yes, I do. Whenever the robot enters a trade, my alert would beep and that is when I would know that the robot has entered a trade.

Q : Do you think that having a trading robot has made your trading a lot more relaxed in a sense?

A : Yes it has because a lot of the time, I may not even be aware that the robot has opened a trade. I will come and check the platform and find that the robot has entered and closed one or more trades in most cases successful ones. As you can see, with the robot, I actually have enough confidence to trade more. I am still going for the 10-pip profit, but the trades are managed better so that I can build the profit if need be.

Q : Does the same go for losses then, in the sense of letting the robot trade more if you have a loss for the day?

A : No. If I've taken a loss then that's it for the day. I don't let him trade again. I'll turn the robot back on the next day.

Q : So pretty much you stick to your original plan?

A : Yes to my original manual trading plan because the discipline to walk away with profits is the most important. The robot just makes it such that I don't need to be in front of my PC anymore to wait for signals. He is picking up signals as they happen and he's entering the trade.

Q : Do you feel like your IT background has given you an advantage in creating the robot?

A : Yes, it most definitely has, as well as some programming skills I developed in my early computing days.

Q : Do you think people like you are much more likely to move to some sort of automatic trading than people that don't necessarily have it?

A : Yes, but even people who do not have that background are interested in robotic trading. In terms of the people whom I train, some of them are not that computer literate, and when they heard about what I was doing with the robotic trading, I've absolutely fascinated each and every single student with this concept. What I've found was in the beginning, when they were trading manually, they would win and lose, but because I was doing so well with the robot, I thought it's quite unfair to not give the robot to these people and hopefully help them turn their trading around and make them successful as well. Everybody is telling me down here that I'm absolutely crazy and that I should be charging for the robot. But at the end of the day, it's all about helping people. As my student you will get the robot with your classes and I can tell you that it has made a phenomenal difference to these people. To be honest, they are not really trading, they are just switching the robot on and off, but I have made it a requirement for them to understand the mechanics behind trading.

Q : Let's continue to talk more about your trading style. Do you usually go into the market with your entire position or do you average up or average down into a trade and stagger your entries?

A : No. Just one entry, one trade and that's it.

Q : What timeframe charts do you look at?

A : Initially, I start with a four-hour, but I take my signals from the 30-minute chart.

Q : You said that initially you learned from your friend and then you read some books afterwards, what has made the difference? Has it been the initial training with your mentor that really taught you most of what you're doing now or did you learn more tricks of the trade later on in books or forums?

A : I learned more from the forums and my own research. It is on the forums where you have guys talking about actual strategies and things that are going on in the markets at the moment. However the bottom line was that at the end of the day, I plugged in each and every single indicator on the charts, one at a time and I would sit and look at this indicator, understand it, analyze it and critique it. If it didn't look easy to me I would take it off and I'd move on to the next one. Through this tactic, I found a group of indicators that I was comfortable with. The next stage for me was then to hone that group down until I had about two or three indicators. Once I had done that and found the indicators that I wanted to use, it was then a matter of tweaking the setting until I got it to point where I was happy that, if X lines up, then Y will most likely happen. I would use the second and third indicator merely for confirmation, and that is actually when success finally came.

Q : So your charts are fairly simple? It sounds like you have about three indicators on them, one primary and two for confirmation?

A : Two is confirmatory. Yes.

Q : Now given that you have developed the robot, do you believe wholeheartedly in systematic trading, or do you believe that there needs to be some sort of discretion as well?

A : There should definitely be discretion as well. In fact, the most important thing about making this robot successful is the fact that you need to manage the robot. You need to be aware of when news is coming out, the time of day and if there is news, then by 9 o'clock, 9:30 my time, I should be out of my trades before the numbers are released. In the beginning, when I tested the robot on the demo accounts, I let him run 24 hours a day. After about two weeks of trading I analyzed all the losing trades and the funny thing was that 90 percent of those losing trades were during times when news is released. That was when I realized that, if I just keep him out of the news, the robot was an absolute winner. So when I started applying the discipline of keeping him out of news basically, that was when I finally became successful.

Q : You hit on a great point, which is that one of the most important things for people to do to improve their trading, especially when they are not doing so well, is to take a time out, go back, and analyze the trades that were both successful and unsuccessful because, more often than not, you will find a common theme of when you tend to lose money and when you don't. It could be one currency pair that for just some random reason you can't trade well. It could also be like in your case, every time data comes out you trade poorly. This is a great tip for new traders. What do you think is more important: indicators or price action?

A : A tricky one but ultimately, speaking for myself, I rely on my indicators.

Q : What was your worst trade ever?

A : My worst trade was when I opened a trade, and just as I opened it, the telephone rang and I had to attend to something urgently. I attended to the matter not realizing that I had not set a take profit or a stop-loss, the trade was wide open. To make a long story short, I came back and I was down about $380 and I got the shock of my life when I saw that. In a state of panic, I just closed the trade and it took me quite a while to recover from that.

Q : Was there any lessons that you learned from this?

A : Yes, I will never, ever trade without a stop-loss and a take profit. It's actually a habit now, where the minute that I open the trade, I will immediately put in my take profits and stop-loss. My trading robot has been programmed that way as well. This is part of money management, which is critically important to a trader's survival.

Q : What about your best trade ever?

A : My best trade was during nonfarm payrolls and actually it was when I broke all of the rules that I have now, or more specifically, before I developed my current discipline. In that trade, I made over $3,200.

Q : Can you tell us a little bit what was happening during that time? Did you have large position on and it moved quickly beyond your 10-pip profit?

A : I could probably have gotten more if I had stayed in the trade longer. But basically what I did was, at 2:50 our time, I opened a buy stop and sell stop, and I just waited, and suddenly the price shot up and my buy was triggered. I was trading I think it was at three lots, which are $30 to a pip. 1–2–3 boom before I knew it [laughter] I was $3,000 up, and I just closed it. I didn't even think.

I just clicked on close and that was it. My profit actually went a bit higher than that. It went up to about $4,000 but by the time I hit the close button and it went through, I was back down to about $3,200.

Q : In terms of the buy stop and sell stop, is it something that you still use right now?

A : Not anymore. I used to only use it for news trading. But like I said before, because of the issues I've had with brokers and their execution around news, I've actually stopped trading this way and have advised my students to do the same.

Q : It seems that you increase your positioning a lot more nowadays to make meaningful profits. Before you said that you had $1,000 so you were probably trading a mini-account, right? Now it sounds like you are trading a regular account?

A : Yes, that is right.

Q : Can you tell us a little about your success, in dollar terms and percent terms over the past few years?

A : I would say, I've been quite successful, but the first few years were very, very difficult. I was winning and then losing and then winning and then making a little bit here and there. Right now, though, I trade the British pound in the early morning and then silver later on. Between those two, I earn enough to sustain myself from trading alone.

Q : That's great. Do you trade every single day except weekends?

A : Every single day, but I have a tendency to not trade on Friday afternoons.

Q : Do you ever hold positions overnight?

A : No, very rarely. On silver though I've had two trades that went overnight I think.

Q : Let's talk a little bit about silver. Why did you start trading that?

A : About four months ago, my eldest brother came to me. Now he's aware that I'm trading currencies, and he said that he wanted to trade gold. I said to him, why would you want to trade gold when you've got all of these opportunities in the euros and the pound, and he said, listen just do me a favor and find out whether the company that you trade with allows us to trade gold. So I went to my trading platform and checked that they certainly had gold. So my brother was the one that started it all. I opened up a chart of gold, I looked at it, analyzed it, and I was quite shocked at the move that gold actually makes. However, I realized that you need a lot more capital to trade gold [laughter]. Silver is cheaper.

Q : How long did you demo trade silver before going live?

A : I demo traded it for a month every single day.

Q : It seems that you typically demo trade for a pretty decent amount of time before actually going live, is that right?

A : Yes, the shortest will be a month.

Q : Why did you decide to teach classes on trading?

A : It started off with three friends and one other guy who was interested, the fourth person was a friend of a friend. If you re-member from the beginning of our discussion, it was only five or six years ago that I was financially crippled and practically broke.

That period of unemployment was a very difficult period of my life. There were some things that occurred back then which sometimes when I think about it, it gives me the creeps, the hair on my arms just starts standing up. So I promised myself that it was something I would not wish on my worst enemy. Yet the funny thing is that I stuck it out, I hung in there and today, in my opinion, I am quite successful. So I felt that it was time to give something back because I am a firm believer that the more you give, the more you will receive, not necessarily in monetary terms, but it could be in all sorts of other ways and I felt one of the motivating things was that if I can do it, anybody else can. Originally, I was going to write a book, but I found it too difficult to put my thoughts onto paper. Also, through my own personal experiences, I realized that in order for the average person to succeed, they are going to need guidance. They are going to need somebody to speak to and that is when I came up with the idea of offering the classes. I basically started with three or four guys who were friends of mine, and when they went live, they started doing fine, and they told their friends about the classes. From there, it's basically taken off.

Q : Do you feel that having a mentor was really that much of an advantage?

A : I think you need a mentor. Somebody who you can speak to because whenever I got stuck and I wasn't sure what was happening, I would be very nervous that night, and I would pick up the phone and call Steve. He would verbally explain to me what he was trying to say through e-mail and that made a big difference.

Q : How long are your classes, how many days a week?

A : The classes are in the evening, Monday through Thursday. That's four evenings and it's three hours per session. What I do is give them an introduction to the trading platform. I use my own indicators that I've developed and basically I show them how those indicators work for different timeframes and how to use them properly. By Thursday, they are generally pretty good with knowing how the platform and the indicators work. Then they need to go back and demo trade, do exactly what I did which is to triple that account, three times over. They will also need to give me their demo account number and password so that I can track how they are doing and see if these guys actually follow the things that I have taught them. We also go through a process of analyzing their trades, especially the losing ones. I will help them figure out why they may have lost money in a trade and typically the problem is that they forgot to look at the calendar for news releases. This is a part of the learning process however and that is basically how I do the courses, and I provide a lot of support afterwards.

Q : So it's a one-week course and the indicators that you've developed, do you send them in a file that they load onto a chart?

A : Yes, the course lasts from Monday to Thursday, and the indicators are sent to them in an encrypted file.

Q : How many people have you trained so far, and what is their success rate?

A : I've trained probably just over 30, of which 16 are currently live. In fact, the 16th guy just went live today. So I'm not going to count him. 15 people have been trading live anywhere ranging from just over a year to three or four months. Out of the 15, 12—80 percent—have been fairly successful. The rest do not follow the rules. They trade on emotion, anger etc., and take the occasional knock. There is one guy who took his account from $500 to $6,000 and in just over a month, he blew it all on one single trade.

Q : It's called greed, isn't it?

A : Yes. Greed is not something you can control in another person. You know your system works, that's the bottom line, period. How people treat the system is entirely in their hands.

Q : Do you think there's a common characteristic amongst those people whom you know just won't be able to make it verses people whom you think will succeed at FX trading?

A : Yes, I think that I've found certain characters who have a difficult time in this market. You can see immediately that they are very gung ho, almost like gunslingers. I'll warn them over and over and over again, Forex is not a game, it's not gambling like in a casino. It's a very serious business and it should be treated as such. It requires a phenomenal amount of discipline. However, sometimes these lessons need to be actively learned by these people. Once they've knocked their heads a couple of times in the live environment, then they will tend to pick up that phone and tell me, "You know what you said in the class? Now I realize what it was that you were trying to say." They cannot see it when we are merely talking about it, but once they've experienced it two or three times, once they've lost money, in other words, they become good traders.

Q : Do you think everyone can be trained? Or are bad habits just too ingrained in some traders?

A : I think that most people can be taught the discipline. Unfortunately, that's going to involve that person probably losing some money before he learns, but because it is his own money, it tends to pull him right once he's taken a couple of knocks. I've seen it with my own guys who have funded an account, lost it, refund it again, lose it again, refund it, lose it again, and then suddenly, by the fourth time, they are up and running and finally trading well. Very few do it right from the beginning. They will blow their account at least once. But these are $200, $300 accounts, nothing too damaging.

Q : How much support do you give them after they've taken your course? A month? Two months?

A : No, indefinitely. I'm available to them over the telephone or over e-mail. We have regular forums in which past students who have become live traders convene to share their experiences, strategies, etc, and learn about new developments I may be working on. It's a good support network as past students share experiences amongst themselves.

Q : What is the number-one rule or tip that you would give to new traders?

A : I think it is discipline, perseverance, don't give up if you don't succeed initially. When you teach a person a strategy or a system, he wins his first trade and he's absolutely ecstatic. He wins the second one, he loses the third one, and suddenly the system doesn't work. It is not that the system doesn't work; it is usually a problem that is easy solve. He probably traded when there was a news release, for example. What people do not want to do is actually analyze those losing trades—find out, "Why did I lose?" They do not want to ask themselves that question. Instead, they just say that the system is useless and they move onto to the next one. But the same thing happens with the next system, and they lose one or two trades, and then they move to another system and the cycle happens over and over again.

Q : How do you help people figure out why they lose?

A : One of my questions to a trainee was, "When do you actually trade?" His answer to me was that he goes to work, he comes home, has supper, spends a little time with the wife, and by the time he switches on his laptop and he gets to trading, it is about 8:00 P.M. South African time. He will place a trade, he doesn't get the profits immediately, and he will leave it on overnight. When he wakes up the next morning, he'll find that he has lost 20 pips. I immediately told the guy that he is trading at the end of the U.S. session, and he's then heading into the Asian session, which is normally quite flat and that is where his loses are coming from. I asked him if it is possible that he could trade between 7 and 9 A.M. South African time because that would mean that he would be trading the open of the European session. So that was exactly what he did, and that was when he started to become successful. It had nothing to do with him or his system, but rather he was just trading at the wrong time of day. Self-reflection is key to becoming a profitable trader in my opinion. You have to consciously make every effort to balance these activities with your daily activities and implement consistency in daily trading times.

Q : Sound like it just falls back to what we talked about earlier, which is going back reviewing your trading and seeing the mistake.

A : I think that people always like to shift blame to someone or something else, such as an indicator not working or the market is reacting weird. They have difficulty admitting that the problem or fault is actually themselves, and I think they need to make mental adjustments to be okay with that. You need to be very honest with yourself when you are trading.

Q : What do you find is the most interesting part of trading itself?

A : I love looking at the charts and doing the analysis.

Q : What's the most frustrating then?

A : Sometimes waiting for a trade setup to occur can be a bit boring and frustrating. In the beginning there was a huge adrenaline rush. You will be waiting for a trade. You can see the signal building up, and it's getting closer and closer. It was like a roller coaster ride. But what I found was that it's not as glamorous as people seem to make it out to be. A lot of the time now I just sit around and watch the screen, waiting for something to happen and sometimes that could take hours, and I would get frustrated. There were even days before I had the robot, where I was away from the screen, and I would come back and realized that I missed the signals. What I find the most exciting to me now is the development of systems, getting them to work, and helping other people become successful.

Q : Do you ever have a problem keeping yourself out of trades? For example if you are trading the British pound and then all of a sudden, the Japanese yen has really big movements, do you feel the urge to participate?

A : No. I have studied the euro / U.S. dollar and British pound / U.S. dollar in particular, and developed strategies for trading these specifically. I believe that every currency pair is unique So I stick to what I know best and have no regrets if I have missed a big move on another pair. To me the bottom line is that I am making money, irrespective of whether it is in the Canadian dollar or the euro or the British pound or silver or gold. It doesn't matter to me where the money is coming from. That is the important thing, and I'm quite happy with the British pound, and I obviously now trade silver as well. To me it all comes back to discipline. When I first started in the market, I would hop in just for the sake of being in the market. If I was bored of waiting, for example, I'll see the signal in the yen, and even though I do not really trade the yen, I'll enter simply because I wanted to be in the market. Then I would lose. And, after having lost a couple of trades, I learned discipline. I'd rather just stay out, because it would take two winning trades to make up a losing one, and I cannot stand losing. I look at it this way, by staying out of the market at the right time, to me that was actually a winning trade.

Q : How is trading currencies different from trading silver?

A : Well the primary difference is that silver moves very, very slowly. You need a tremendous amount of patience, because silver might only move 4 or 5 pips in two or three hours, but each point is worth a lot more money. I am earning $50 for every pip that's it moving. So, even though it's only moved five pips, in the last three or four hours, for example, that's $250 to me. So I'm quite happy with that, but it takes patience.

Q : So are you ever competitive with your students or your brother in terms of trading?

A : No, I only compare myself with myself. I was taught from quite a small age to always give of your best, and my dad always used to tell me that even if you think that you're the best, you are probably not. There's probably somebody, somewhere out there who is better than you. So you always need to strive to be better. I think that is where he instilled in me, the passion to learn as much as I can. The passion for traveling, meeting other people, learning about other cultures. What I've found was that with the silver now, I've got the indicators, I've proven the indicators work, and yet every single day I am still looking for something to make it better and that just drives me.

Q : Do you feel like you have changed a lot of your systems or strategies along the way?

A : It has really been fairly small changes, just little adaptations as I've discovered new things.

There's one more thing that I want to talk about. When I started teaching people in the beginning, I realized that there was one thing that is terribly wrong with many new traders, they tend to open demo accounts with $50,000. These people will start trading this amount, and they will make money or they will only incur small losses, because the bottom line is that it is very difficult to blow $50,000. Then these people feel confident and open up a live account with $300 and they start to lose money. It may be because they do not have enough capital to withstand the same amount of stop-loss or they cannot take as many lots as they could with a $50,000 demo account. Either way, they are trading differently and it has a huge negative impact on how they are doing live. Therefore, I think that it is extremely important to ask for a demo account with a balance that you plan on funding with when you go live. This way, if you triple your account, three times over like I teach people to do, you know that you are playing with the same amount of capital and there should be no major surprises when you go live. That to me, is absolutely critical.

LESSONS FROM HOOSAIN HARNEKER

Triple Your Demo Three Times in a Row

Hoosain Harneker has not had an easy life. Being born in a country that was formerly segregated by race, Hoosain worked hard to earn enough money to start a partnership. When that partnership turned sour, he was left with nothing. It took him six to seven months to save up enough money to start a $1,000 trading account. Yet his struggle may be the key to his success. Having gone through so much difficulty, Hoosain has become extraordinarily conservative. When he persuaded his wife to let him give trading a try, he knew that $1,000 was his one and only chance to prove that he could make trading a career. That is why Hoosain made it a rule for himself to triple his demo account three times in a row before actually trading live. Although this rule is exceptionally hard to follow, both in terms of patience and actual results, it is one worth implementing because it forces you to develop a trading methodology that has a substantial chance for success in real market conditions. For anyone who is serious about trading and who has the patience or discipline to earn your stripes before heading off to battle with the markets, this is a trading rule worth following.

Focus on Your Pip Target

Compared to many other traders, Hoosain's 10-pip-a-day goal is also extremely conservative because, in certain cases, this is no more than the spread of a currency pair and is a fluctuation that can occur within a blink of an eye. However at 10 pips a day, five days a week, four weeks a month, that adds up to 200 pips per month or 2,400 pips a year. At those levels, the numbers are not conservative at all. There are many different ways to make money trading. Some traders in our book aim for 200 pips a day rather than

200 pips a month. Both of the methods are sound, but for short-term traders who seek instant gratification, Hoosain's methodology may actually be more suitable. You can always alter your trading size. On one standard 100,000 unit lot, 10 pips are worth $100, but on 10 of those lots, they are worth $1,000 a day. Focusing on the point potential may be more intelligent than focusing on the dollar amount.

In order to lock in profits and to increase the probability of success, Hoosain also uses trailing stops. For example, if his trade is up by 8 pips and goes back down by 3 pips to positive 5 pips, Hoosain's robot will kick in and automatically lock in the profit. Once again, these singular pips may seem tiny, but we already know that Hoosain's conservatism has paid off.

Practice Regular Self Reflection

One of our favorite pearls of wisdom from Hoosain is his practice of going back and analyzing his trades. When he first started trading, there were times when Hoosain would incur a string of losses. In those cases, he would go back and revisit his trades to see if there was any pattern to those unsuccessful trades. We practice this as well. Even when we do not face a string a losses, every week we will reanalyze our trades to see how we could have improved them. This may involve things like timing trades differently, perhaps avoiding trades around certain news releases or tightening up the stops. In fact, in our trading, we have found that when trades go wrong by more than 70 pips against us, they will end up in a loss 90 percent of the time. Therefore, what we learned going forward is to limit the majority of our stop-losses to 70 pips. When you reanalyze your own trades, you will find ways to improve your own trading results.

CHAPTER 6

THE WISDOM OF EXPERIENCE

FRANKI LAW

Meet Franki Law, the man who turned $200,000 Hong Kong dollars (HKD) into HKD$6 million. Having been in the business for over 20 years, Franki is a big believer that success comes with experience, and time. A technician at heart, he ranks price movements on an A-B-C scale, not in terms of complex indicators like Elliott wave patterns, but in terms of potential profit opportunities. He identifies a trading zone, commits to it and scales down as long as the zone holds. His relaxed, simple and philosophical approach to trading has served him well and we were delighted to sit down with him for an interview in his office in Hong Kong.

■ ■ ■

Q : How did you get into the business of trading?

A : I started in 1986 and have been in this business for over 20 years. When I first started, Hong Kong just released the Hang Sang

Index futures. The only other product available for trading besides the stock index futures were gold futures. Unlike the wealth of products available abroad such as oil, foreign exchange, merchandise, and bonds, what I had to trade were Hang Sang and Gold, both of which did not have very high volume. After the 1987 crash, I wanted to trade something else, so in 1988 I started trading currencies and later on I returned to trading stocks as well.

Q : What sparked your interest in trading? Was it something that you learned in school?

A : Twenty years ago we did not have the opportunities that many people do today in Hong Kong, so I only finished high school and never had to opportunity to go to college or get a CFA or CMT designation. The good thing was that this left most people on the same playing field, with equal opportunities. Everyone started at zero. Even if you did get the opportunity to go to college, although there were economics classes, there were barely any classes that talked about investments. When I started in the industry, I started in the financial markets doing administrative work. I didn't seek out financial markets—but that came more by chance, and shortly after I realized there were many opportunities in the financial markets. That was when I changed my job and decided to become an investment representative. I was a broker who specialized in futures and then later on in currencies and stocks. Only after I became a broker did I begin to trade for myself. That was not until 1988 because, unlike some people who enter the industry with a pocketful of cash and are looking for investment opportunities, I saved money first and then used a portion of that money to trade, which is why I did not begin trading immediately. It took me two years to save up the money to do so.

Q : Did you work a full time job while you were trading?

A : Yes, I did on the side. My primary job at the time was as a broker and financial advisor.

Q : How long did you trade stocks and oil?

A : Up to the present; Although since the beginning of 2005, I switched away from brokerage to focus more on education and I trade stocks and oil on the side.

Q : When did you start your own education company?

A : I started the company in 1992, but throughout that time, I was working as an investment advisor. It was only in the beginning of last year that I put my full-time focus into my company.

Q : How much did you start trading with?

A : In 1988, about $50,000 HKD, which would be considered quite a bit in today's dollars, and is the equivalent of two years of savings.

Q : Was trading easy for you in the beginning or did you feel frustrated at the start?

A : Yes, it was definitely frustrating. In the beginning, I did face a lot of failure. I think that when it comes to investments and trading, in the beginning it's a cycle of failure, followed by success, followed by failure again and success again. But the last step is either success or failure, which is the same as life. You are faced with many success and failures, and my later successes come from the experience of my failures. This, too, is a repeated cycle. Even at times that I think I may have succeeded, I hit a stumbling block, which becomes another learning experience, and that has really been all part of my training to become a successful trader.

Q : What encouraged you to keep on trading when you had failures?

A : Well, there is a very unique characteristic of trading, which is that the feeling of success and failure comes quickly. Today you make a trade and it becomes a loser, but tomorrow is another day. So, when I make a bad trade, I forget about it, go to sleep, wake up and start all over again tomorrow. Success is also very fulfilling, which is the main thing that pulls me back into the market. In other jobs or industries, the feelings of success and failure may not be as strong. When it comes to trading, every day, you get to experience the feeling of either success or failure. For people who like the feeling of success and drive, trading presents plenty of opportunity for fulfillment.

Q : However, there are many people who face big failures that make it difficult for them to have the confidence to trade again. How do you prevent this from happening?

A : Personally, after many mistakes, I have learned that the most important part of trading is using stops because, at bare minimum, it allows you to control your risk since bad trades are unavoidable. Let's take a casino, for example. There is little chance that you will be able to win 10 out of 10 bets. As long as you control your betting size, however, it will allow you to retain some of your capital to play the game the next time around.

Another thing that I don't like to do is to average down and post margin calls. There are many people who will go long a currency pair and keep injecting money into their accounts if they get margin calls and buy at even lower prices in hopes that a rally will help them to recover their entire account. For example, if you are long 10 lots, if the price falls, you add 20, if it falls again, you add 30 etc. Although the ability to recover quickly may seem extremely attractive, it is very dangerous and it is something I will rarely use. I feel that if I keep on posting money into my account to meet a margin call and add into a losing position, I am essentially at the whim of the market. I can only hope that the trade moves in my desired direction. But I am stripped of my decision making power. Perhaps the price movement would have called for a short, but since I am buried so deep in the long position, I can only let the market take me where it wants to. So what would I do if I got a margin call? I would close my position and wait for the next clear opportunity or setup to get into the market because it avoids letting the market dictate my profits and losses and allows me to be the decision maker once again. I get to choose when to get into the market, what product, and what size and this control is very important to me.

Q : How long did it take you to realize that stops are important?

A : It was something that I realized later on. I remember the first trade that I lost money, I did not learn that lesson. The second trade, I didn't as well but by the third losing trade, I finally realized the importance of using stops. In addition to stops, there are other methods that I use to reduce risk. They include spreading out my entry levels so that I can spread out my risk as well as diversifying by product or entry levels. If I am very confident, I could put my whole investment into one entry, but I will scatter my exit levels. If I am not as confident, I would spread out my entry.

Q : How long did it take you to develop a strategy that worked well for you?

A : In approximately 1998 when I started making changes to my trading style. So as you can see, it took approximately 10 years of success, failures and essentially gaining trading experience for me to get where I am today. Although this may seem like a long time, since then I've had 10 years to act effectively on these experiences—which would be post 98.

Q : Why did your strategy change?

A : After a series of failures, you want to change yourself because the right direction to look is forward. And the other reason for the change is age. Before you are 30, you are very aggressive. If you have $300, you could risk the entire $300. But after 30, you become more conservative. The younger you are, the riskier, the older, the more conservative. So I believe people change with age, which contributes to the reason why I began to change my trading style in 1998. After experiencing many different types of markets, I became more mature and realized that I shouldn't risk all that I have, and I should save some on the side. If I make a bad trade, I have learned to just give up on the trade rather than pressing further in hopes of making a quick recovery as I may have done when I was younger.

Q: So you only started to make serious money after 1998?

A: Yes. By that time I developed my technique and system. How much you make really depends on how much you invest. But if you have a good system, even if you make one bad trade, you can feel confident that your next ones may still lead to success. Your system and technique are very important. Getting into a good trade really involves having a good eye. None of us can guarantee that, so it is important to learn how to analyze the markets and to have a trading plan.

Q: Have you ever taken any classes that teach you how to create a system or read charts?

A: When I started to get into the industry, there weren't that many classes available. These days, investment classes have become far more popular in Hong Kong, and the desire to learn more about investing has as well. But 20 years ago, this was not very popular. I read newspapers, financial magazines. I used Reuters, read charts, price levels, which was the way I learned myself.

Q: What is your normal trading day like? How often do you trade?

A: I prefer a longer-term style. I will pick a direction, probably based upon last night's charts and then determine my entry point based upon economic data and technical levels. I look at country news or political news, but I don't give much weight to it because, for example, if I am analyzing the Middle East situation, any information that I read in the paper will probably not be as up to the minute or as in-depth as the information that big banks or large investors may have. Information can be bought, so I am sure that there are people who know a lot more than I do. But if those people do something, the market will move, so if I look at the charts, I will see the activity. I may not know why they are moving the market the specific way, but I do know that people are moving it at the moment. This may give me enough information to enter or exit the market vis-à-vis a breakout or breakdown or a bounce off the average. This is the most common technique that I use to trade. I will also look at economic data such as upcoming interest rate movements, whether the U.S. will raise or cut interest rates, whether the U.K. did so overnight, etc. Interest rates are extremely important in the FX markets. I will also look at charts and use both of that information in combination.

The way I look at things is that on a normal day, a currency probably moves 100 pips. If you capture 50 pips during the day, that is already considered very good. If you capture 80 pips, I would consider that A-cup. Fifty pips is C-cup, and this is a good way at looking at it to determine when I should stop trading. C-cup is pretty good, I am generally happy with it, B-cup is even better, A is the best, but rare and is basically a long shot.

Q : Do you look at charts first, then economic data or economic data first, and then charts?

A : I will look at charts first because if you do, you can see what kind of trend is happening in the various currency pairs. This can also be a neutral point that you work off of. As for economic data, I use it on a much more short-term basis. For example, let's say that I got into the market and there is an important economic release due out tonight, I will consider whether it will most likely hurt or benefit my position. This is secondary, though. I think that the trend and the direction of the trend are most important. I will only look at data as to how it can impact my position.

Q : How long do you usually keep your positions open?

A : On a short-term basis. I have tried to day trade. Day trade has two meanings to me. The first is that I can earn a large amount of money if the move happens in one day, so I would pocket that. For example, if I am long dollars and the U.S. dollar rallied 300 points, I would definitely pocket the money because 300 points is far beyond what I may have considered for a daily move. So I would take it as a day trade and bank the money. On the other hand, if I was long dollars and the dollar is not able rally, and I have some small profits like 10 or 20 pips, I may pocket that money as well.

The thing is, when I go into the market and enter into a position, I will not think about whether this will be a day trade. To determine how long I will hold a position, I look at the charts to see how long previous trends have lasted and how long the current trend has been in the works. In these situations, I would be perfectly comfortable holding a position for as long as a month. When I hold positions for a month, one of the most important things that I will always consider is interest. There was a time when I felt that U.S. interest rates were very high. So I went long the U.S. dollar against the Swiss franc and Japanese yen because, if I am holding the position for a month, I will know that at least I will earn the interest. If I felt that the outlook for the U.S. dollar is weak, I would short the dollar against the British pound because at the time I would earn interest going long pounds against the dollar. So I will pick a direction where the interest is favorable to me. This is important for longer trades because the amount can be significant. The interest that you earn is increased by the usage of leverage so it can be a large amount. This is exceptionally important for medium-term traders. For short-term traders, interest is not important because there is only a limit to how much interest you would end up paying out.

Q : How long did it take you to figure out the importance of interest?

A : Not too long after I started trading. The great thing about the FX market is that you have a choice. I can pick to earn or pay

THE WISDOM OF EXPERIENCE

interest. If I didn't have a choice, I would have to pay the interest, of course. However, because I do have a choice, I would definitely pick to earn interest. I can go short or go long dollars and still earn interest. It's just a matter of which currency pair. It's not always easy because some pairs have narrow interest rate spreads and others have wider, so you may not always know which one to pick.

Q : What currencies do you trade the most?

A : The Swiss franc. I will spend the most time there. I like it because of the larger volatility. The euro is good too, but sometimes the volatility is not as big. When I trade, I usually will look at price, charts, and overnight Dow Jones activity. I think this is enough

Q : What type of equipment do you use?

A : I will use basic, free charts. I think that trading FX these days is much better than in the past. Back then, more sophisticated people would use Reuters, but that can be very expensive. I was also previously sponsored by Reuters to use it for over a year. But afterwards I did not opt to pay for it myself. When it comes to information these days, there are many places to get it for free and during that time you can see how the price moves, which is as reliable as it gets. Reuters, sometimes has false prices. Like the highs and lows may be indicative and not actually executed prices. I prefer to watch the dealing station in real active times because then I can see more reliable prices that are probably being dealt at the moment.

Q : So you don't think that an average person needs very expensive equipment similar to what banks have to be successful?

A : I think that it is not necessary these days. In the past it was. But in the present information is more fluid, so it allows you to avoid paying up for those services. Also, I don't think that people should not get it just to save money, but because many of the cheaper or even free resources out there are sufficient if not better. Capital is important when it comes to trading and there are some costs that should be made initially, such as a fast computer and connection, but other things are not as necessary.

Q : Sometimes the timeliness of certain services may pale in comparison to Reuters or Bloomberg. Is this a disadvantage?

A : Usually you know in advance when data is going to come out or when speeches will be made. Sometimes you have scenarios like 9/11. But that is very rare. I don't feel the need to know the data the second or even minute it comes out. Most services will release it shortly afterwards and you can watch the price for the reaction. If you are really worried about the risk, you could call in and put a stop or something. When there is a large unexpected event, there is not much that we, as small investors, can do about it. We find out as quickly as we can and the key is to focus on reducing risk on the back of those events—to put in stops as often as possible. Most investors cannot afford a Reuters or Bloomberg, so the key is to focus on finding your most reliable news sources and then watching the price. Sometimes the price can lie too because it can be late in updating, so make sure you look at a few different charts.

Q : What time of the day do you trade?

A : I don't really split between times. Usually I prefer at night because it is more relaxed and quiet and, as such, I have more time to look at the charts in finer detail.

Q : The afternoon in Hong Kong is basically London open, and the evening is the U.S. open. So is it better to analyze the markets then because there is more activity?

A : I think that certainly is a reason. If the market is moving a lot, you get to see a lot more information and understand the currency's reaction more. Sometimes watching the markets may require a one-hour, two-hour analysis, or just a quick glance at the charts. You can even set alerts. What I like to do is to use a price quote beeper that shows how prices are moving. This is great when I am sleeping because I don't like to have to wake up constantly to check the price quotes. You can also put alerts on your computer, but you may not be able to put that next to your bed like you can a beeper. Instead, with the beeper, I can set the price levels that I am watching and it will alert me when the price is hit. When the alarm rings, I know that something unique is happening and I can go look at my charts to see if I want to do anything. It's impossible for me to watch prices constantly, especially if I am in a meeting or teaching a class. It is also impossible for me to bring my computer with me into the meetings as well. So a price beeper is a perfect tool for me to use to keep on top of the markets.

Q: When did you start using the beeper?

A: In the '80s. These beepers were available before the '90s. They have changed a lot since then, of course, and are very inexpensive and cheap to use. On a monthly basis, here in Hong Kong, it can cost $300 HKD a month. Now one thing—these beepers are convenient and inexpensive, but you cannot rely on them 100 percent. Sometimes with wireless connections, updates can be slow, especially if the market is moving very fast. It definitely won't be as fast to update as your cable Internet or DSL connections. So the beepers should only be used as a secondary support tool. In typical scenarios, it works well. But if there is a major interest rate decision or a political development, it can be a bit slower because the connection speed can be a bit slower.

Q: Typically what timeframe charts do you use?

A: I will use daily charts and minute charts. Daily charts are for direction to see where the trendline is pointing. If the daily charts indicate that the currency pair will rally, I may want to avoid making shorts on a shorter-term basis. The daily charts can show the general direction. I use the minute charts to determine whether the price is the best price to get in at. If I am looking to buy into a trend, I want to get a nice price, which is really the benefit of using shorter-term charts. If the minute charts show short-term weakness and the potential for a 20-point dip, then that could be a 20-point better entry for me.

Q: Do you think one-minute charts are really more reliable and better than five-minute charts?

A: I feel that the one-minute chart gives you a closer more instant look at market behavior and is a truer reflection of current market activity.

Q: Have you always used the combination of daily and one-minute charts, or is that something that you discovered later on?

A: It's definitely a technique that has evolved. I feel that when it comes to trading, one is always evolving whether you realize it or not. It's all about change for any investor, including myself, Right now, if you ask me if I have the best strategy, I may say yes. But in a year, things may change and a scenario that hasn't happened in the past may have happened. As a result, I may have to react to that as well. It's all about challenging yourself to adapt to the changes.

Q: Do you feel that the changes along the way have been big?

A: I think it really has been a small evolution along the way and not a big change. Training yourself to be a good trader is not like rebuilding a house, where you can completely strip the old house and its foundation and start from scratch.

Q : There are some people who start as a trend trader and then switch to become a range trader or vice versa before they find their true trading style. Has this happened to you? Have you always been a trend trader?

A : I think that I have always thought in the mentality of a trend trader, just not so perfectly and with as reliable trading strategies. Most people are this way with the things they do. For example, if you like martial arts and kung fu, you may begin to do some of the motions, but at that time you may not know or consciously care about whether the motions are karate style, taekwondo style or jujitsu style. Only after you learn and practice more and more and become a true student of the art do you realize that your motions may actually be taekwondo and not karate. The same is with trading. Some traders may start out trading one way, maybe as a momentum trader who rides the wave of price or a reversal trader who always tries to pick a top, they may not realize what category they fall into until much later on.

Q : When you first started trading, how many hours a day did you trade for, how long would you hold your positions? Has this changed?

A : As for how long I would usually spend trading, I consider every time I check my quote rates on my beeper as part of trading. Every day I do look at the markets, more so at night. Generally speaking, the time that I spend at night sitting down and really analyzing the markets is usually under an hour. The reason is because usually when I have already identified the major trend in the market from a broader scale, I already know what I am looking for on the charts on a daily basis. That is, if the trend is still intact, is it losing momentum, or has it already been compromised and ready to reverse. Some people find trading currencies very difficult because they feel that they have to spend a lot of time watching the markets since it is open 24 hours a day. I don't think it should be the case. When I trade, it is usually very relaxed because all I do is spend a little time every day looking at how the market has moved and how that movement plays into the overall trend and from that I have usually identified the key support and resistance levels, which I then enter into my beeper machine. Any levels within the support and resistance zones I am usually very comfortable with. The only times that I need to keep an eye on the market is when my support level is breached in an uptrend or resistance level is breached in a downtrend. But regardless of the direction of the trend, I will usually check my charts if either the support or resistance zones have been broken to see if I need to react to it.

This is the main reason why I think trading is very accessible and easy for individuals. All you need to do is to make sure all of your eggs aren't in one basket—diversify, identify a direction, and figure out what the top resistance level and bottom support levels are. Movements in the market on a daily basis are very normal. If there were no movements, I would probably not want to trade. I just don't become obsessed with the market. I want to wait for a good time to get into the market and go with the movements. Ten, twenty, thirty pips on fluctuations are very normal. If I become nervous when the market fluctuates 10, 20, or 30 pips, that may be more of a problem with myself than with my position. This, of course is if you trade like me and look for big moves. I am only worried when it moves beyond my predetermined amount—i.e., breaks a key level—and that is when I will revisit my position to see if I need to make changes. Therefore, even if you have a full time job, you can be active in the market as well. Just have some sort of alert system either via e-mail, which you can set up some charting packages to do, or subscribe to a beeper like I have. It doesn't require you to watch the market 24/7.

Q : How many pips do you look for in an average trade?

A : Usually I look for at least 75 to 100 pips. The good thing about currencies is that there isn't much cost involved. If I trade a currency pair with a 5-point spread, I view that as my cost of trading and will usually be satisfied with making 50 to 100 pips, which is quite lucrative for a 5-pip cost. If the currency pair has a wider spread, I will usually look to make more pips than that.

Q : What is your stop usually?

A : It really depends on whether I am looking for a shorter-term or longer-term trade. But usually what I like to do is to exit in increments. If it moves 75 to 100 pips, I might stop out a portion of the position, if it continues to move another 75 to 100 pips, I might exit another portion and so forth. I really like this exit strategy, and it is something I have only started using in the past 10 years. However, I only do this when I still believe that my directional bias is correct. Keeping a portion of the position allows me to retain the ability to turn this trade around. I have used this technique in the past year and it has worked out for my trades on many occasions. So I may put one stop at 100 points, another at 200 points, and another at 300 points.

I do the same thing with profit targets. I will begin to slowly take a portion off the table in increments. If I make 100 pips, I may close out a quarter of my position, if it moves another 100 pips, I may take profit on another quarter and so forth. This basically prolongs the life of my trade in the market which I think is important for trend trading.

Q : So it seems like you always trade in multiple lots then?

A : Yes, I have quite a bit of speculative capital dedicated to trading currencies. When I trade and have confidence in my analysis, I may put my entire speculative capital into the investment but manage my exits more aggressively by spreading them out.

Q : When you trade, do you usually focus on one currency pair at a time or will you hold positions in multiple currencies?

A : I usually trade one currency pair at a time because if I trade too many, I will not be able to focus on my positions. So if I am trading Swiss francs, I will only focus on the franc. Then if I want to move on to yen, I will wait until I exit out of my franc trade before taking a yen position.

Q : What kind of leverage do you use?

A : Usually the maximum leverage offered. In Hong Kong, that is 20 to 1.

Q : When you first started trading, did you use your savings, or did you borrow from the bank?

A : It was basically my savings. Personally, I do not believe in borrowing money to fund my investments. I use my own funds.

Q : Do you have some sort of monetary or pip target every day or week?

A : No, I do not have daily or weekly targets. The main reason is because I do not want to stress myself out. If you have a daily or weekly target, you are making trading a necessity. That is, every day, you are forcing yourself to look for a trading opportunity even if there may not be one. I prefer to wait for an opportunity and then take it. I don't want to be forced to trade to meet a target. I would rather wait for an opportunity or setup to occur and then to act on it. If I see opportunities, I may trade more. If I do not see an opportunity, I will opt to preserve my capital and wait. I feel that having targets could actually erode your performance.

Q : Have you ever traded full time?

A : Initially, I was an investment advisor. So trading was not my full-time job or focus. Only in the past few years, after I have been successful, have I switched over to giving education courses while trading at the same time. As you have mentioned, there are indeed people who trade full time. For those who do, I suggest they look more at the longer term. That is, to have a quarterly instead of a daily target. This allows you to more flexible. For example, if you need to make $30,000 a quarter, you can revisit your records every month to see how you are doing to meet that goal. This way you avoid the situation where you have a $300 a day goal and because you lost money yesterday, you end up overtrading because you need to make $600 instead of $300 the next day.

Q : What about life expenses? Like rent, health care, and the like, how do you deal with that?

A : Well, I am fortunate enough that I do not have that many expenses. I own my property, so I do not have to pay rent. As for spending, I do not have high expenses, so that is why my stress is not that high. As for my education company, there are expenses, but the income from the business is relatively steady, so there is no major problem. To me the most important thing is that when it comes to my trading, I do not have stress. No stress to meet a goal, no stress to make money to pay my rent so I do not feel like I have to force myself to trade. Therefore I have no need to make any quick cash. I can sit with my position and trade only when opportunities arise.

Q : Do you do your own taxes?

A : In Hong Kong you do not need to pay taxes on your trading profits. But at the same time, if you lose money, you cannot use the losses to reduce taxes. This is as far as I understand, but an accountant would know the details far better. This is for stocks and currencies. Property/real estate gains, you have to pay taxes.

Q : Did you have a mentor when you first started?

A : I had colleagues in my company that taught me the basics.

Q : Did you ever join a support group?

A : No, because 20 years ago there wasn't that many advanced services for trading. Support groups did not exist. These days I will sometimes attend a lecture, but not really take classes because now that I have been in the industry for 20 years, I feel that I have enough experience that I do not need to take any of the classes.

Q : Do you recommend classes for new people?

A : There are a lot of things to learn in the markets, but learning yourself could involve a lot of time and a lot of brick walls. You may spend time looking at tools that may not be right for the market that you want to trade. These days, there are many classes available which help start traders on the right foot and ease their learning. But don't expect to take a class no matter how expensive it may be and be successful right away. The class will give you knowledge, teach you techniques, help you to develop a trading plan, and through this knowledge you will learn the product's characteristics and after that you can learn to develop trading techniques. A class helps people to accelerate their learning, take the first step. But just accelerating your learning will not guarantee success. If it did, everyone would pay a few hundred dollars for one class and never go to work again. No one will teach you the main secret to trading. It is a matter of how aggressive you are at learning and your talent at picking up the information.

Q : Do you have a number one rule for trading?

A : Yes. Stops. The number one rule I have is to use stops and to diversify your investments and do not be afraid to lose. There will always be risk. There are many people who analyze intensively for hours, days, or weeks until they find a trade that they have 90 percent confidence in. But there is nothing that can be 90 percent right all the time. As long as you find something that may only be 80 percent right, that is good enough because it still means that it only has a 20 percent likelihood of being wrong.

Q : What about fear of losing?

A : I think that the more you are afraid to lose, the more unsuccessful you will be. You will be overselective and find that you have missed opportunities. You need to analyze and do your homework. But you also need to be willing to take the chance, to take the risk. If you are wrong, that is okay as long as you have a stop in, your stop will be taken out, and your loss is limited. Maintaining limited risk is better than missing out on what otherwise could be great opportunities. Making sure what your worst-case scenario is at any time will help you manage your trades better, which will ultimately lead to more success.

Q : What was your most memorable trade?

A : It happened two years ago. I took a trade and was able to make 40 percent in one week and a bit more. This was in August 2005. At the time, I was long 5 million U.S. dollars/Swiss francs. I added 2 million later, totaling 7 million. Then I held them both at the same time for eight days before getting out at a 40 percent profit. At the time, U.S. dollars/Swiss francs was range trading and it was nearing a key support zone, I checked my charts and saw a minor breakout and felt that it was a good point to enter into the trade. I initially bought at 1.2487, then I went long again at 1.2485. I exited the whole position at 1.2737, which was the fastest time I exited out of the trade with such large profits.

Q : What was your worst trade?

A : It was in June 2005. I lost close to half of my investment. I was long 5 million British pounds/U.S. dollars and then added another 4 million. I had small profits at the time, but then got greedy and added another 5 million. Then the market reversed and collapsed and because I was long so many lots, I incurred huge losses. The problem here was really my greed. It caused me to let a winner turn into a loser.

Q : How did you recover your confidence after this?

A : Winning and losing are all a part of trading. If you believe in your system, you shouldn't let it get to your confidence because you will be able to trade again and hopefully make the money back. Even though I lost half my capital, I still had the other half, so I had the capital to recover my prior losses. I think that capital preservation is most important.

Q : Did you learn something from this trade?

A : Definitely not to be greedy. If I have profits, I now look to pocket them. At the time, I was hoping for a big ticket winner if the position moved in my favor, ignoring the risks. It's a mistake I won't make again. At the time I lost close to $200,000 U.S. dollars.

Q : When you look at charts, do you add indicators?

A : Yes, MACD, moving averages, DMI. My charts are generally very simple—only a moving average on top and then maybe either the MACD or DMI on bottom. If there are too many things on the charts, I think it's confusing. I don't think you need to put too many things onto the charts. It's important to analyze when trading, but because every indicator is different and may give different entry signals, you can get more confused rather than more clear. I don't rely on too many indicators. Picking a few key ones is enough.

Q : You have already said that entries are important, as well as scattered exits, which do you think is the most important?

A : I think entries are the most important because if you enter well, then it gives you a good price to work with. But I also think that exit is also important because many people will enter in the market, have profits, but because they do not exit properly, the profits will turn into losses.

LESSONS FROM FRANKI LAW
Cut Your Losses, Retain Control

For Franki Law, trading is all about retaining control. Our favorite piece of advice from the Hong Kong–based trader is to make sure that you never lose control of your position because if you do, you will also lose your power to make intelligent decisions. Franki believes that it is extremely dangerous to average down or post margin calls on a losing position. Although you are lowering your average entry price, requiring a smaller price movement to return to breakeven, every point move against you also becomes even more damaging because of the increased position size. At this point, you are essentially at the whim of the market and can only go where it takes you. Even if, based on your analysis, you wanted to take a trade in the opposite direction, you may not be able to because you are paralyzed by your losing position. Therefore, sometimes the smartest trade to make may be the hardest one. If you cut your losses, you not only end the pain, but you also regain your decision-making power and can examine the market from an objective point of view.

Averaging Down Increases Risk, Averaging Up Decreases It

Instead of averaging down, Franki averages up. In fact, many of the traders that we have interviewed also trade this way. By averaging up, you are actually lowering your risk because you are risking profits and not original capital. Franki also tries to milk his trades for everything they are worth by scaling out of his positions. This prolongs the life of his trades and allows him to capture as much of the trend as possible. The way he exits is based on what he feels is the potential of a move, which is his methodology of ranking movements. What we like about Franki's style of trading is the fact that he ranks the potential movements of a currency. For example, if prior breakout moves have lasted for 400 pips and the current move has extended by 100 pips, you can consider that the move is only beginning to run its course and may elect to take off 25 percent of the position just to bank some profits. If the move has extended by 300 pips, then the move is nearing its potential. At this time, traders using a ranking system may elect to take off 75 percent of the position. A small percentage of the position is kept on with a trailing stop in case the current trend has the momentum to extend beyond 400 pips. This way, you are riding as much of the move as possible while also locking in profits along the way.

Rank Your Profits

Day traders may also find it useful to employ a ranking system. For example, if a currency pair has a daily average range of 100 pips, trying to bank all of those 100 pips on a given day may be very difficult. Aiming to bank 30 to 40 of those pips on a day trade is very feasible, 50 to 70 pips may be harder but still possible while 80 to 90 pips may be extremely difficult. This could give traders a frame of reference of when to take profits on their day trades by controlling their greed.

CHAPTER 7

THE TREASURE HUNTER

INDI JONES

Indi Jones—an alias—is a self-confessed treasure hunter who flies around the world looking for hidden gems. Spending six months trading from a beachfront condo in the Caribbean and six months trading from an emerging market country every year, he lives a lifestyle most of us can only dream of. Having passed on a cushy job at a major bank, Indi started his career in the New York commodity pits earning $16K per year two decades ago. He trades extreme sentiment and takes positions in the market when no one else wants to. His forte is trading options for volatility as well as directionality. His motto is to press the trade when it moves in your favor and to always know your maximum loss limit. This discipline and eye for intelligent and unique trades have resulted in an impressive record, as Indi turned $25,000 into a million dollars before he was 30. He is a true professional and an extremely creative trader.

We were delighted that he agreed to share his ideas with us on his brief layover in New York as he was headed down to the Caribbean for some fun in the sun.

■ ■ ■

Q : We are excited about having you participate in our interview series because your story of success is particularly interesting. Let's start by talking about your background and how you got into finance and trading.

A : My education in finance and trading began in my junior year at New York University. We went on a class trip to the commodities exchanges. I looked at the gold pits and the crude oil pits and I thought to myself, "Wow, this is kind of where high finance meets professional sports." It looked like an exciting way to combine my interest in finance and economics with something a little bit more exciting. I saw some guys making a few thousand dollars in a few minutes in the gold pit and then, maybe a half hour later, I saw a similar episode in the crude oil pit.

Q : How long ago was that?

A : It was 1986.

Q : So why did you pick finance and economics as a major? Was it something that your parents encouraged you to study?

A : No, actually, I loved finance since I was a little kid. I used to ask my mom to get me two newspapers, one she didn't have a problem with and that was *Newsday*, so I could read how the Yankees did, and the second one was the *Wall Street Journal*, which she could not understand because nobody in my house was involved in finance. So she used to get me the *Wall Street Journal* and *Newsday* every day from when I was about 10 or 11 years old, and I just became really fascinated with finance and economics from that time on. I loved to study trends. I used to read the commodities sections when I was a kid and I guess I related it to some type of sports score.

Q : Given your interest, did you ever try trading before you went to college?

A : No, I didn't try doing any type of trading until college. That's when I started, and that's when I got my baptism under fire. Shortly after that class trip, I decided, well, hey, I'm studying finance, economics—some of these guys on the floor looked like street thugs—maybe I can outsmart them with a college degree. So I opened up a trading account and started trading these commodities. I basically put in my whole net worth, which was about $5,000 and that wasn't enough to meet the account minimum at the time, so my father put in $5,000 of his money.

Q : How did you convince him?

A : I don't remember how I did that sales job at the moment. But I guess he kind of liked me and thought that the kid can now get some practical experience and see if he knows what he's doing. I had also made some calls during my teenage years, like crude oil is going to go up or the dollar's going to weaken, and maybe he heard some of these and they actually happened, and he thought, "Well, you know, let's let the kid roll the dice."

Q : So your whole family was very supportive then?

A : Yes, they were very supportive, especially my father, 'cause like I said, he had to open the account, too. I think we had a joint account because he had to open it for some reason. It might have been the net-worth thing, or maybe I was under 21 at the time. There was some reason why we had a joint account. It was in his name and my name and we opened it up. I put in $5,000 of my money, which was everything I had, and he put in $5,000 of his to top it off to meet the account minimum, which I think was $10,000 at the time.

Q : So tell us about your very first trade. Did you do a lot of research, or were you so excited about opening the account that you just wanted to put something on for the sake of it?

A : No, I didn't do much research, and I made probably every mistake in the world because I couldn't wait to put on the trade. I mean that account couldn't get opened up fast enough as far I was concerned. Low and behold, of all things, I decided to dabble in coffee. There was some type of crop report coming out on Friday afternoon. So, on the day before, I took a position in coffee based on what I thought was going to happen in the crop report. Right away I made a host of mistakes, as I later realized that it's very risky trading before a crop report. You don't do that, definitely not as a newbie. To make matters worse, I had a midterm exam in marketing the next day at NYU, and I didn't understand all the orders at the time such as stop-loss or limit orders, and most importantly I didn't understand what an OCO order was. It's a *one-cancels-other order*. I had this theory at the time that the crop report was going to be bullish, the market was going to open higher, maybe two to four cents, and I would get out. Alternatively, I would have a stop-loss in, maybe two, three, or four cents below where the market was trading in case it didn't move in my direction. But I was worried that day. I didn't want to put it in and that was really stupid. I didn't want to put the stop-loss order and not take the profits because I was afraid that it would go as high as my profit target, take me out of my position, but then I'd get stopped out and end up with a new position. I didn't want to just put in the target without the stop and didn't know what a one-cancels-other order was and, as a result, I had no orders, just an open position. So I took my exam, ran out of the exam hall to the library, and found that coffee had opened two cents higher and then went limit down after the crop report and I lost like $8,000. I lost all my money and about $3,000 of my father's. [*Authors' note:* Indi here refers to a very common trading order used in almost every financial market—the OCO. One cancel other order allows the trader to enter the position with both a stop and a limit order attached. If either one of the price levels (the stop or the limit) is reached and executed, the other order is automatically cancelled. His ignorance of the OCO left him unprotected in the market.]

Q: So how did you break the news to the big man?

A: I remember a couple of things that Friday: I was going home on the subway and on the train back to Long Island to my parents' house, and it was the only time in my life where a train was coming at me and I actually considered possibly jumping in front of it. It was the first and only time in my life I ever thought about suicide. But I had hit such a low I couldn't believe what I did and every single step of analysis told me what a shmuck and idiot I was, and now I had to go explain this to my father. It wasn't bad enough that I lost all of my money, but I lost some of his too. Surprisingly, he was actually very good about it because I was sitting there and he came home and asked me how did we do today [laughter]. I was speechless for a moment and then I explained the whole thing to him and he was pretty forgiving of it and understanding. He then left me alone and about two days later he just asked me what did you learn from all this. So then I went through the list of how I did everything wrong. That you can't trade when you're taking exams. You've got to put in orders, you've got to put in stop-losses, and you have to learn all of your orders before you do things. I also told him that you have do more homework on the trades, research what's going on, and don't trade before crop reports on your first day. That's one of the riskiest things in the world that you can do. So that was pretty much my baptism under fire.

Q: What happened next? You had $2,000 left in the account, did you continue trading or did you stop?

A: We stopped trading that account, and it was a year or two later when I actually opened an account on my own with what I had, which was like $5,000. I opened an account that allowed me to trade shares, options, and also let me buy options on futures. I traded a little bit of that and by then I learned a little bit more. I was also much more defensive. I think I might have made maybe $300 on it over a 6- to 12-month period. After that I graduated from school and wound up getting a job on the floor at the commodity exchange as an order clerk—which is pretty much how everybody starts out. I'll never forget that story. It was the summer of 1988 and I had two jobs offers. One was from Citibank as a Forex trader and the other was as a clerk on the commodity exchange. At the time, the Forex job was offering $24,000 a year and the clerk was $16,000. Back then 24K was a good starting salary for someone out of college. For someone earning 16K, it was pathetic if they had a college degree. I remember coming home that evening and my mom said, "Well, how did it go today?" I said, "Pretty good. I got two job offers and I picked one." She goes, "Oh, okay. Well, when do you start at Citibank?" I said, "No, I'm starting on the floor next week. Then she asked: "Did you learn anything at school, one job for $24,000 another one for $16,000—come on, the choice is obvious." Then she asked why we were paying all this money for school [laughter].

Q : When you were on the floor as a clerk, could you trade for yourself or was it forbidden?

A : It was forbidden. You had to do your job, and my job was to take orders from customers. It would have been a conflict of interest if I had positions on as I was trying to service the clients. My primary responsibility was to take their orders, cancel their orders, report their fills, and not be trading my own accounts or anything like that. I got really lucky, you know the stock market crashed in 1987 and there was a pretty much a recession on Wall Street from 1988 to 1989—people were not hiring aggressively. I got lucky in that I got offered a job by someone I didn't know on the floor. What I found out about the floor was that there's two kinds of people down there and I hate to say it, but this is what I saw. There were really nice, good people who are losers in the markets, but you know they would be your best friends and they would loan you their last buck to buy lunch if you did a bad gold trade or something. Then there were a bunch of rich, ruthless jerks. That was the kind of the delineation between the two types of traders on that floor—it is a very competitive environment. I got lucky in that through chance I just happened to get a job with a guy who was rich, who knew what he was doing in the markets, who was making money, and was also actually a nice person who cared about your career, not just how much money he could make off you working for him. It was just the luckiest thing that happened to me. One of the reasons I took that job on the floor instead of working with Citigroup is that he had promised me if I studied the market and learned it, if I picked it up quickly I would be in the ring trading within 6 to 12 months.

Q : That's pretty fast!

A : Yes, really fast, most people take three to five years. So I jumped at the chance because I wanted to go as quickly as possible into the trading side, I didn't want to be answering phones all day. So this really excited me about the job and I'll never forget what happened next. When you're on the phones, you make friends with the people next to you. They are your competitors, but you are also chatting about what you are doing this weekend, what you are doing with a girlfriend, and this and that. So about three months into my job, a so-called friend of mine was next to the silver pit with me and the market was really slow and it was getting time to go home for the weekend. All of the sudden he looks at me and he's like, "Indi, what are you doing down here, you've got a college degree"

Q : Did most clerks not have college degree?

A : No, a lot of them didn't actually. So he said what are you standing down here getting underpaid, answering telephones for? When you could be doing something else *upstairs*. You know, at an investment banking firm or a trading firm or something like that. I said to him, well these guys promised to put me in the ring

169

in about 6 to 12 months, and all I heard was this sheepish laugh. Then I thought, "Oh no, so being told you will be put in the ring in 6 to 12 months is the same thing as someone telling you that the check is in the mail." I felt like I had been had and thought that I'm probably going to be down here for three to five years answering phones unless something changes. But I stood behind this trader every day for 6 months and afterwards would pick his brain clean. I was his clerk, so I asked him why are you doing these trades, why are buying this, why you selling that? Low and behold, believe or not, about 9 to 12 months later I was in the ring trading sugar and coffee options. I was getting my revenge on some of those guys, and that's how it started on the floor.

Q : Did somebody on the floor stake you?

A : Yes, the guy I worked for also had shares in different trading companies. So he owned shares, sometimes big interests in a trading group on the sugar exchange, and one on the oil exchange, and back then there were about five different commodity exchanges on one trading floor in the World Trade Center building. So one corner of the building was the cotton exchange, one corner was the coffee, sugar, and cocoa exchange, one corner was the COMEX gold exchange, one corner of the building was the New York Merc Crude Oil markets, and then in the middle was a small little New York futures exchange that traded stock index futures and, I think, the CRB index. So he had shares in a company that was trading on the softs, which are coffee, sugar and cocoa, and as soon as that opening went up, I went for the interview with the director of that company, which was at a local bar, as most of my commodity interviews were. After a few beers and probably several questions about sports I got the job [laughter].

Q : So first you were taking orders and just fulfilling orders?

A : Yes.

Q : How much longer before you began to take positions?

A : As I mentioned earlier, I started as a clerk and then it took about 9 or 10 months before I got into the ring, and I started trading a company account. I was so excited by that. You go into broker training for about a month before you're going into the ring. Part of your day is spent on the phones taking orders, but the other part is to go over to the pit that you're going to be trading in and observe for an hour every other day or so. Then maybe twice a week you have classes after the markets are all closed. You go into the pit that you're going to be trading in and they do simulated trading and teach you how to do open outcry, which is really a fun and a thrilling process, and how to quickly get your mind ready to execute orders and multiple orders when the markets are falling and rising—also how to cross trades and execute buy and sell orders at the same time. So that was really thrilling, and I was really loud and vocal in it, and so was everyone else. Then, when it comes to your first day in the trading pit you see every newbie, who was very loud in training, is basically standing there with their arms crossed. Except for me of course, I had to go wild. I start yelling and screaming and making markets and doing trades. I remember one of the other newbies from the class looked over to me during the second or third day in the pit. He was like, "What the hell are you doing, do you know exactly what you're doing, yet?" I was like, "No, but I'm just trying to react to the order flow." Then low and behold that relaxed feeling paid off because in my first month trading open outcry, I made $40,000, and I thought okay, now it's going to happen. I'm going to be the next George Soros, this is how it's going to start.

Q : The reason it happened was because you were just reacting to order flow? That is you were basically fading the offers, buying the bids and the market was relatively quiet so you were able to make the spread?

A : It was a little bit different then, the market was pretty busy. So I was fading orders, market making, scalping in and out, and when everything netted out, I was buying options and hedging it. So I had basically a long volatility position, which will be profitable if the underlying moves significantly. So I was making money two ways, first scalping and collecting on the bid offer spread, which was paying some bills, and then building that into a long-term, long-volatility position as the market was going crazy. Option volatilities were getting more and more pumped as the gyrations in price increased, and then I thought, I'm going to take this strategy and run with it until I become billionaire. Naturally, about a month or two later, I had lost all of that money. Volatility contracted [laughter] and, of course, then everyone really wants to hit you on the options at that time.

Q : Once you started making bids, there is no way to offset it, right, because nobody wants the other end of it?

A : Nobody wants the other end of it when volatility is contracting. So I got stuffed and probably lost all that I made plus about another 40 or 50 thousand. My equity swings were going wild.

Q : Who's money was it?

A : It was the trading firm's.

Q : How much of a line did they give?

A : I don't remember exactly, but we pretty much had access to funds. I mean millions, if you wanted it. But they were watching you and every few days you'd be meeting with a risk manager.

Q : Were they screaming at you when you started going from plus 40K to zero to minus 10K, minus 20K?

A : They weren't really screaming at me. They were very happy with the first month, obviously. They didn't really warn me about being long the volatility. I guess they thought this guy knows that now's the time to be long vol. They did mention it, at one stage, that my equity swings were getting a little bit too wide for what they do. They said we told you to buy and sell options and they looked at my position and, let's say, sugar was trading at 10 cents at the time, and they said, hey, you are long the 10-cent calls, you are long on the 11-cent calls, but in the 9-cent calls you should sell something. Don't just buy every strike [laughter].

Q: Long strikes all across the board right?

A: Anyway, at the end of the year, I tried to grind my way back, and I'd been in the ring for six months since, I think I had got in May 1989 or June, and by December that's the yearend. So by the first month, let's say it was May 1989, I made 40 grand and then the second month I lost 20, and the third month maybe 40 and then treaded water back and forth. But by the end of the year I was down about 20. It was time to go in for a review, so I figured, "Okay, well, I'm fired. I'm out of here." So it's the end of the year, and I'll never forget it, I go into the interview and the director sits me down and he looks across the table and he's like, "You had a pretty good year." I'm like, "Oh, cool. They got the wrong file [laughter]." The way it worked was that you had a base salary of $24,000 plus 20 percent of the profits that you made. So I asked the director, "What's my bonus?" He said, "No, you don't have a bonus, you're down 20,000, but you had good year for a first year." He said that most of our guys get killed in their first year, and he said that you were active so you should have lost 100 to 200,000 dollars this year. I was like, uh, okay, and from that day on I just decided all right, Indi, you are either going to have to learn how to do this like a professional and learn money management skills, not just shoot your mouth off by saying taken and sold. Otherwise next year, they're probably not going to be as forgiving. If you are down again, you'll be looking for another job doing something you probably don't love as much as this, because trading was exciting for me.

Q : So how long did you trade in the pit?

A : I traded for that company for three years.

Q : How were those years? The next year, when you said you were going to get serious about money management, what were your equity swings like then?

A : Very controlled, and I started to make anywhere from $100,000 to $300,000 depending on how much opportunity I was given. When the markets threatened me by going against me and I didn't know what was going on, I would really play defense. Really cut back.

Q : What would that mean when you played "defense"? Could you cut your positions?

A : I'd cut my positions. In other words, if I was long vols, and I owned several strikes and the thing went against me and wasn't turning for whatever reason, I'd cut the trade, take the loss, get out.

Q : Did you then try to make money scalping?

A : Yes. You could make money scalping, but not all of the time. When the markets are slow you couldn't. If the market got really dead or slow I'd leave the pit. One of the areas where I find my trading is horrible is when the markets are dead. I do one thing that is stupid. I want to trade, open my mouth, or, in the electronic format, buy and sell stuff on the screen and then wind up with a graveyard position. I get the crap that no one else wants just because I couldn't keep still, and now I will probably die with this stuff.

Q : What would you do to avoid that?

A : Get out of my positions and then get out of the pit.

Q : Where would you go?

A : I would just go into the lunchroom or go downstairs and look at where other markets were going. Maybe go over and look at some other market on the floor that I wasn't a member of, but see what's going on there. Basically, I would just get out of that area where I was going to get tempted to lose money.

Q : How long would you take a break for?

A : As long as it took. However, you've got to be careful. You can't be working for a company and play pinball all day down in the pizza parlor because the markets are slow. So I would go in there and see what was going on, if I saw that the quagmire was starting again, I would either stay in the pit and just shut up, or see if there were any new pretty clerks on the floor. I would have some other way of amusing myself besides trading commodities or bidding and offering on these options. It was only when the markets go crazy that you find big wide spreads, you find gaps, and you find things that are mispriced. So I kind of wait for that, cherry pick, if you will.

Q : Did meeting with a risk manager every few days, help your trading by having accountability because you had to report to some-one your results?

A : No, really that's an internal process. Most of the risk managers, the people I've dealt with, they're usually failed traders or someone who doesn't really have the first clue about what's really going on. They can yell at you after the fact, but they can't offer you constructive advice. It's an internal thing. You have got to come to terms with the fact that you are going to be a professional trader, that you are going to manage your risk, and you are going to study these options or these strike prices or the relationships for them so that you can quantify your risk. You must come up with your own methodology on how you are going to calm down and control risk, and be professional, and try to be the house in a casino instead of just a player. It's a really an internal thing. These guys can help you a little bit. But a lot of them don't have that much better insight than you do, and none of them are as motivated as you are in terms of trying to make money and be successful in the business. That's what I found, they're not going to be your savior, so you better do it yourself.

Q : Was your trading style *organic*, was it basically something you learned yourself, or something that you modeled off somebody else?

A : It was a combination of things. When I decided to become professional after that first year of the $20,000 loss. I ate, breathed, slept, and drank commodities. I read everything about the markets. I would read the *Market Wizards* book about Tony Saleba, and tried to understand what he was doing. Okay, I don't want to get too technical, but he was doing butterflying in the front months and back spreading in the back months, and scalping in the middle to pay for the whole thing. So I looked at that idea. I started to remember what my mentor in the business was doing when I was standing behind him and he was trading gold options and things like that.

Q : What was he doing exactly?

A : He was lucky back then. You were able to get conversions done where you were able to buy puts, buy futures and sell calls and lock in profits and link butterflies for zero [a butterfly strategy links a number of option positions in hopes that the underlying will remain in a narrow trading range] and sell them out to the order flow for a buck or something.

Q : So string a hundred butterflies all together, so if one of them made a hit, he would score?

A : Yeah, and other things like that such as linking butterflies for zero, combined with cashing in on being able to trade the bid-offer spread, and having a string of butterflies on and one of them, was going to be in the money. Gold was less hectic and less volatile in the mid- to late 1980s than it was earlier.

Q : Was he trading strictly options?

A : Yes.

Q : Or was he trading other instruments as well? Like hedging with the underlying?

A : He was hedging with the underlying. We all were.

Q : Mechanically, where was the underlying trading, was it trading right next to you, how was the hedge done physically?

A : We had an order taker in the futures ring that worked for the company. So I would be in the option pit and let's say I bought 10 put options and the delta was 0.5 and the market was trading at 10.60. I'd immediately yell to him, "Greg, buy me five!" And then he'd buy five futures against the put options I had just bought, and then he'd report back something like, you know you bought them at 10.71 and I'd yell FU or something [laughter]. And then right after I bought 10.71, it would drop back to 10.60 [laughter].

177

Q : Now you currently don't trade in the pit. So how long did you actually spend trading for the company in a pit?

A : I worked for that company for three years and, at the end of the third year, I'd saved enough money to buy a seat. I bought a seat on the cotton exchange because one day I was literally laying down in the sugar options pit because it was one of those periods where nothing was going on in the market and this had been actually going on for a month or two and the market was just horrible and I'll never forget what happened next. I was laying down, literally looking up at the ceiling, and I heard a roar from one of the quadrants, like a riot had broken out or something. I ran over there and my company had given me a cotton exchange seat as well, which I never used. I went over there and there was a crop report and this was in 1991, I think. There was a crop report in orange juice and the orange juice market went up 40 percent in one day and the place was crazy.

Q : Was there some kind of freeze in Brazil or something?

A : It was a crop report that everyone miscalculated. Everyone expected the crop to increase and, for some reason, the crop materially decreased because of some citrus aphid or some bug or something and, of course, the whole ring was short along with the market going into this report and it was pandemonium. They had security guards, and if you did not have a cotton exchange badge you could not go walk through that quadrant. Whether you were going to the bathroom or going to lunch, you couldn't go there. I had the badge. So I went in the middle of the pit and it was pandemonium, yelling, screaming, insanity. This is what I loved and I couldn't help it, but I started reacting to order flow [laughter]. Then I thought, "Okay, idiot you better go downstairs and run some options theoretical values before you start shooting your mouth off in here." I did and then went back in there and it was lot of fun. Now the problem was that we already had a prop trader trading orange juice and I was the sugar guy. But, I thought, this is exciting and he didn't mind that I was over there so I traded for a few days there, scalped, made some money, but it was really this guy's turf and I didn't want to step on his toes. So I went back to sleep in the sugar pit. Near the end of the year, I thought to myself, after this year, you have enough money to buy a seat on the cotton exchange for yourself and you have some money left over to put in your account. That place is going to be cooking for six months afterwards, I mean, they just dropped a bomb over there and re-verberations are going to go for at least six months till that thing dies. Why don't you take a shot on your own. Instead of making 20 percent of what you make, make a hundred. So that's what I did. So near the end of that year I told my firm that I was going to be leaving them and that I would trade the last month of December as hard as I could for them, which I did. I told them that they really should have me in orange juice because sugar stinks. That place was still gyrating every day, and they said, okay, you can go over there since the other guy didn't mind. What was great about that, too, is that I was still trading for this company, but I was learning things about orange juice and was also making friends with some of the other brokers over there. This way, I wasn't some new strange face who showed up on January 1st, 1992.

Q : So you could cash in on order flow when order flow came to you?

A : Yes, and I had more ammo because I was still trading for the company backed by millions, whereas in a few months, I was going to be just me with my little $25,000 in my account. So, in 1992, January 1, I went on my own, started trading orange juice on the cotton exchange, and I had a net worth of $25,000 and the clearing firms were so afraid of me, I could tell every day, every morning that they just had this look like, "Now listen idiot, if we lose $1,000 because you lose $26,000, we will hunt you down." [Laughter.] They watched me like a hawk. If an option went too far in the money, they forced me to exercise it no matter what. They were nervous about me. It eventually ended because that year I actually turned that $25,000 into over $250,000 trading on the floor.

Q : Was most of that 250K a function of scalping or a function of your directional calls?

A : I think the main part of it was two things: In the beginning I was just scalping because I didn't have a lot of capital. You know 25K is not a very big stake. So I would pick my spots and try to arbitrage things or find butterflies. Sometimes I'd lay butterflies out there for credits, so that's even better than zero and I'd string some of them. At one stage, after OJ went up to about $1.60 or $1.70, I thought that it was overdone. Back in the '90s we were in a deflationary decade, so I thought, well, it's only a matter of time before this thing crashes and dies, and I started putting on some positions basically.

Q : You bought some long-term put positions?
A : Yes.

Q : Like spreads?
A : I bought puts and sold some calls, creating collars or fences.

Q : With the underlying or without the underlying?

A : I would hedge the underlying. But the beauty was if the position blew through the put strikes, it kicked in, and I was long puts and short the market to a degree. I mean, I hedged everything but left a little leeway. The reason I liked the trade was that at the time there were huge volatility skews, calls were trading at volatility levels 5 or 10 percent above the puts. So I was building up the positions with a great theoretical advantage and with the thought that, when this thing crashes, I'm going to underhedge it. I'm not going to buy back my deltas as quickly as I should because markets usually drop much faster than they rally, and I knew the whole world was long now and the whole thing had changed, and I thought it was just a question of when the market did a cliff dive. We were in the deflationary '90s, and I had seen how the guys in gold used to get burned every time it rallied too high, and I kind of thought the same thing would happen here in OJ. There were some newspaper articles, like Jimmy Rogers was in *Barron's* one weekend saying this OJ market is unsustainable because Brazil was growing a zillion orange trees or something like that. Which was eventually true, then destiny kicked in and OJ crashed.

Q: So you took $250,000, and then did you leave or continue to trade OJ?

A: No, I stayed with them, I traded there until 1997. The thing that made me leave the market was the best trade that I ever had. It was in orange juice as well, and it was the freeze that never happened. This was February 1996. We had gone through freeze season and if a freeze happens according to what I studied in the charts, they usually happened in December and usually right around Christmas Eve. We went through this period, went into January and there was no cold weather and nothing was going on, and so the option volatilities were plunging, they went from like 40 percent down to 20 and I had never seen option vols at 20 in orange juice. So I started doing back spreads while other guys were crushing out of the money call options for May delivery. They figured that freeze season was over, volatilities are going to collapse, orange juice was never going to go back up to $1.30 to $1.50—let's nail these guys on these May calls. So I'd buy, and then I'd back spread them. I would try to do back spreads for zero cost, so I'd sell at-the-money calls and buy whatever strike I could get out of the money where I could buy two of them and be zero cost in terms of option premium. I thought to myself that even if we had a big down move, it wasn't a problem and that this position would work too because if we did get some type of spike, some type of freeze, my twice-as-many calls would kick in.

Q : The only time it wouldn't have worked is if things stayed the same?

A : Yes, or if we had a slow rally, I would have gotten hurt. But I would check my risk every day. I'd run scenarios several times during the day to see what my worst-case scenario was and how big my problem would be and could I live with it. Then I remember it was a Sunday, and it started snowing in New York like I had never seen it. There was three feet of snow or something like that.

Q : This was what month?

A : February 1996. I woke up that Monday morning and I thought, oh this is beautiful. There was a freeze that hit Florida during this whole snowstorm and I felt like this was a Christmas gift come late and I must have been a good boy last year. I remember the market being closed that Monday because New York was snowed in or it was George Washington's birthday. But when I came in the following day, the market was called to open 5 percent higher and it did. It shot 5 percent higher and I was long and, the next day, we came in and it was called 5 percent higher and it opened 5 percent higher, which was the limit at the time. By then I started scaling out of the position. You just naturally want to get out of stuff. You're ringing the register. You're seeing money that you might want to spend some day [laughter]. It was hitting the account, and by the end of that day I was still slightly long futures and slightly long options, but I was out of probably about 85 percent of the positions. I rang the register on it. By now it was on the TV. One friend, whom I hadn't heard from in awhile, phoned me to say, "Hey Indi, you're trading oranges. I saw the orange on CNBC with the icicles. Did you catch it?" I said, "Yeah, and I was on the right side, don't worry, I caught that move." By now it was the third day. The opening call was about 3 percent higher, and I had a problem with that because, I was thinking, wait a minute, it's all on CNBC now, the orange with the icicle is on the TV. I was thinking that all my friends are calling me up about it and the market only opened up one-and-half percent. So, I thought, this doesn't feel right. I didn't know if it was trader intuition or my bull alarm. Something was going off and I just said, I'm getting flat. So I got out of as much as I could and now the market's barely higher. I'm standing in the ring and I'm confused now. I'm very confused because this is not like it was in the last two days and then all of a sudden a light bulb went on and I had a dream. But after the dream I began to feel more conviction now than when I walked in on Monday morning. I had this vision then, a dream: There are these guys that come down onto the floor every now and then. They are Florida citrus guys and they're these old Southern gentlemen who are very smart. They're very wealthy and they control the orange juice business in south Florida and I had seen them many times on the floor with the greatest tailoring jobs, the greatest suits, some of them fly up in their own private planes, and I had this vision of one of these guys on the balcony of his mansion overlooking his orange groves with his cordless phone who knew that the whole freeze was bull and he was phoning his New York brokers telling them, cap this thing, sell this thing, short this thing. Basically, what was going on in my mind was that this is what the smart money is doing. They are saying, "Sell, damn it." I figured that guys like him must be selling, and I have to get in on this especially since I had just had a nice score in the market. One of the things that I do is, if I've just made some money and if I still feel I'm in sync with the market, is that I step on the gas. I would be a horrible high school football coach in America today because, if my team is up 90 to nothing at half time. I'd be trying to figure out ways to bury these guys 300 to nothing by the fourth quarter. That was how I was thinking on this day. I was up 90 to nothing at half time, but I want to kill. I want to make them cry. I want to win, you know, 300 to zero. I decided that I'm going to do whatever I can in futures and options to sell the hell out of this market with my fictional smart Southern friend. This guy was a ghost basically, but I wanted to be with him. I wanted to trade with my imaginary friend. So I started selling and I did enough futures and options where, if the market took out the high for the day and I was going to give a stop order to one my brokers in the OJ futures to take me out, I would only have lost about 40 percent of what I made on the up move over the last two or three days. I decided that I wasn't going to do anything until the market went to unchanged or lower and a few minutes later the market went to unchanged and I went hog wild and sold as many futures or options or whatever I could do. Just a gasket went off to get short where my risk was that if the market took out it's highs for the day, I would have lost 40 percent of my equity on the last three days. So I put the trade on and about 30 or 45 minutes after that, the market was down 6 percent and about two to three days later, it was down another 4 or 5, or about 10 percent from where I sold it. I made another killing, catching it up and down, and I decided at that stage, a few days later, that I had just made a killing and I was going to take the rest of the year off. Why should I become a rat on a treadmill chasing the cheese in front of me until I croak? I said to myself, go out, hit the clubs in New York City, relax, enjoy yourself, become a playboy—why make more millions, why? You don't need them, so I decided alright, I'm getting off this treadmill now and I wound down my positions and, in about March or April of that year, I left the floor and pretty much never went back.

Q : Was it an easy decision for you to just leave the markets? How did you pull yourself away from making more money?

A : No! I never thought that I was leaving for long term. I thought I was going to leave for about six to nine months, party in New York City, go out to the clubs with my friends, call up my high school friends, college friends, go skiing every weekend and come back the next year. So, to me, it was just like taking a long break. I thought I was the luckiest guy in the world. I could take a nine-month vacation. I mean, who could do that? I was 29, 30 years old, and I was just going to enjoy the nightlife in New York City and maybe go on cruises and go to the beach and do whatever I wanted for about a year and then I'd get serious again and work. Well, after about three months of the so-called playboy lifestyle, you find out your college buddies are all getting married, they all have kids, they all can't go out every night. They have to work the next day, they wake up at 5 A.M. and commute from wherever they live in New Jersey into New York City and you find that you get bored pretty quickly. That was when the idea of the Emerging Market hit. A few years earlier I was at a good friend's wedding there, I took a look at their markets with the thought that I'm going to come back there and trade their commodity markets some day and then I forgot about it. I thought to myself, rather than goof off for nine months, why don't I start a new business, which will fail because 90 percent of new businesses fail, and I'll go over to the emerging market country and just hang out and party there. Look up my old friend there and start a new business.

Q : What year was this?

A : 1997.

Q : So what was your new business?

A : To trade commodity options on the Emerging Market's futures exchange. They didn't even have them yet, but I did persuade them to list them a few months later and that first year was really tough. I think I traded from June until December 1997. It was broken up a bit because I went over there for three months, got semi-homesick, and came back for a month or two and then went over there again. I think I made like $24,000 during that time.

Q : Were you doing this pretty much by yourself?

A : Yes, by myself. I signed up with a brokerage firm over there and then the exchange was going to list these new commodity options and nobody knew what to do with them. They said look, if someone puts up a bid, you put an offer, if someone puts up an offer, counter with a bid. And I said, are there any restrictions on me, like how far away I do the options and they said no. We just want to see two-way markets. We don't want to see someone put an order in that never gets answered. I said alright I'll do that.

Q : What type of commodities were they trading?

A : Agricultural. They were trading corn. That's their staple food product, which they also use for animal feed. Wheat and sunflower seeds and soybeans also.

Q : So were on you on the floor of the exchange?

A : No, it was electronic and that was bizarre. Here I was—I went from New York City, the financial capital of the world, the most sophisticated financial battleground where everything is done by yelling and screaming and spitting on people and poking them with pencils and here I go into the third world and it's all electronically integrated. It was the weirdest thing.

Q : So that must have been different for you, since what you were doing mostly was reacting to flow. Electronically it must be very different from hearing people yelling and screaming. How did that work?

A : Oh man, it was terrible because you're right on the floor. I could hear people yelling and screaming. Hearing the noise level would get you up. On a computer screen there's nothing. I remember times I'd be reading the newspaper and all of a sudden I'll look up and I'd see my screen blinking indicating that the market's limit down or something and I'd been asleep through about a 30-pip drop in prices where, as in the old days, if I was on the floor you'd definitely hear that and you'd react to that. So it was a little bit different.

Q : Did you have to change the style of your trading then?

A : Yes, I'd have to set up alerts on the computer to make a noise, and I would use various indicators—oscillators to determine when it broke out to a certain level. My computer would start making noises or something and that would wake me up.

Q : So you'll stay with the same strategy, but you'll just use mechanics to make sure that you were awake and alert while you're following it?

A : Yes, correct.

Q : Were you trading in an office?

A : No.

Q : It was from a brokerage house?

A : Yes. But remember, this was an electronic exchange. It could be traded from anywhere. Currently, I am trading from a beach house in the Caribbean, because after I am done trading I love to swim, snorkel, jet ski, and soon kite surf.

Q : Were there other traders around you that were doing the same thing?

A : There were other traders trading for the brokerage house, but they were trading mainly the stock market and also the stock index futures.

Q : Socially—was it a relatively isolating experience to trade against a screen rather than a ring, that is, very, very social and very loud?

A : Yes.

Q : Did that kind of take you back a little bit?

A : It did, but you learn how to market strategies to people. On the floor, it's just you reacting to people. You say, "Hey, how are you doing, what are you looking to do?" It's much more vocal and in your face. There you become much more introspective, and what you have to try and find out is who are the players, what do they want, and can you come up with some type of product or strategy that will give them what they want, but will have some type of option related theoretical advantage for you.

Q : So that is how you would try to attract some of the institutional order flow to you by creating all of these option strategies for them.

A : Exactly. Then you advertise on the screen, not by yelling and jumping up and down, but whenever someone puts in a bid that you're the first guy to offer. That will eventually lead to a phone call like, "Hey, I notice you're trying to sell here. I'm trying to buy here. What can we do?"

Q : Let's talk about what kind of equipment you used. What was your setup?

A : My belief is to use the best stuff that you can get. So I travel around with a Bloomberg terminal with real time data.

Q : So you have a Bloomberg Anywhere?

A : They've even done something better for me, before Bloomberg Anywhere was invented, they did not want you traveling around with any of these things, but they did have the facility. That was only for their salespeople mainly. So they'd give you Bloomberg Professional on your laptop, which they hated to do. In fact, I tried to get it through London, and they said they would do it for me for six months. I had some shares in a energy trading firm in New York that had several of the Bloomberg Professional stations in their offices. I said, I travel around—can you give me the Bloomberg Professional on my laptop? And don't try to sell me an actual terminal. I don't need a desktop terminal. I go through airports. They eventually did, and they gave me the Bloomberg Professional as you guys would have with the four screens. But I have four boxes on my laptop. I have to toggle between what I want to look at. So they gave me that and I use TradeStation. I also use different option pricing software pieces that are custom made for me by programmers. I use different people in financial engineering to help me model how the option pricing surface should look. What the advantages are in the current one versus the historical.

Q : So, all of these functionalities are on one laptop?

A : No, I travel with three. In fact, it drives people nuts. I literally run around the world with three different laptops. One has my Bloomberg, my TradeStation, all of my data and back testing stuff. Another one has all of my option financial engineering analytics, and the third one is a dealing screen.

Q : So when you are trading all three are up in front of you?

A : All three are in front of me.

Q : The dealing screen, how do you deal now? Do you have a broker?

A : I've got brokers who set me up with direct dealing in the exchanges overseas, and here in the states I use Interactive Brokers,

TradeStation securities, the different ones here that give you the online access. My favorite is Interactive Brokers.

Q : Let's talk about Interactive because many readers use them. When you're trading option exchanges in the U.S., you're now able to make bid/ask. Do you use that facility when you're doing Interactive? Are you sort of trading typically like a Market Maker these days or more or less a customer?

A : No, I'm trading more as a customer on Interactive. What I'm really doing there is, I develop strategies where I'm mainly doing a lot of stuff like buy-writes. A *buy-write* is a covered call strategy in the options market where I buy an underlying share and then sell at-the-money or in-the money calls against the share position. The most recent ones were in the energy shares. This was in 2004, 2005—Conoco Phillips—I would buy shares, write options against it and let it get called away.

Q : Companies with big fat dividends?

A : I would do that, but that doesn't work anymore. I had a great time with the Canadian oil trusts about two years ago, where you'd be able to buy the oil trust, write an option that's in the money, giving you like 10 or 20 percent downside protection plus a little bit of time premium, collect the dividends, and write your way to prosperity. That no longer works because they've all appreciated a lot. Also I don't know if the open interest is thinner or whatever, but a lot of times recently, maybe about six months ago, I used to get exercised right before the dividend date. So you would lose your share at a very critical time. That was another problem and now there is a change in the tax laws in Canada which is going to put that whole thing out of business. It's not going to work anymore, but that's how I'd use Interactive. In the foreign markets, I'm usually trying to act as market maker, a facilitator of deals.

Q : Can you tell us about how you start your trading day now that you trade as a customer? Do you read news, do you rely mostly on your back-tested models?

A : I trade a lot of foreign markets, so on a typical day, I wake up at weird hours. I wake up about two in the morning and I look at the market to see what's been happening, see any news, what could be changing in the world or in the commodities or shares that I'm trading. Then I jump in about an hour later and I start executing stuff in the foreign markets.

Q : Do you read local papers?

A : Oh yeah.

Q : So your focus is still very commodity driven, this is your core domain of expertise?

A : Yes.

Q : When you are talking about foreign markets, are you talking about foreign commodities markets? Do you look at foreign equity markets, but sort of find commodity themes within there as well?

A : That's what I'll do. It will be either foreign commodity markets or usually domestic or foreign share markets that have a commodity theme to it.

Q : So you're reading the news and you've been trading an hour into it. Now are you focused and sitting in front of screen for the whole time?

A : Yes, without a doubt.

Q : So you don't go and do other things?

A : No.

Q : Do you find that commodity-driven stories are much more news affected than pure stock stories, pure equity stories? In other words, if there's a big piece of news on that day that is commodity related, it's going to have a continuous impact on the commodity markets versus the stock market where we can't tell if the stock will have a significant reaction to an economic release?

A : Yeah, I have seen that. What I've seen with the news-driven events in shares and what I've seen with the commodity is when you get a news-driven event like a crop report, it usually has a sustained impact that could mean you're in an interesting period for three months, six months or so. With stocks, and I've seen it mainly with earning-related news so there's a slight difference here but the earnings-related event to a commodity stock is usually a one move and that's it. It moves 20 percent and that's it. It's readjusted.

Q : So you are focused, you're sitting in front your screen. At what point do you start looking?

A : I trade very intensely through the first three hours. Then it's usually about six in the morning or so. Then I'll stop.

Q : Let's go through the first three hours. Very intensely means how many round turns a day?

A : Sometimes it could be small like a 10, 20, 30 contracts, but usually a few hundred. There are some days when I'll trade a thousand contracts.

Q : More important than even the size is how many trades do you do during those three hours? Are those quick succession of trades? Or do are you usually building one position that you let go at the end of that session?

A : No it's quick. I'm getting in and out and doing things and reacting to what's going to on.

Q : So you're moving between 20 to 100 round turns during that three-hour period?

A : Oh easily, easily. Yes. It's active and intense.

Q : You could be holding these trades for minutes at a time literally?

A : Oh yeah. I don't recall if it was last night or the night before, but I got in and out in about two minutes on a trade.

Q : Do you feel like this is the same way you were trading when you were in the pit? Very quickly? In and out scalping? Or have you changed?

A : It's very similar but the electronic element is slightly different than open outcry. There are no computer, phone, or fax that can react as fast as a human can react in an open outcry pit. I mean, I could literally do three things at once in open outcry, and I'm lucky to get one guy on the phone in electronic trading. So, I mean, I could be hitting bids in the pit, yelling at my clerk to get another guy who had an order that was resting, that I want to hit, and hedging myself immediately in open outcry within a microsecond. To do that electronically, to get one person on the deal, you got to phone them, then you got to execute that, then you have to key it in, and if you're like me, and sometimes not so finger friendly, you've got to study, buy 10 futures, go.

Q : Most of the contracts that you're dealing with are still phone-based transactions, they're not pure electronic, straight-through processing?

A : What I find in the foreign markets is that it's electronic, but a lot of it seems like an over-the-counter Forex-type thing. Where you're also talking to the guys and kind of just booking a deal through electronically, especially with complex options spreads.

Q : When it's not simply an outright position, and you have to do lots of different spreads, is it very difficult to do it purely electronically?

A : You got it.

Q : How do you find these brokers—usually by word of mouth or do you have connections? This must be particularly difficult in the foreign markets.

A : You pretty much go there and they get flushed out of the wood-work. They'll see you on the screen offering or bidding. They'll phone the brokerage firm that you're trading with. That firm will contact you and say, "Hey, we're getting calls from this broker. They want to do this structure, are you interested?" Yes. So that's pretty much it and you go to whatever functions are there, like if there's a hedge fund conference. You go and meet all of the people. If there's agriculture conference somewhere on a new commodity exchange, you go. A lot of these exchanges or a lot of these associ-ations have their annual meeting, where the official business gets done and then afterwards there is a party. You go to the party, even though you might not be able to vote at their board or whatever, you go to the party afterwards, and you meet a lot of the people in the markets.

Q : Now that you're trading by yourself, do you ever have people that you speak to on a daily basis? Or are you pretty much doing it on your own?

A : I always try to talk to a lot of different people in the markets.

Q : Every single day?

A : Yes. People whose opinion I respect, and also there's the proverbial dumb money. I think it's valuable information. You want to talk to as many people as you can and decide whether you're going to trade or fade these guys today, It gives you a huge amount of information. For example, if the markets first rally today because a crop report came out and it's looking good, and you've talked to four people, two really good traders—who say, "Yeah we're bullish, we'll get long today."—and two guys who are slow behind the curve—and they also said it's obvious that it's going higher today—and all the sudden the market starts acting really bad at the end of the day, that might give me the guts to go short or to bet against these guys or to squeeze it on the downsize.

Q : So a lot of sentiment work goes into your analysis?

A : Yes. I want to talk to people in the market every day. You try to pick the people who you think are the most sophisticated traders, but you also get sentiment from a broad spectrum of people.

Q : It sounds like most of your strategies are in and out, in and out, do you ever carry anything overnight?

A : Yes.

Q : Is it in a different portfolio, same portfolio, and/or different broker?

A : Yes. I'll describe it as briefly as I can. I have one limited liability company that I set up for my aggressive trading. That's where the fast-and-furious stuff is going to be done and that is my trading business. Then I have two other accounts that I use, which sometimes are as frenetic as the trading level. But I would characterize them more as my investment accounts. In the trading account, I can have stuff held anywhere from a second to a few minutes. Sometimes the nature of the option market is such that you'll have stuff on for a year or so because you put them on, and you just can't get out of them. So that's why I would say anything from a few seconds to up to maybe a year maximum. Then, on my investment accounts, that's where it's a more buy and hold. I wouldn't call it exactly that because I'm a trader, but it's more longer term. I might even have structures that I end up holding for two or three years.

Q : These structures you're talking about, are they essentially complex option and futures strategies that have some sort of either positional or volatility bias to them?

A : With the structures I've found some great securities. Two of my favorites are betting on the Japanese stock market using the Nikkei MITTS, the Market Index Tracking Securities. These are great because they have option-related properties, bond-related properties, and allow you to take a very long-term, safe bet on the Japanese stock market.

Q : Structures actually mean unique instruments that you find across the world, which contain lots of different properties of the common instruments that we have in the United States?

A : Yes. I'm doing one now that's more along your line of business, I'm bullish long term on the Asian currencies. I just think that at some stage one of the ways that these imbalances are going to get cured is the Chinese currency and all the tag-a-longs, like Japan, and Singapore, and Malaysia, are going to get stronger as well. It's been hard to pick that thing. The currencies acted really badly earlier this year, which was surprising to me. So one low-risk way that I've decided to take advantage of that is to buy one of these securities where it's got five Asian currencies in it. It's trading at a discount to what the bank is going to pay in 2008 when it expires. So the way I've structured it is I'm either going to earn 4 percent a year in the basket of Asian currencies, or make big on the appreciation and interest. The basket has the Korean won, Taiwan dollar, Australian dollar, Indian rupee, and the Malaysian ringitt, and I roughly added up the rates and saw that if I hopped on a plane and went to the different countries, the rates would not be much different. Singapore's interest rate is about three, Taiwan is like one or two, Thailand is like six, and I found out that if I physically went over there and opened up accounts in the four or five different countries, I would get about the same yield, but waste money on a plane ride. So I bought this security, which is going to pay me 4 percent plus the rate of return of these currencies, which is a great low risk way to play the Asian boom, and if it never happens, I'll make 4 percent in dollars, which is not the end of the world. I'm going to hold that for two or three years.

Q : How do you discover these hidden gems across the world?

A : I read everything in terms of investments letters, and I talk to a lot of different people in the business. It fascinates me. This is a treasure hunt to me and I'm Indiana Jones. I'm not looking for the Holy Grail. I'm looking for good investments. I want to go around and find treasure just like Indiana Jones. I'm not looking for great artifacts. I'm looking for great trades. And I'm going to hear that from people and from newsletters.

Q : Can you tell us how many newsletters do you subscribe to?

A : One of them that I think is really great is the *Gartman Letter*. I subscribe to that. Another one I subscribe to is *Grant's Interest Rate Observer*. Some that I've subscribed to in the past include Harry Shultz's letter and Richard Russell's *Dow Theory*.

Q : Would you say 10 or 20 newsletters then?

A : I'd say about 10 newsletters.

Q : Do you also read blogs on the Internet now?

A : Yes I do, I go into all the investment chat rooms to see what's hot and what's not, and what I want to trade with and what I want to fade against. So, yes, that's part of the sentiment stuff. In fact, there's a huge glaring gap in sentiment, especially overseas. They don't have the bulls/bears consensus like they do here. They don't have the Daily Sentiment Index.

Q : What about the *Commitment of Trader's Report*?

A : Well, the *Commitment of Trader's Report* they also don't have. You need to gauge sentiment a little bit differently over there, and one of the good ways is the blogs or talking to a handful of people every day. Finding out what sentiment is like in those markets is basically the same as doing an informal poll.

Q : So it sounds like you spend about four hours trading every single day?

A : At least.

Q : And then three or four hours doing research and reading, and contacting people?

A : My trading day could be anytime. At a minimum, it's going to be about three hours, most of it trading. It could also depend on if I'm doing stuff first overseas and then moving to the U.S. markets. If I'm doing a campaign of buying Canadian royalty trust and writing options against it, that could maybe extend my day longer. Sometimes I find opportunities where you can arbitrage the S&P MITTS and mark their strikes against S&P futures and options. So it takes time to build that type of thing. In that scenario I might be trading three hours overseas, maybe about another three or four in U.S., so seven or eight hours of trading total. Then each day I've got about an hour or two minimum of preparation. I look at what my positions are, what do I look like, what are the risk scenarios of what I'm doing. What trades do people want to do, I have to risk study them and see if can handle this in my option book, etc.

Q: You're still making sure what your worst-case scenarios are every single time.

A: Yes.

Q: Before you place the trade on?

A: Yes.

Q: During risk analysis review, do you have any hard-and-fast rules per trade? For example, do you say, I never want to lose more than 5 percent of my equity in any given trade? Do you have any kind of formulas that you follow internally to always control your risk?

A: When I'm doing the trades, in those options scenarios I don't actually have a fixed fraction of my capital that I'll commit, but I look at the risk versus the reward ratio. In other words, when I'm right, what's the amount of money that I'm making given my scenario? When I'm wrong, what's the amount I'm losing? The amount I'm the losing—can I live with that? I mean, is this an earth-shattering thing? Or is this a percentage of capital that is devastating and mind-blowing to me in terms of intellectually being wrong and stuff—but it's not going to put me out of the business?

Q : Is there any percentage number that you could lay down that would be just psychologically hobbling? On one trade?

A : Yes. I don't like to lose more than 5 percent on a position or any amount of capital that I'm committing. So, if I'm in some type of deal and this is threatening my account equity by five percent, warning bells and warning alarms are going off. I'm not quite interested in putting myself in that situation. You guys had asked what is your number one rule of trading and it actually occurred to me, this might have been about a year ago I was on a business trip in the Caribbean and the movie came on, *Million Dollar Baby*. I think Clint Eastwood would be a great commodity trader because he told the Million Dollar Baby that rule number one in boxing is to protect yourself. And I think the same is true in trading, if you love trading. If you want to trade, your capital is everything. So if you want to be a great trader, you have got to protect that capital. No capital, no trading, no life and its the same whether you want to be a Million Dollar Baby in boxing or a Million Dollar Baby in commodity trading, I think it's the same thing—protect your capital. I don't have solid formulas or Kelly formulas, or betting things like that. But I do study what I'm risking on each trade, what the risk reward ratios are. What my worst-case scenarios are, and is it strategically threatening to me.

Q : Now along those lines, how often do you revisit your earnings? Do you pay yourself on a weekly, monthly, yearly, or quarterly basis?

A : I'll tell you how I deal with it honestly, I get paid w-e-a-k-l-y [laughter]. Very weakly. In other words, I live below my means. It's like I said, capital to me is the most important thing, I want to be in the trading business, that's what I know and love. So what I do is I pay myself as weakly as possible. I think that you asked about how you deal with the pressure to make money. I think that the pressure on a trader to make money is what kryptonite is to Superman. It will hurt you. I am not aware of any market wizard who thinks that putting pressure on themselves to make money is a good thing. You have got to get as far away from that as possible.

Q : Yet how do you pragmatically resolve the need to have spending cash with the psychological necessity of not worrying about that in order to be successful?

A : All I can say is the following. I don't put any unnecessary pressure on myself to make money. You have to meet your daily expenses, you have to meet your medical bills, you have to meet your insurance, you have meet your basic life expenses, put food on the table. If you are going to go into trading and you can't do that, then don't go into it. Don't live on a shoestring. Meeting your basic life expenses is one margin call that you have to meet and don't think otherwise because you can't live in a cocoon. I wish it were different, that you could isolate yourself in cocoon, not have medical expenses, not have basic life expenses or insurance and trade until you became profitable, but the world isn't like that.

Q : If you were to give advice to a starting trader, how many months of daily basic bare bones expenses would you recommend he have, aside from his trading capital, in order for him to give it a fair shot?

A : I never looked at it that way. When I went into trading in the ring for myself, I knew that this was now a time where I could end up with no paycheck. I started coming up with contingency plans—if I wasn't making money in the ring or if I lost my $25,000 capital, what would I be doing? It was stuff like friends lined up who were loading UPS trucks at night making $8 an hour and I had them put me on a list there, where in a month or so, I'll be doing these trucks and I'll be back making a living again. So I had fallback provisions where, if trading didn't work out, I was going to pay the bills by doing things like delivering pizza and unloading trucks.

Q : You are much older now, so has your perspective changed on that?

A : Well, I've been fortunate now where I built up capital and what I've done is compartmentalized my life. So I put stuff in trusts or charitable foundations, things that I can't touch, things that you can't sue me for, things that, if I blow out trading, they can't get. I now have stop-losses on my life in terms of assets, which are better than working at UPS or delivering pizza. That will deliver me at least a living if I go out tomorrow and totally screw something up on a few hundred lots or few thousand lots or miscalculate something and then lose everything. I'll still be able to live.

Q : Do you have a goal in terms how much you're looking to earn every day?

A : No. I just think it's crazy when people always say, for example, "I'm going to aim for $300 a day." "I'm going to make a billion dollars this year." You know, to me that's nonsense, I mean, we live in an uncertain world you cannot quantify these things. You're not selling encyclopedias door to door in a market. You're not selling Amway products. I mean you don't know what's going to happen in the markets. You don't know what opportunities will be given to you and whether you can capitalize on them. What I've seen in the markets is this: We live in an uncertain and ever-changing world, and it's been like that ever since I got into trading and even now it is. What I have found out is that opportunities come along from time to time. Some of them you're able to capitalize on and expand your capital. What I try to do is the Million Dollar Baby thing: protect my capital at all cost. Analyze it, check the worst-case scenarios, check the risk/reward ratio, try to set yourself up so you're not committing more than 5 percent of your capital on any one day, trade, deal, or whatever. And then wait for these opportunities to come along, because you will find them. If you are patient, you'll see a time where you're in the zone and the markets are behaving just like your script says it should—now let's give it gas and try to build up some equity and then, when it comes back to the situations where I don't know what's going on, things are getting too uncertain. Then you turn to protecting your capital, maybe even go to cash and just clear your head. So that's how I deal with it, and for me to tell you, oh my goal is to make $300 a day, I mean, yeah, that's nonsense—or if I want to think big and think positive like Donald Trump and make millions of dollars a year. That's just nonsense to me to either way understate or overstate your goals. I mean maybe 10 years ago I used to do that and I would tell my dad this year is starting off really slow, I think I'm going to struggle to make a $100,000 trading on the floor this year. But I might end up making $700,000 that year. Then there'd be other years where I think, oh, this year is great, I'm going to make a killing, I'm going to make probably a million this year and I end up making $150,000. I just found that it is ridiculous to think that way.

Q: Your sense of forecasting your own equity is the worst?

A: It's the worst, it's horrible. Some people take this stuff seriously though, which brings me to another war story: Several years ago I was on the floor of the New York Commodity Exchanges and there was a prominent trader who used to work for Richard Dennis of the Turtles fame. I overheard him talking to his clerk about a chart of his account equity, and he was going on and on about how perfect the chart was and how this could mean that new highs in his account equity were just around the corner. Well, I couldn't resist, and so I went up to these guys and asked: "Wow what chart is that because I want to sell the heck out of that market?" He looked up at me as if he wanted to kill me and then exploded at me with every curse word you could imagine. I mean this guy really believed in this stuff.

Q : Any other worst trades?

A : No. The baptism under fire coffee trade, that's the worst. Anything worst than that and I would not be here today talking to you guys about trading, if I were in your office today, I would be asking you guys something along the lines of who ordered the Big Mac [laughter].

Q : Do you average down into a trade?

A : This is going to cause some controversy—but a qualified *yes*. Let me stop the controversy though as much as I can. I realize as much as anyone else that averaging down has led to some of the biggest debacles in our industry. The idea of averaging down is where if you are buying an asset and then it goes against you. You start buying more. You are getting hurt by reverse compounded interested. Not only are you wrong, not only is your net worth declining, but you're also increasing your risk. Now I know that is a recipe for disaster and most people should not even do it. However, there is one other thing that's been happening in the past few years and that is you identify a great asset class that you want to own for whatever reason. You're thinking about buying it, and you're sitting there and sitting there, and because of the world we live in and the amount of money that is going into these markets, all the managed money as well, and the amount of people who are using black box or some type of trend following system designed to basically exploit trends. You might be watching this asset class with a whole bunch of other trend followers. They're going to get into the asset class make it go further and further away from you. You have a choice to make because you may think that this is a great asset class that I want to own it. I hope to own it at lower levels, but the trend guys are in there and they're pushing it and pushing and it's getting away from me. I've got to buy some now and get some exposure because the worst thing you can ever do is be right about an investment, researched it, it's correct and it goes dramatically in your favor and you're not even on board. I mean that's going to lead to huge underperformance or maybe losses for the year. So they're going to get in, you're going to get in with them, and the Achilles heel of every trend follower is this following sentence: You cannot pick up a trading book without reading it. In fact, you've heard it all before. To be a good trend follower you've got to cut your losses and let your profits run. In that statement is the Achilles heel of their trading strategy. They're going to cut losses, which means they're going to take a lot of whipsaws and they're going to let their profits ride, which means they've got to suffer huge drawdowns before they get out of their trades. Let's focus just on the cut your losses side because that is what is applicable to my averaging down. What happens is that I'm going to get in with all the trend followers and you then have the reaction, which is then going to cause the trend followers to further that reaction by cutting their losses, which is going to create more pressure on the down side. At that stage I may relook at this thing and say, "You know, it still looks like a great asset class, I still want to own this thing for whatever reason." I know it's gone against me, but I have to commit more capital here. Usually I'll let it drop two, three, four days against me, and I'll wait for it to show that the trend is going to continue before I pull the trigger again.

Q : You wait for prices to stop going down and going against you?

A : Yes. I'll give you one example that I use. Technically I've seen and I've tested on Trade Station that markets that are in good uptrends and followed by trend followers, have anywhere from two-, three-, or four-day price drop correction, which is, in my mind, a reflection of the trend followers cutting losses. If the trend is over, this might not apply. But frequently what I've found is that the trend is going to reassert itself. What happens is the market eventually takes out it's high the day before and, let's say, we had a three-day correction. So you had down moves day one, two, three, and on day four I'm watching and I'm thinking, "Are they out? Are they out? Are they out? I don't know. I don't know." I've reevaluated everything. I've probably spent hours thinking about if I'd do this trade again and all of a sudden it takes out yesterday's high. At that point, most likely, I'm going to start to execute and buy and basically this is my averaging down. I figure that this trend should now snap back, it should continue, the trend should go up and at that stage, I do tighten up my stops. I will look to suffer less standard deviation risk because, by my logic, this should be over. We've just had a pretty good standard deviation correction in prices—I think that the trend followers are out. If this is a real trend, it should reexert itself. If it doesn't now, I'm out because I've doubled up and I am in a risky position. If it goes wrong, not only do you have a move that is one standard deviation worse than I thought, we're now exploring standard deviation two, so I'm out.

Q : Do you find any drudgery about this business?

A : Well mainly the recordkeeping, the data you have to keep. You have to keep your data in meticulous tick-by-tick format or daily data points. You can't miss a day. You've got to update all that stuff. You have to keep your records correct. I'm trading many different markets. I might have positions on in 10 different markets and reasonable option positions against them in maybe five, So now I've got to make sure that not only are my positions correct in the accounting on the statement but in my computer, too, and that I'm monitoring the risk correctly. That I find just tremendous drudgery and the end of the year just getting all the files all together for tax purposes is a mess. You know the shoe boxes and the reams of data and going through it and seeing what I did and didn't make on this or that trade.

Q : Do you do your own taxes?

A : No. Too complicated.

Q : You trade a lot of foreign markets. Do you have tax accountants in every country, some are not specialist in all the markets, so do you have a lot of people whom you seek advice from?

A : Yes, I do, and the tax laws for trading and investing are complicated in and of themselves just here in the United States.

Q : They get infinitely more complicated when you go overseas?

A : It can get more complicated overseas. There's some planning that you can do for the U.S. stuff. Try and find someone who specializes in accounting for traders. Don't go to HR Block and don't go to some generic accounting firm that might be great in the basics but they don't know how to do taxes for traders. You are also going to have to delineate your trading between what's your real active stuff that you're doing versus what is you more passive investment activity. Then, when you go overseas, it's hard enough just to learn our tax system—to try and learn the foreign ones are almost impossible. So my advice to you is that your best bet is to try and take advantage of double-tax treaties. I talk to experts who structure my investments in these countries by either using America's double-tax agreements or they will set up our business in a country that has a double-tax agreement in the country that I'm going to be investing in. It just simplifies everything and keeps it all governed here. I would urge people to really get with a professional because the laws are complex, they're always changing, and if you make a mistake, any amateur auditor from the IRS will get your records. I mean it's all on paper. It's very easy to go through your records see what you did wrong and even if you did it wrong honestly, you're going to be looking at higher taxes, penalties, interest, and things you don't want.

Q : Okay Indi we've been at this for a while and it's getting time for lunch. How would you summarize the most important parts of this interview? Please feel free to add anything we may not have covered.

A : Gordon Gekko said that lunch is for wimps [laughter]. All traders are different, but we can find some common ground. First, I will start at the beginning. Every great trader who I have ever read about has had the baptism-under-fire trade. You know the trade which occurred early in your career, where you nearly blew it all and the event becomes a type of soul searching exercise where you decide whether or not you can continue in this arena. If you are a slow learner like me it actually happens twice. My warning to all traders is that this will happen to you. What happens next is up to you. Vince Lombardi, the all-time-great American football coach, said, "Its not whether you get knocked down, its whether you get up that counts."

Second, focusing on the money and or pressure to make money eliminates a large pool of potential traders from ever becoming successful traders. I was lucky in that I was born to parents who instilled in me at a very early age that they would love and respect me and elevate my self worth no matter what my net worth was. When I first started trading, I felt psychologically invincible because I knew that if I totally blew out trading then I could at least count on two people who would always be there for me no matter what happened. Thank you, Dad and Mom.

As time goes on, I try to surround myself with people: friends, girlfriends, investors, etc. who do not pressure me to make money. I am not aware of any successful trader who feels that putting on massive pressure to make money will enhance their trading. We all know that getevenitis—you know, the disease of getting even with a market that just took some money from you—is the most expensive form of revenge in this business.

In another vein, you wouldn't think of getting in the boxing ring with Mike Tyson and then focus on the belt you could win. You would be knocked out in no time because you would be too busy staring at the belt you could win instead of on the task at hand. Don't focus on the prize. Focus on the process. Similarly, Mr. Miyagi would be a great trader coach because he taught the Karate Kid to not focus on the karate or the black belts, but on the process itself. He would show him how to sand da floor, paint da fence, wax on, wax off. Embedded in that disciplined learning approach was the attainment of black belt proficiency in the art of karate. So my advice is to go out there and wax on and wax off—meaning focus on the process. Each trader is different in this regard.

THE TREASURE HUNTER

Third, go out and watch the movie: *Million Dollar Baby* and listen to Clint Eastwood's rule number one for becoming a Million Dollar Baby: "Protect yourself!" No capital, no trading, no life.

Fourth, you need intellectual freedom and flexibility to be successful in this arena. Go back and reread the part of this interview where I described the best trade I ever had. Jesse Livermore once said: "Our job in speculating is not to be on the bull side or the bear side, but on the winning side."

Finally, there are two pieces of advice in commodity trading legend which has been passed down through the ages as gospel. One: "You must cut your losses and let your profits ride!" Two: "Losers average losers!" Both are conceptually correct, yet the logic of both has been blown out of proportion, if not twisted, over time. Today it is considered a sin for any self-respecting trader to not cut losses quickly, sometimes too quickly. Today it is also a trading sin to average losing trades. We need to reexamine these ideas with a greater level of maturity and sophistication in order to continue to be able to win at trading in the future.

In 1974 Muhammad Ali in the "Rumble in the Jungle" against George Foreman in Kinshasa, Zaire, used a strategy in boxing that was considered a boxing sin at the time to become Heavyweight Champion of the World against great odds. It was the so called *rope-a-dope strategy*. The theory at the time was that lying on the ropes was wrong because it exposed a fighter to more punishment than if he moved around the ring. This did not discourage Ali from using the strategy against Foreman. Foreman was a harder puncher than Ali. Most analysts felt that Ali would have to stay away from Foreman to beat him. Instead, Ali started to lie on the ropes by the end of the first round and used the ropes for the rest of the fight. Foreman's strategy, which was totally obvious (just like cutting losses and letting profits run in trading) was to cut off the ring, get Ali to the ropes and hit him. Since Ali was willingly lying on the ropes, Foreman would plant himself in front of Ali and punch as hard as he could. Foreman landed constant blows to the body, but due to Ali's focus on protecting himself had trouble landing to the head. Ali scored on Foreman with an occasional jab or series of jabs as Foreman tried to reposition himself or catch his breath. Foreman began to tire from all this activity (in trading terms, getting repeatedly stopped out and then trying to reenter at worse levels) and from the occasional punches he was taking from Ali (in trading terms, the actual capital losses related to the stops getting hit and possibly not being able to reenter at favorable levels). Foreman was visibly finished by the end of the fifth round and eventually knocked out in the eighth.

If Clint Eastwood can take great trading advice and apply it to boxing, perhaps I can take great boxing advice and apply it to trading. The greatest boxing advice I could find inverted a boxing sin and converted it into a favorable outcome against great odds. This advice came from the greatest boxer of all time, Muhammad Ali. Thank you, Muhammad Ali, you have always been a hero.

My commodity trading version of rope-a-dope is to take a commodity trading sin. That is, not cutting losses quickly and then making it worse for a brief period of time and space—but don't expose yourself too long—by adding to the loser trade. I have found that in the long run I am achieving better results, behaving with better discipline and emotional control than the people who mindlessly cut losses too quickly and won't even consider averaging down to improve odds. Warren Buffett once said, "I buy a stock I like for 100, it goes to 90, I still like it, I buy more. How is that more risky?" Just like Warren Buffett, I also have trouble perfectly timing trades. This strategy has at times enhanced my performance in spite of my initial poor timing. It definitely involves superior discipline and emotional control—try it sometime—than someone who allows themselves to get whipsawed too soon out of a perfectly good trend. My risk is increased for only a very short period of time and movement. Be careful about exposing yourself for too long. My opponents are getting tired out both in terms of physical capital and mental capital due to the fact that they got thrown out of a good trade too quickly and now must try—and I emphasize *try*—to reenter later, most likely at higher prices, and with less real capital and less mental capital than when they started. Constantly getting stopped out and trying to reenter trades is very tiring from both a mental capital and physical capital perspective.

Please, don't take trading lore for granted. Step back and try to take a more mature and sophisticated view of how to achieve results. "Whipsaw is for losers!" Did you ever consider that? If so,

I hope you will find your own version of the rope-a-dope strategy. You will need to first understand the concept of value for buys and possibly the concept of hysteria for sales as well as the concept of margin of error for both buys and sells. I wish you all the best of luck in your endeavors. Thank you all, and now let's go to lunch.

LESSONS FROM INDI JONES

Protect Yourself, Protect Your Capital

The most important pearl of wisdom from Indi Jones is how trading relates to boxing. According to Indi, the number one rule in trading is the same as the number one rule in boxing, which is to always protect yourself. "No capital, no trading, no life," he states succinctly. So how do you protect your capital? Always know your worst-case scenario. Before you place a trade, figure out what you are willing to lose in terms of points, ticks, *and* dollars. Check your risk/reward ratio and make sure that no one trade has the potential to destroy your entire account. As a general rule of thumb, Indi Jones does not like to lose more than 5 percent of his equity on a single trade. This way, even if the trade becomes a loser, he can still survive to take another swing at the market.

Along the same lines, always have a backup plan. When Indi first started out, he knew that if he lost his $25,000 starting capital, he could find a job loading UPS trucks at night in less than a month. As time progressed, he was able to build up some savings, which allowed him to set up stop-losses on his life. In case he ever had a major trading loss, he was able to put money away in places that he could not touch, such as trusts or charitable foundations.

Take the Risk, Take the Plunge

Once you know your risk, you can take the plunge. One of the worst sins in trading is to be right in your analysis, have the asset move dramatically in your favor but not be on board for the ride. In some cases, when a breakout into a new trend occurs, there could be large extension moves with little retracement. In order not to miss the trade, Indi will initiate a probative position just to get some exposure and then if it retraces against him, he will look for opportunity to add to that position. The key, however, is not just to add blindly. If the asset does retrace, the retracement can last for two, three, or even four days. What Indi will do is wait for the price to show that the trend will continue before taking the plunge again.

When You Are in Sync with the Markets, Keep Pressing the Trade

Once you are in sync with the market, step on the gas. Indi Jones' most memorable trade was in orange juice, where he made money on the ride up as well as the ride down. Having banked profits when a snowstorm sent orange juice prices skyrocketing, Indi was looking to flip his trade and sell when prices failed to extend their rally after CNBC started showing pictures of oranges covered with icicles. Having made significant profits over the past few trading days, Indi stepped on the gas and sold the commodity aggressively. Yet before doing so he knew exactly how much he wanted to risk. At worst, he was not willing to lose more than 40 percent of the money that he made on the move up. This is an extremely important tip to remember if you are going to press your luck in the markets—never risk all of your profits.

Be Aware of Market Sentiment

Indi always has his pulse on the sentiment of the market. Every single day he speaks to many different types of market players and reads at least 10 different newsletters. If market sentiment is very one sided and price acts the other way by breaking a significant support zone, for example, it may be a good signal for Indi to bet against the consensus. The flush out can last for days if not weeks in the commodity markets, especially if it's a news-driven surprise that confounds market's expectations. You, too, can keep on top of the overall market sentiment by reading newsletters, blogs, mainstream media, as well as looking at the *Commitment of Traders Report* that provides information on commercial and noncommercial positioning.

CHAPTER 8

THE NEWS JUNKIE
ROLAND CAMPBELL

A veteran of the technology bubble, Roland Campbell likes to practice the Warren Buffett way of trading, which is to trade only what makes sense to him. This tactic has served him well, as he went short stocks with negative earnings and long stocks with positive earnings before the stock market collapsed in 2001. Since then he has moved to trading currencies, employing much of the same fundamental-based trading that he did in stocks—albeit on a shorter-term basis. Roland's strategy is to trade news flow, but only news flow that catches the market off guard. When everyone is wrong and getting stopped out, that is when he wants to be in the market. Fading market sentiment and psychology is a very important aspect of his trading and one that has proven well for him. He looks for big moves based on misaligned sentiment, which is how he once managed to turn $60,000 into $100,000 on one single trade. Crediting part of his success to the Chinese practice of Feng Shui, Roland believes that the comfort of his trading environment helps him stay focused and relaxed when he trades.

We took an afternoon to talk to Roland over the phone and he was kind enough to share his tricks of the trade.

■ ■ ■

Q : Can you tell us a little bit about yourself?

A : Sure. Actually I don't trade full-time. I do it on a part-time basis so that makes it a little easier for me. It takes the pressure off because I have a steady income. My work is scheduled such that I'm able to trade the markets just about all the time. I would say most days during the week or any time there's market moving news, I'm available to trade it. I work a lot of Saturdays and Sundays, so I don't have to make a certain amount of money. I feel like I've done well because of that. If it was my only source of income, it would be a little bit scary, but it would still be manageable.

Q : So what do you actually do as your full-time job?

A : I'm a systems engineer for a large bank. My work doesn't relate in anyway to trading.

Q : Were you ever exposed to trading when you were younger?

A : I basically came across it by myself. My family is very, very conservative in that regard. They believe in saving money, just putting it in the bank. My dad does have a 401(k), but that was about it. So it wasn't discussed very often. It was actually when I moved to San Francisco during the tech boom, to take a job there. Everyone around me was trading stocks such and I felt completely lost. I didn't know what was going on. So I felt like I wanted to be involved in those conversations and started doing my own research and finding companies that I liked. Once I found those companies and started learning a little bit about them, I would invest small chunks of money in them.

Q : Your education background is in technology, but did you ever take any economics or finance courses?

A : I did, but those were just required courses. I took nothing beyond the required education.

Q : How did you figure out what kind of stocks you were interested in trading?

A : For the most part I knew I wanted to trade in and out, so I wanted a stock that had a lot of volume. I traded the big tech names in the beginning, mainly through word of mouth. Actually I caught the market right about when it was breaking. So I learned a lot about shorting stocks at that time, too. I was able to come out pretty well in the market and kind of step up to the plate when other people were dumping.

Q : So you mean shorting, right? How did you learn to do that?

A : Because I'm always very pessimistic. I saw all these companies out there and thought, "How can they be possibly making money?" I looked at the balance sheets of most of them and they weren't. They were losing money. So I said, "Why doesn't everybody short the stock?—I don't understand." So I would short the stocks that weren't making money, buy the ones that were, and see how it all fell. And it turned out really well. I would just cover the shorts and then put more money into the companies that were making money—like banks—those were my favorites back then.

Q : So you traded the Warren Buffett way by making sure that the fundamentals lined up?

A : Exactly.

Q : So how long were you doing that for?

A : I started that in about 2000, that was when I really started trading. I did a little bit of options trading as well. Similar strategies, though.

Q : In the beginning was it all about fundamental analysis? Did you ever look at price charts?

A : In the beginning it was all fundamental. I didn't really know anything about technicals. I hadn't gotten that far along.

Q : How much did you start with?

A : Probably $5,000 to $10,000 in that range.

Q : Was this your savings or money that you borrowed?

A : It was actually savings. But it was my first time trading. So obviously any little hit hurt. Now that I'm more experienced, I realize I probably shouldn't have been trading that money.

Q : In the beginning when you first traded stocks, you did well. Did that streak continue?

A : Actually, I feel like I got extremely lucky in the beginning. That was probably a curse because it hooked me into the markets. I was up 10 or 20 percent in a few days and I thought, "I'm meant to be in this market." Within a year though, I blew up the account because I just traded too fast, too hard in the beginning.

Q : After a few months you were overtrading?

A : Right. I was trading too often, that was my problem.

Q : What's typically your style? Are you someone who gets out of trades by the end of the day? Or do you end up holding them for longer?

A : Back then I would hold. If it was a good strong fundamental company, I had no problems holding them for a couple weeks. But on the side I would do the little tech plays in and out within an hour of two, and those caught up to me.

Q : So what was your return like in the beginning?

A : Let's see, that first account I basically blew up in about six months. So then I opened my next account, promising myself I wouldn't take the risk because I stood in front of a lot of very strong companies and tried to short them, like Expedia, Krispy Kreme Donut, and just got crushed. That's where most of my losses came from, two or three very bad trades.

Q : What do you think got you? Did you use stops? Or was there just so much volatility?

A : I wasn't using stops when it comes to the stock market, I've never used stops, ever—even on a short, which was probably a bad move [laughter].

Q : So about six months later you blew up your account. What made you want to get back into trading?

A : Right. I just felt like I'd made several big mistakes. I hadn't really listened to anyone in the market. I just thought I knew how to do it. I didn't want to listen to anyone, and didn't feel the need to diversify. But I also didn't want this portfolio that just grows 5 percent per year. That didn't interest me because this was money

I wanted to play with. So, when I went back in, I was a little more conservative, I did a little more research on the company I would trade in. I realized if the stock dips, I don't feel bad buying a little more, whereas before I would just exit out.

Q : When did you introduce options trading to the mix?

A : Quite honestly, I got bored with the low volatility in the stock market. Just after the big crash it just seemed like nothing really moved and the stuff that did move everybody was playing. So I wanted something that had more action and was more of a challenge and, of course, options fit the bill. I don't claim to be an expert, but I got so lucky with my first trade in options. I bought 30 dollar options and I sold them out for a 1,000 percent profit.

Q : How long did that take?

A : I was hooked [laughter]. That was over one-month and it was a stock that you wouldn't think would move. It was amazing, I just got lucky [laughter].

Q : How were you introduced to options? Did you take a class or seminar to learn how to trade them?

A : Well. our company actually gave us stock options, and I was so curious about what it meant to have stock options. I started doing research and figuring out what options were. I thought, "Hey I could use a put and call to help me out in the market, to hedge against different plays." So I started using them especially for companies that I thought were going to have the high level of volatility coming up like the release of drug studies. Stuff like that actually worked quite a bit for me.

Q : Were you worried about things like time decay?

A : Yes. The time decay did kill me in the beginning. I hadn't really factored that in. It took me a couple of trades to realize what time does and I found myself holding some options that ended up being worthless, of course.

Q : Did you change anything in terms of your trading strategy when you started trading options versus stocks or were you doing them in tandem?

A : I tend to do both of them in tandem. One would hedge the other. To be honest, I haven't really traded very much in the options market, probably only about a hundred times. So I don't have a lot of experience there, but I mostly use it for a hedge. Eventually, though I sort of lost interest. I was doing well, but I got more interested in my job and I said I'll just throw some money in the account every once in a while and play with it. I just had too much going on. But then I found currencies. That's when everything changed for me. I realized that was my passion. I would start trading and I couldn't pull myself away from the computer. I knew this was it.

Q : How long ago did you discover currencies?

A : It's been about three years.

Q : How did you learn about currencies for the first time?

A : Quite honestly, I just did some research on the Internet. I was curious about it. I traveled a little to Asia and Europe. So I was aware of currency exchange. But I didn't know how people actually traded it. I did a lot of research online. I read a couple books—basically taught myself. I couldn't find anyone that knew anything about currencies, quite honestly.

Q : Did you trade currencies based upon fundamentals like you did stocks? Or did you introduce technicals into the picture?

A : I actually mixed them. That's when I really started getting into the charting. I would say I traded the majors primarily at first. I traded euro/U.S. dollars almost exclusively for the first few months just to get a feel for the pair. Then I started seeing a lot of volatility in the Japanese yen, so I wanted to trade it as well. Mostly I would trade the majors. I tried to stay away from the crosses because I didn't really understand how they were working.

Q : Can you walk us through the thought process of one of your trades?

A : Well, I am contrarian just about all the way. When everyone is bullish, I'm normally looking the other direction. I always like to look at a psychological level that seems to be a big mover, and I like to be in the market around that time. If it's a solid figure, 1.25 in the euro/U.S. dollar, for example, I want to be there when the market sells through that level. I realize that there's risk there, but technically I know a lot of people are getting pushed out of their positions at that level. I want to be the guy selling at that point if the market's moving down. If the news pushes it through a technical level, that's just fantastic, and everybody's going the other way. I know they're trapped because I've been there.

Q : How do you manage stops then?

A : I'm very careful with placement of my stops. I really don't like to use them unless I'm going to be away from the computer. If I'm in front of it, I want full control because I want to make the decision right then. I have a general idea every time I place my trade where my stop will be. But I don't want to just leave it hanging out there for anyone to pick off.

Q : How often do you actually end up staring at the screen, because it sounds like you trade pretty actively?

A : I do. See, I just don't consider it work. So it's not big deal. I put my laptop up in front me, turn on the TV, and I'm watching both at the same time. I would say if it's an active day, maybe that window from 2 A.M. until 10 or 11 A.M. Central Time, which is an excellent time to trade for that eight- to ten-hour window.

Q : You're up pretty early, you're up overnight, basically.

A : I'm awake when there's volatility. I can feel it, and it wakes me up.

Q : What is a typical day like?

A : I wake up at around 2 A.M. I'll watch the markets. If it's relatively quiet, then I'll go back to sleep for a few hours. I prefer to trade from 2 A.M. to 4 A.M., get a few hours sleep, and then the U.S. news normally comes around 7 A.M. my time and that's a good time to be awake and ready to trade. The first thing I do when I am ready to trade is, obviously, glance at the numbers see where the market is trading. I want to know if it moved while I happened to be asleep. Then I will read over the news, various market reports. I'll start looking at the price charts, see what it did overnight, where are the highs, where are the lows. I start getting an idea of which pair I want to trade and start watching it and planning an entry ahead of time. Of course, I know in advance when all the news is coming out. So if there is a big news item, I won't position in front of it, normally, I'll wait for it to come out.

Q : So you are day trading during that time?

A : Normally I'm in and out within the time I just discussed. Sometimes I'll hold a position. It really depends on why I entered

221

the trade. If the trade is still viable, I will stay in it. I don't have a problem holding it overnight.

Q : Do you go in all in one shot or do you tend to average in to get a better price on the move?

A : That to me is absolutely the key to my success. I average in on every trade I make and I average out whenever I exit. I have a tendency where, as soon as I buy a currency, it will dip 10 pips. Before I would get upset, but now I love it because I feel like I can get in at a better price, so I hope it dips another 10 pips. I know the price I want, so I will average into that price.

Q : How many times would you average into a trade?

A : Normally four's about right. If it goes much further than four average downs, I have to start considering whether this is the right trade to be in, but 9 times out of 10 that strategy works for me.

Q : You average out as well, right?

A : I most definitely do. I tend to get rid of half of it and then bring my stop on a quarter of it up to a nice amount of profit, then bring the stop on the other quarter just to my entry price.

Q : How much leverage do you use?

A : Fifty to 1 or 100 to 1. Just depends on which account I'm trading in.

Q : Do you care about carry or interest rates? If something has a high negative interest rate does it matter to you?

A : It does to some degree. I won't short something that has a super-high interest rate right before they're about to do the turn because it will cost me a ton of interest. However don't worry about it too much. I mean, I bought the British pound against the yen a while back and enjoyed getting that interest. But to me the market moves so quickly that it ends up meaning very little to me.

Q: Are there certain currencies that you might avoid trading?

A: I avoid the British pound/Japanese yen now. I don't know why I wanted to trade it that day. I have to be careful to pull myself away from those because they look very interesting sometimes.

Q: What about currencies that are your favorite?

A: Oh, I love to trade the New Zealand dollar, that one has a personality of its own. So I can trade maybe euro/U.S. dollar and it's not really acting right, it's not doing what I want it do and I can take my mind off that trade. Go over and trade "Kiwi" and it's just a different animal. I enjoy trading that.

Q: What type of timeframe charts do you like to look at?

A: It obviously depends on the trade. But right before a news release, I normally like to look at a five-minute chart and see what ranges we have been trading in. Where are people's stops at? Where am I looking for this market to go? Where do I want to get out if I get into trouble? So normally the five-minute is the one I like to look at.

Q: It sounds like you talk a lot about news. Do you feel like you're usually positioning for news or reacting to it?

A: Normally I position after the news. I tend to go for the meat of the move, I don't care about the beginning and I don't care about end. I tried to catch the beginning of a move quite a few times and ended up with a losing trade. Nowadays, I let the news come out.

I let the market move in its direction. I watch for the pullback, make sure it's not a reversal, and then normally I'll move in on that pullback. If it's a reversal I'll go short, if it's just a pullback I'll go long. On 7 out of 10 trades that's a successful move.

Q : What kind of resources do you use for news?

A : CNBC—but I also have another news feed that I use through my brokerage company.

Q : Do you have to pay for any extra services, or does it tend to be pretty low cost?

A : It's fairly low cost. I haven't pulled the trigger on a big investment yet.

Q : Do you pay for your news service provider?

A : I do, but I use a free charting package.

Q : Do you feel it's necessarily for a trader, a new trader, to have fancy equipment and resources?

A : I think people need to start out learning the markets. I don't think that paying for that stuff up front is important because you probably don't know how to use it yet. So I would say no in the beginning. But later on paying $50 or $100 a month for a service is well worth it.

Q : What about your equipment and set up? Do you have one screen or three screens up at one time?

A : I use a variety of laptops. I do a lot of traveling so I have four laptops. Normally I have two or three of them on at once with different accounts up. I have different brokerages. So it's just easier to have them on different machines so I can access them quickly. That's one area I feel strongly about investing a lot of money in because you can control that aspect of having the best computers, the best Internet connects, that's all controllable. So if I can control those, I want the best and I think I do have the best right now.

Q: In terms of various brokers that you look at, is there a reason why you feel you need to look at so many market markers?

A: Yes. I think each one has its own thing that it does well. The one I use now is very good. They execute orders well during the news, but the spreads are a little bit high. So in times when there's no volatility or low volatility, I want to make a trade and maybe it's in a currency pair they don't offer, I have another market maker that I use.

Q: So basically you may alternate depending on who gives you the best price on your trade, right?

A: Correct. It's alternated based on best price. But it doesn't necessarily have to have the best spread because one of my brokers has a variable spread the other is a fixed spread account. So, depending on the news that I'm trading, I'll use one or the other.

Q: Do you trade other products right now? Or just exclusively FX?

A: FX and a little bit of gold. I still have long-term accounts in stock. But I don't trade those too often. Sometimes I'll pay myself that way whenever I have a good month. I'll take 10 percent out of my currency account, send it over to my long-term stock account, and just throw it in there and invest in something.

Q : Do you have a weekly profit target or do you just look for trends and wait for the account to build?

A : I honestly don't have a pip goal because I don't want to pressure myself. I already have enough pressure. At the end of the month I know if I'm trading well, and I know when I look that statement what it's going to represent. So I do want a month-over-month gain. It doesn't have to be 50 percent, but as long as it's 5 to 10 percent over last month, then I feel like it's been worth my time and effort.

Q : Let's say you have a handful of bad trades, at what point do you decide to stop trading?

A : If I am having a bad streak, I'll try to change currency pairs. I'll try to look at myself, analyze myself, figure out what I'm doing wrong. I've had 5 to 10 trades in a row that just have gone against me and I'm not sure why. At that point I did take a couple of weeks off. I paper-traded for a while. I went on vacation. I did a few other things, and when I came back I was fresh. I was ready to go. I missed the markets a lot and got back in there and I was ready to go.

Q : Do you ever review your trades to see if there's a common mistake?

A : I probably should, but I don't. Once a trade is over, it's over for me, and I don't want to relive it [laughter].

Q : Throughout the week, how many trades do you think you actually make?

A : I would say probably 5 to 10 a day, so maybe 50 to 60 a week.

Q : That's pretty active. You mentioned that sometimes, when you make profit, you put it back into your stock account. Do you pay yourself in any other way?

A : I pay myself in equipment. I'll go out and buy something nice—maybe a better computer. Last year I traveled to Asia because I made a lot of money on the yen, so I took myself to Japan. I would take a small portion out of the account—and normally it's less than 10 percent of the profit, so it's very little.

Q : How is your performance now?

A : It's been very good. This is one of the best years I've had. I just feel like I have a grip on the market. I can feel how it should it be traded, and once you get in that rhythm, you can just feel when the market is going to move. To me it's about market psychology, knowing what other people are doing and trying to take advantage of that. I've been on the wrong side of many trades. I want to make sure that I'm not on that side and I'm on the side that's taking the money out.

Q : So you don't think you've changed anything in terms of style?

A : The main thing I've changed is incorporating market psychology. I never used that before. In the past I would simply see that the euro dipped, so it must be on sale and therefore I'm going to buy it, which was a very poor strategy in the beginning because, as you know, once a trend starts it normally continues for quite some time. So, in the beginning, I would make those mistakes. I wouldn't get on the trend. I would fight a trend all the way. Now I try to follow the trend and take it where it's going to go. But if everybody gets on board, that trend does mature and I know when to get off.

Q : How do you gauge psychology? Do you look at the COT [Commitment of Traders] reports or just watch price action?

A : I do look at the COT report. But I really like to watch the price action. Particularly around the figures or anywhere that I know I would have placed my stop if I was on the other side of the trade, those areas tend to make you the most money.

Q : You said you tend to go in the direction of a trend and you like to be in the meat of the move and not the beginning or the end, but do you buy ahead of the number? Let's say we're going from 1.27 to 1.26 euro/dollar and it breaks down, do you tend to just go ahead and buy at 1.26, assuming that it will reverse? Or do you wait for some sort of signal of a reversal first before getting in?

A : Normally I like to watch the level break and I'll get in right about when it's breaking through that figure. This can be very dangerous; it tends to move back up against you. But like I said, I think 7 out of 10 times, once that level is breached, you may get a minor pullback, I'll add more to the trade and it generally continues in my direction.

Q : So basically you pick key levels, right?

A : Right, the key levels are imperative.

Q : Do you have any alarm alerts in case something happens, or your levels are breached, when you are asleep?

A : Yes, I certainly do. I normally sleep very close by my PC. Some people think it's strange. But I have my laptop open right beside me. I also have a plasma TV that I can glance up at just to see the numbers real quickly and fall back to sleep.

Q : Spoken like a true trader. How does your family feel about this?

A : Oh, they think I'm crazy [laughter]. They didn't understand at first. They thought I was spending probably too much time doing it. But I'm not married and I don't have any children, so that helps a lot. I still visit my family and they're aware of the number of hours I spend doing this. After I explained the market to them and how it works, they have, in fact, become pretty interested.

Q : So have they started trading as well?

A : They haven't. I'm trying to train my sister to trade, but we'll see how that turns out.

Q : Do you have any trading buddies or do you pretty much do this by yourself?

A : I do talk to a few people. I try not to let them influence my trade ideas because it just seems like you know the market is always changing. So if I told you to go long the dollar right now, you know, four hours from now I could be telling you to go short. So I try not to make any predictions. But I do discuss the markets with a few key people. We talk about things, but we never discuss exactly what we're going to do. We just talk about the economy in general.

Q : How often would you talk to them?

A : I would say that we probably brainstorm or talk markets once a week. During my downtime, I do enjoy reading trade ideas on different forums or online bulletin boards. I normally don't take any ideas from them, but I like to read what the consensus is, what everyone is thinking, and I may go against that or I may go with it.

229

Q : So forums are where you go most often for some interaction with other traders, right?

A : Right. That's the part that I enjoy, just the interaction with other people who are doing the same thing. Trading can get a little lonely [laughter].

Q : Have you ever attended seminars or participated in any courses?

A : I really haven't. I've wanted to go to a few, but just haven't found the time.

Q : Given your experience, do you think it's important for new traders to get formal training.

A : Obviously they have to start small. For me to learn I had to lose money. So people say trade a demo account to get started. Yes, if you want to learn the mechanics go ahead and open a demo account. But if you want to really feel what it's like to be in the market, open a $1,000–2,000 account, get in there, trade some mini lots, and start to learn what it's like to get stopped out, how to take profits. The most important thing is to get in there and start educating yourself because the market will teach a lot. Then, later, I think you should read some trading books.

Q : So practical trading is what you suggest people do to learn the ropes?

A : Right and they have to start small. It is very different to trade a demo versus a live account. I've tried to trade a demo account and it loses my interest. I just have to have money on the line to really pay attention and focus. I've done a little bit of paper trading and that's fine when I'm in a down streak. But when it's time to trade, I want to be there—to have real money in the market.

Q : Let's talk about your results. You said you've done very well in the markets, what was your return like in the currency market and in the stock markets?

A : My stock account I did pretty well in. I was able to double it in 2002. At that point I got a little more conservative, and then I started dabbling in the currency markets. I felt like it had higher leverage. There's a higher amount of money to be made. So once I learned a little bit about it, I put a couple thousand in the account, started trading it, and didn't take long to blow that one up. I did it again, started trading it, just like I trade stocks, got it up from $2,000 to maybe $7,000 and then blew that one out.

Q : I'm surprised you didn't lose your confidence.

A : No [laughter], I knew I didn't know what I was doing. So the third time was the charm. I put in $10,000 this time and started trading, actually drove it down to around $5,000 and then all of a sudden I switched, things turned around, and I started having successful trades. They would be small, $400 to $500, but they would build. I would just check the statement at the end of the month and realize, "Hey I made 70 percent. That's pretty good." Just over the course of the year 2005, I went from $5,000 to over $100,000. Well, the amazing part was I was sitting in an Internet café in Thailand and I was trading. It was an NFP [nonfarm payroll] day, I had like $60,000 in the account, I put $40,000 to work, the trade went my way, and I realized when I closed out that day I had a $100,000 in my account, and I thought, I'm on vacation. I'm enjoying life. I just tipped everyone in the Internet café and bought everyone drinks and it cost me $10. So I was very excited, but I got a little scared once I had that amount of money in the account because that was a lot for me at the time. I took some of it out and moved it into my longer-term account and just kept going for that goal of getting it back to 100,000 and I did several times. So my goal is to always keep each account around that the level and to pull the excesses and put it somewhere else.

Q : Do you trade a lot from different places around the world?

A : I do. I love to trade on the road. The time difference makes it a little difficult when I was in Asia, trading NFP on a Friday night. That felt very strange. But I do best trading on the road when I've had time to kind of breathe and get away from things. I remember before I made that trade in the NFP, I was sitting in the Starbucks café just thinking about the trade and what I planned to do. I wasn't looking at any charts, I had just planned in my head, and when it happened the way I thought it would, I just executed. It was like mechanical.

Q : Do you think finding the perfect entry is more important than managing your exit?

A : I think you need to have a good entry. I always know where my stop is, my risk level. That's planned before I even enter into the trade. But as far as profitable exits, take profits, I tend to leave those open. When it's going my way, and I'm satisfied, I'll take most of it off the board and let the rest of it set up with profitable stops from there on.

Q : How did you learn about technical analysis and different indicators?

A : Well, as you know, some of the indicators are actually the same as in the stock market. They're just used a little differently. I do have a technical analysis book that I tried to read through.

It's so difficult. You know the basics are all I use—MACD, RSI, stuff like that, moving averages. But once again, the key to me is psychological. You have to know what other people are doing and just get a feel, a taste for the market because those technical levels won't mean anything if the market doesn't want to go there.

Q : What's your favorite indicator?

A : I would have to say Fibonacci. I prefer using those for defining and testing resistance levels and supports.

Q : Are you more of a systematic or discretionary trader?

A : Definitely discretion. I couldn't do system trading. It's too monotonous. I have to choose how I want to enter, where I want to enter, the environment I want to enter in, so definitely discretionary.

Q : Given you background as a system engineer, have you ever considered trading systematically?

A : I guess the reason I don't is I get too bored at work [laughter]. So I don't want to do the same thing at home.

Q : When you are doing your currency trading, do you typically have one currency that you're trading at a time or will you have positions in a few different currencies at the same time?

A : I would say two is the max. Any more than that and it gets to be too much to follow.

Q : Do you care about correlation between the two pairs? For example, the British pound/Japanese yen and euro/Japanese yen pairs which may be very strongly correlated.

A : In general I'll trade pairs that aren't very correlated. Like I said, I do trade the British pound/U.S. dollar or euro/U.S. dollar quite often. That's the normal one. Then if there's not a lot of action there and there's more news coming out in the commodity currencies, I'll go over there and trade it because often times they'll move when the majors don't.

Q : What do you find is the most interesting thing about trading?

A : Just that basically you can dictate when you decide to trade and work. Some people don't want to wake up at 2 o'clock in the morning and trade, some people love to. I mean, I can't think of anything I'd rather be doing from 2 to 5 o'clock in the morning. Everybody else is asleep. I'm up making these great trades. It's a fantastic market. It can be very exciting. I try not to get too emotional one way or the other. But you do get excited, especially when you trade well. It's very rewarding at the end of the day. There's a statement telling you whether you did or did not do good. Whereas at a normal job, you're told if you did a good job or not and it's not based on the numbers you produced.

Q : Yes, it's very tangible. So what was your best trade ever? Most memorable?

A : The most memorable was definitely the one we discussed because I was in an Internet café and I was kind of nervous, hoping that the connection doesn't drop in this place. I'd actually gone all around Bangkok testing connections to see which ones were strongest and which cafés were quiet. So finally I found one I liked, found an end computer, and when the NFP number came out, I just jumped all over it. It was exactly what I was expecting and key levels were broken. It's been a while, so I don't remember what they were, but it was about 120 pip of profit on a good amount of money. So it was at least a $50,000 profit and that sticks out.

Q : Now, did you make so much money because you went all in or did you keep on scaling?

A : I kept scaling in.

Q : Was it a one-way move at the time or was it a lot of retracement and then continuations?

A : Well it jumped initially and it pulled back, I want to say like 20 or 30 pips, and every time it pulled back I just kept loading up. I knew from the get-go what my limit was. I was willing to risk 10 to $20,000 on this trade if it didn't work out.

Q : So you had a hard monetary stop then?

A : Right. This was one time I did put in a stop because normally I just watch the market. I was afraid that the Internet connection would drop [laughter].

Q : What's your worst trade ever?

A : Wow, that would have to be another NFP. That Friday I got in on the wrong side of a British pound trade and it went against me. I was basically frozen like a deer in the headlights. I just didn't exit when I could have gotten out for maybe a 30 to 40 pip loss. I ended up getting out for 100. So, of course, I was in a bad mood and I didn't handle things properly. At the time, I went out and bought the pound, leveraged myself really high, and then turned off my computer. I came back it had reversed another 100 pips, and I ending up losing like 200 pips that day senselessly, just because I didn't control my emotions properly.

Q : Was there a lesson there?

A : Yes. I told myself that I wouldn't let the emotions get the best of me, I wouldn't just sit there idly, and I will never turn off my computer again and hope that the trade will turn back my way. The problem was I didn't have a plan. At the time, I bought in before the news and that's one of the things I don't do now. But it was kind of like a guessing game back then because I felt I was so lucky but now I don't do that, I don't need that little part of the move.

Q : Do you always have a plan before going into a number?

A : I have a plan. Obviously I don't know what the number will be. But I'll say okay if the number is this amount, then I'll go short—if it's this amount, I'll go long. I will also keep in mind the price action and how the market responds to it and what is the market doing prior to the number coming out because, if there's dollar weakness, it doesn't matter what that number is. Sometimes it can be fantastic for the dollar. It will continue to sell off even after great news. So I'm always watching the price action.

Q : So when you are trading what is the most you've lost pipwise?

A : I've been down more than 100. But I don't like being down more than 100 pips at any point. I would say normally 75 to 80 is about where I call it quits.

Q : In terms of your trading style, do you feel like it's changed at all?

A : Definitely less aggressive because I can trade a larger number of lots. In the beginning, I would trade two or three. Maybe now I'll do 20 or 30. It just depends, so I need a smaller amount of move to actually pull that profit in. I try to only take the trades that I think are going to be successful.

Q : Do you find that you spend a lot time trying to keep yourself out of trades?

A: Oh that's a problem [laughter]. I have to pull myself away from the computer on Fridays, especially NFP. I'll have locked in $5,000 to $10,000 for that day, and I literally have to turn off the PC. Otherwise I'll try to jump on another move. One thing that I love is to go into the weekend on a winning streak. Today was one. It gets you really energized for Monday's trading. If you go out with a poor trade, you spend the whole weekend thinking about things and you come back Monday in general as a negative trader.

Q : Do you hold positions over the weekends?

A : I try not to, actually. I don't mind holding it over night. But over the weekends I prefer not to.

Q : What's the most humbling trading experience for you?

A : Wow. I would say probably either that pound trade or another trade where I got a bad entry, and didn't pay attention to what the market was trying to tell me. I was trying to fight the market. I thought I was right, and I would just say, "Well I can buy 10 more lots or I'll buy 20 more lots." I'll force the market in my direction—and once you realize that you're not moving the market one bit, then it's very humbling.

Q : So what's your number one rule of trading?

A : My number one rule is don't overleverage yourself. Don't get into a position to the point where you're margin is called. You need to always have some ammunition on the side because you never know when that trade is going to start turning in your favor and a lot of times that's a great time to add to your trade. You've been down 50 to 60 pips, now all of the sudden you've broken through some key support, you know you need some ammo, and you don't want to be sitting there thinking, "Wow, wish I could buy." So it's money management. You have to have that money available at all times.

Q : So you encourage people to average into winning trades then?

A : Absolutely. If it's going in your direction and your plan is working, there's no reason not to cut those pips down and make it that much easier to make profit.

Q : Do you feel like you ever compete against yourself or against others when it comes to trading?

A : I always feel like I'm in competition against the big players for some reason, that it's me against the big guy. I'm very cautious, not to disclose what I'm doing, and it may sound paranoid, but I just always feel that especially when I have a lot of lots in the market that someone's out to get you—gunning for you. I feel like I'm always competing against someone. Rarely do I put the pressure on myself and say, well, I have to get this number of pips.

Q : What kind of pips do you look for on an average trade?

A : I'll tell you I only need maybe 30 or 40 pips to have a successful trade because I like to trade larger amounts. I prefer to do that than to hold something for 100 pips.

Q : You mentioned earlier that you might trade multiple lots, so do you do any stop management with the different lots?

A : I definitely move the stops up. If a trade is working, I will take some money off of the table by moving my stops up. As it moves more into my favor, I'm going to take more off, even if the adjustments are made in a few small pip increments. Sure there's a higher likelihood of the stops getting picked off, but that's part of the game. It could also drop another 50 so I'll just keep moving those stops until they get hit because that's what they're for, which is to get hit.

Q : Is there anything we didn't talk about that you feel other traders might be interested in hearing?

A : I don't know if they'd be interested, but one quirk I have is that I really feel like Feng Shui plays a part in my trading. The way I have my trading room set up makes a huge difference in my opinion. I went from losing quite a bit to making successful trades, partially based on my environment.

Q : That's interesting, how did you change it?

A : For one thing I was facing a different direction. My room was set up to where people would enter from behind me and watch over my trading and sometimes I wouldn't know they were there. Now it's facing the other way, and I can see everything that's coming towards me. I'm just a lot more comfortable. I have greenery in the room. Everything feels much cleaner and crisper and I can trade. So, as I was saying, when I was searching out Internet cafés to trade in, whether it was Japan, Thailand, or wherever, comfort was an important factor. I want to sit to the side of the room. I need to ensure that all these things function the way I like them to.

Q : Did you learn that from someone?

A : Picking up Feng Shui was just a part of being in San Francisco. I was around a lot of people who taught me about healthy living, so I applied the same things when I started trading stock. I looked at my setup and thought, that's true, my trading room is not the way I want it. So I started changing things around and you'd be surprised at the differences. I like peace and quiet. When I enter a trade or exiting a trade, the TV's muted out and I'm fully focused especially right before news. Once I'm in the trade, I know there's nothing I can do to change it. Then I'll put on other distractions because I don't want to think about the market 24/7. I can glance at it and see what's going on and continue with the rest of my life.

Q : Now, in terms of taxes, do you do that yourself or do you have someone do it for you?

A : I did it myself last year, but this year someone else is going to do it [laughter].

Q : Any plans of ever trading full-time?

A : Yes. It seems like every time I go to work, I ask myself why am here? And my coworkers—they're aware of my successes in the currency market—they ask me the same thing. You should trade full-time, but things like health benefits are stuff that is really worth thinking about. Right now I have the flexibility to work only three days a weeks, I get a full-time income. It's hard to walk away from that.

LESSONS FROM ROLAND CAMPBELL
Fading Market Sentiment

Some of the smartest traders that we know are *fade traders*. Typically called *contrarians*, these traders will step into the market when moves have become very extended and sentiment has become extremely one-sided to take a position in contrast to the prevailing market opinion. For example, if the market has become so dollar bullish that mainstream media starts printing cover stories about the strength of the currency, instead of buying the greenback on the surrounding euphoria, contrarians will sell it in anticipation of a market slump since they realize that sentiment has likely reached its peak. This is exactly the way Roland Campbell trades because, when everyone is bullish, he is looking for opportunities in the other direction. One of the most dangerous yet most tempting ways to trade is to jump into a market move when everyone is talking about it. Oftentimes this is right before the exhaustion occurs and the market begins to reverse because everyone who wants to be in the position already is. Therefore, at those points, fading the prevailing market movement may be far smarter than joining it.

Go for the Meat of the Move

The most important technique when looking for a reversal is to look for the price action to confirm your opinion before getting into the trade. Market extensions can often reach further than most people can imagine, especially faders. Therefore, arbitrarily picking a top or bottom can be very frustrating as well was very unprofitable. Roland's focus on catching the meat of the move rather than trying to pinpoint the exact beginning or the end of the move is the key to his strategy. Having experienced the damage of top or bottom picking with no clear price support, Roland now waits for news to come out, let the market move in its direction, make sure it is not a false move and only at that time, enter into the trade.

Average Your Entry and Trail Your Exit

With every trade, Roland averages in and averages out. Although averaging down can be a mug's game, the difference for Roland is intent. He knows the average price that he wants before he even places the trade. He also knows when to get out. If the price moves against him and goes much further than four average downs, he will usually abandon the trade. Not every one can get the trade right 100 percent of the time. On the flipside, he tries to get as much out of his winning trades as possible by averaging out. In order to do so, he will first lock in profits on half of the position, trail his stop on a quarter of his position and leave his stop on other quarter at breakeven. When market reversals occur, the moves can be just as powerful as the trends that preceded them. The use of trailing stops allows medium-term traders like Roland to ride as much of the meat of the move as possible.

CHAPTER 9

THE GREAT ADAPTER

TYRONE BALL

One of the most remarkable aspects of Tyrone Ball's story is his uncanny ability to adapt and succeed in some of the most treacherous market environments in recent history. Trading Nasdaq stocks almost exclusively, Tyrone has been able to navigate and prosper through a variety of changes in the market, including the vicious bear market decline in the early 2000s and the introduction of decimalization, which compressed bid/ask spreads and destroyed many profitable trading strategies. While the vast majority of his colleagues have fallen by the wayside, Tyrone has found new ways to extract profits from the market. Although his trading methods remain relatively simple, his flexibility and refusal to be satisfied with the status quo make Tyrone one of the most consistent and successful retail traders we've interviewed. He talked to us from his home office in Illinois.

■ ■ ■

Q : What is the market that you trade?

A : Primarily Nasdaq.

Q : Are you strictly a day trader, or are you a position trader?

A : I would say 98 percent day trading. Occasionally I'll take something overnight.

Q : Most people we talk to usually don't like to take anything home overnight either. Let us start by getting the basic background story from you. How did you get started in trading? What triggered your interest? Was it your family, or was this something you came across yourself?

A : You want the shorter version or the longer version?

Q : The longer version.

A : Okay. Well, I've always had an interest in the market. Growing up, my father was always dabbling with his stock portfolio, and I would poke around at the time with a very small Schwab account.

Q : That's very common. So you traded a little bit in high school, then you went to college. Did you focus on finance or a completely different subject matter?

A : I knew I was going into business and I did my undergraduate in finance and went on to get an MBA as well. But I always thought I'd be more on the brokerage side of things. I interned for a major financial services company and it worked out very well. I actually built a nice book of business while I was in school.

Q : You had a Series 7 while you were in grad school?

A : They let me get my Series 6 and 63. I was doing life insurance planning, variable life, and variable annuities. Any mutual fund business I'd refer to the rep above me. It was a great experience. I learned how to run your business while going to school. Most importantly, it provided a solid foundation and work ethic which I applied to my trading career.

Q : Did you cold call a lot?

A : The first year I did a heck of a lot of cold calling and figured out that is the lowest percentage game out there. I worked hard and learned to work a little smarter as time went on. Going to school full time and working 30-plus hours demanded I learn to manage my time efficiently.

Q : What did you do differently in the second year to help you build your book?

A : I really started hammering referrals. I'd get in there and try to do the best job I could, give the best advice, do the most for the client, and then ask them for referrals. Instead of beating up the phones, I'd ask them who their five best friends are and call on them. So that's where I thought I was headed out of grad school.

Q : And then what happened?

A : Well, I took my wife, who at the time was my girlfriend in the spring of '99, down to see my best friend, my childhood friend who I grew up with. He was living in Houston at the time. When I got there, he had all this day-trading material on his coffee table because that's what he was going to do. He was going to quit his job, cash in, and go trade full-time. So I started reading and then I felt guilty that he was taking time off from his job to cater to us.

So I suggested we check out a couple of nearby offices and that's how it all started.

Q : So you went along with him on a trip? When you walked into one of those trading operations that were so common in the late '90s, what was your initial reaction?

A : My jaw hit the floor. I remember the first office, I think Momentum.

Q : How big was the room that you walked into?

A : It wasn't real huge in terms of bodies, but it was a full shop. I don't know the head count—under 50 I'm guessing. I just remember the branch manager showing me the trader P&Ls by noon. I thought, "Are these monthly or yearly P&Ls?" [laughter.] I said, "Wait a minute, all you got to do is play this game?"

Q : Like playing a video game, right?

A : Right. I mean that was essentially how it was advertised. So I just went and started checking out more shops after I got back to Illinois.

Q : Were you living in the suburbs of Chicago or the city proper?

A : At that point, I was six hours south of Chicago, in southern Illinois. I went to school at SIU.

Q : We can't imagine many day trading shops around there.

A : Right, nothing. So I just called around and asked, "Where's the closest place I can go try it?" and it seemed like it was Chicago.

So I called a couple of buddies and they said come on up. I figured I'd give it a try, and they offered to let me live free for six months on the couch.

Q : Great deal.

A : I cashed out everything. I had a house in college that I bought as a repossession from a bank, fixed it up, cashed it out. And that, along with my savings, was my day-trading ticket.

Q : How much was your seed capital when you started trading?

A : I had around $75K liquid at that point, and I think I put $40K or $50K in my first trading account.

Q : You left the other $25K for monthly expenses. You had no rent, so basically you were just paying food?

A : I helped out with bills and chipped in some, I could have funded more in the account, but I like not having my back against the wall, psychologically.

Q : So how was your girlfriend feeling about this little venture at the time?

A : She was probably skeptical, but she had seen the Houston offices as well. I was really interested. I thought if it works, great, if not, I can sleep at night knowing I tried it and just go back to being a broker. That was the game plan. Okay maybe it was a small setback financially if I lost some money, but no family, no kids and no mortgage; it was an ideal time in my life to try it.

Q : What about your parents, any feedback from your parents on starting this up?

A : They've always been really supportive—probably more shocked than anything. But they weren't really scared that I was going into hock and might lose everything. They thought it would be a good time to try it as well.

Q : You have a $40,000 grub stake. You have $25,000 in the bank for expenses. You're living on the couch and you walk into a trading firm in Chicago, what happens then?

A : Oh it was horrible [laughter]. I went to interview at all these different shops and pretty much went with the one that didn't charge a seat fee. The shop I chose claimed they gave some good training before you started trading. So I thought great because I know nothing. I knew a little about fundamental and technical analysis from college, but not enough to be a professional trader. So I was hungry to learn, and I was also conservative with my capital. Some of these seat fees were $500 to $1,000 bucks a month, which I thought was just crazy. In hindsight, I probably would have been better off going through a different shop that charged a fee.

Q : Why?

A : Because the shop I ended up going to had so many IT problems.

Q : So execution was terrible. You were not able sometimes to get in and out of positions because the computers went down?

A : Oh yeah, it was just misery. I mean [laughter] the worst place to come in. The traders there were more swing-oriented, I think, just because maybe the software wasn't lightening fast like some of these other shops, where the guys were just in and out, in and out, moving thousands and millions of shares per day.

Q : They would hold positions for an hour or two, sometimes even overnight?

A : Yes. Guys were holding stocks for weeks. At the time, that was the thing to do and they made thousands of dollars [laughter]. So it was a horrible place to start, but it all worked out.

Q : How long did you stay there?

A : [Sigh.] Let's see, I stayed there probably a good two years.

Q : Really? As tough as it was, what happened in the first, let's say, two months? Were you down substantially?

A : Training class was me and probably 10 others. This was pretty common. There were probably more than 100 people in the firm, but it was a revolving door. New blood rolled through weekly. For every one guy who was hitting it hard, there were 10 or 15 leaving. Everybody from my class was gone in a couple of months. My training class had a big thick manual and a lot of stuff I probably shouldn't have even been taught because it clutters the thinking. And when my trainer got done, he said you're going to trade next to me for the first couple of weeks. So I would put on 100 to 200 shares, do nothing crazy, and after about a week I was like, "This is nuts." These guys around me were throwing around big size, trading tech stocks, making all this money. I was just prodding around, not really making any money. So my trainer had to go to Austin for a week for training [Laughter]. And after he left, there I was putting on a thousand of everything, and it was a horrible two weeks. I was holding stuff overnight, doing everything I shouldn't have been doing. When the branch manager walked up, I'd hide my position blotter. I'm like, "Oh, everything's fine." He's like, "Are you sure?" Yeah. He'd walk away. Of course, he knew the P&L of everybody in the whole firm [laughter]. But, yeah, I took a bath my first three to four months where I probably drew down close to $20K—half my account.

Q : That's still not bad given the fact that you were trading 1,000 share lots. At that time stocks were dropping a point a minute, so you could have been hurt much worse.

A : Yeah, well mostly everything was going up five bucks every hour [laughter]. Yeah, this was fall of '99.

Q : So, you would get long and strong, just buy everything, and hope the market would rescue you?

A : Yes, but the stuff I was willing to get into wasn't that good. It wasn't the big name stuff, and I didn't know what I was doing.

Q : What kind of stocks were you trading at that time and why did you choose those stocks instead of the high flyers?

A : Good question. Probably because they were the cheaper price, and I thought I could get maybe 1,000 or 2,000 shares on when there was only 2 to 1 buying power. So it was a big thing if you wanted to trade Qualcomm or Yahoo!. They were all premium stocks at that time and tied up buying power. Additionally, the moves were vicious to an inexperienced trader. So I was hunting smaller, techie stuff. But obviously I didn't pick the right ones [laughter]. The first four months were misery in terms of trading, and I had no business trading.

Q: What were you thinking throughout that time? Every day you would come back home, you'd be beaten up, what was going through your mind?

A: Horrible. I'd come up here [Chicago], and I was losing a lot of money. I could have been back home earning money, growing my other business, and know what I was doing. It just didn't make sense. So I said, I'm going to draw the line in the sand, if it gets to this point, I'm just done.

Q: So what was your time stop? Was it six months?

A: Well I think I started in August, so I was going into the end of the year and I figured somewhere through the holidays and maybe an extra month beyond that would be my max if it continued the way it was going.

Q: What made you keep on going?

A: I got lucky [laughter], extremely lucky. I started building a little portfolio of these tiny biotech stocks—$3 to $5 stocks—a few thousand shares of each. You could hold stuff like that, and I was getting margin calls here and there. But there was a service that met your margins calls for x amount of dollars [laughter].

Q: This sounds like the traders book of what *not* to do.

A: Oh yeah, to the T. I mean, I could have written that book. So yes, I got lucky. Things really started booming, late '99, early 2000 before the bubble burst in the spring. Suddenly these teeny little things started running I was jumping on these trades and just holding them instead of getting in and out of them.

Q : How long were you holding them for?

A : Usually from all day to maybe a couple or a few days. At times I held them for a few weeks.

Q : How big were the runs? Let's say it was a $3 stock, how big would it run in two to three weeks?

A : Anywhere from 3 to 7 to 10 bucks or something.

Q : So you had a chance to sometimes triple your initial stake?

A : Yes. I probably went from somewhere in the ballpark of a $30K account in 1999 to $120K by February 2000.

Q : And was this primarily based on holding positions in these tiny biotech stocks that really started to run and were able to quadruple your equity?

A : Right. That was a big chunk of it and some tech stocks. Better guys trading around me held 15 to 30,000 shares by just holding it, and I'm like, "If they can hold that much, I can surely hold 3,000." I might make a few points on it, which at the time was huge. So that's kind of how I fit in the game. I still had no business being a trader.

Q : That is a good story, you hit the lottery.

A : Small lotto.

Q : Now you are very decently capitalized. You're at $120K. We're in February, but we are on the precipice of the largest dive in Nasdaq history. So what happens?

A : Yeah, it was high times, I was walking tall. I even started giving my roommates some rent money [laughter].

Q : Were you finally ready to leave your couch?

A : Yeah. Actually, you can only stay on a good couch for so long [Laughter], longer than I should have. Obviously the bottom fell out, and it didn't kill me. But it put a little crimp on the easy money. I had maybe lost 10 or 20 percent drawdown from highs, but nothing I couldn't recover from.

Q : At that point, it was an utter, sheer collapse. Did you learn to take losses? Or did you simply not put on large positions?

A : Yeah. As I saw the bubble pop, something inside me said, "Relax." Everybody was still buying them, and it would sort of bounce here and there. But overall, guys were just getting crushed left and right around me. It was pretty sad to see. There were guys—kids that made a million, two million over the last year—and they were just giving it away at an alarming pace. The bells and whistles went off at that point, and I started to look around the firm and look for guys that weren't big traders taking these huge swings. I tried to find anybody who was making consistent money. There was one guy. He kept pretty private, but a nice guy. So I got to talking to him. He said he always made around five grand, day in and day out, no matter whether the market went up or down. He said, "I'm not going to make $20K or $50K like that guy sitting next to you. But I'm never going to lose money." I said, "Wow, how do you do that?" [laughter.] So that was when the light went on and I said, "Okay this guy is an actual trader, not a buy'em and hold' em and hope for the best guy." He's actually trading stocks up and down. I never really went short anything prior to that point. If you wanted to trade—scalp—them both ways effectively, you had to put on some conversions to enable selling on the downtick.

Q : Let's just step back and explain what conversion is. At that time you would basically be allowed to buy a put, right?

A : Yeah, it was a married put.

Q : A married put that would allow you to short the stocks because you would be synthetically always long. So he sort of taught you that there were two ways to go in the market—that you could make money on the short side. So did you sit by his desk, observing him for a while?

A : No. Once in a while I would watch him, but he was a pretty private guy. He sat on the floor, but it was always hard to tell what he did. He just traded a few stocks he liked, looked at the chart, and if it moved around every day for a few points, it's probably a good one that you can get in and out of and trade up and down. So I picked about four or five names to put conversions on. BroadCom, Seibel, and Brocade were three of them.

Q : Very familiar names.

A : Yeah. I just started trading like 500 shares of them, up or down. The first couple weeks were horrible because I was teaching myself. I probably lost five or ten grand trying to do this.

Q : Prior to this you're basically building positions. So you're not really having too much daily turnover. You're not doing a hundred round turns a day, right?

A : No, I wasn't.

Q : So now you slow down the size. You go down to 500 shares. Clearly you have to do a lot more turnover to generate revenue. How many round turns a day were you doing and were commissions starting to become a much bigger factor on a cost basis at that point?

A : I was doing 50 round turns. Ballpark.

Q : Right. At a 1,000 shares, how much commission were you paying at that point?

A : Oh, it was horrible, a penny and a half maybe. I'm trading at a third of that now [laughter]. Every hundred-thousand shares was $1,500 bucks.

Q : Right.

A : Outrageous, but we were making a lot more money because we were still trading in fractions.

Q : And fractions made it a lot easier to flip over. So, for the first two weeks, you're trying to get the feel of it. It's a lot harder than it looks. What's going on there?

A : I was thinking maybe I made a mistake, maybe this guy is just really good and he's got some secret that he's not willing to give up, because this is pretty hard. But the more I kept doing it, I kept figuring out little things. I think it was more building a familiarity with the stock. How the stock moved and really watching what the overall market was doing in tandem. These stocks were pretty highly correlated. So I would just short them, hold some wiggles, and learn how to catch one or two point moves.

Q : How long did it take you to become profitable?

A : A month to six weeks.

Q : How much risk per trade would you allow yourself at that point?

A : Well, there were occasional ones when I got stubborn. But usually around a half point, I was getting out for sure—if I could.

Q : On those occasions when you got stubborn, what's the worst loss you took?

A : Doing regular scalping probably a grand or two. I did get stubborn with overnights sometimes—that I would do on the side after I had built up my account. Those were my worst trades. I ended up losing 10 or $20K, on some overnight positions.

Q : So you would give back, sometimes, a week's worth of work on an overnight trade?

A : Yeah, and I would ask myself, "What am I doing?" I can make money every day, why am I doing this overnight business? And a few months later I find myself in another one,

Q : What was the thing that attracted you to the overnights?

A : I think it was just the charts were so beat up and had these huge ranges, and I tried to go in and bottom-pick some stuff.

Q : Except they kept going down. Did you average down on those trades?

A : I would on occasion. But most of them were smaller-price stocks, around 20 bucks. If they were at $150 and they came down to $20 or so, I thought, "Wow, how much how lower can they really go?"—and I found out [laughter].

Q : You found out it can go to zero [laughter].

A : I never held something to zero. But I held stuff definitely way beyond where I should have got out.

256

Q : So, when you were day trading, would you go for a half a point to a point on your winning trades for these 500-share positions?

A : That's pretty safe to say. At that point I'd say a lot of my money came from the open, where stuff would just scream two, three, four points either way—sometimes both ways within an hour- to two-hour period. So that was probably where 80 percent of my profit was coming.

Q : And did you learn to read the open? You learned how to successfully trade the open, which is what gave you the profitability edge, is that right?

A : Yes. I knew it was essential. If you were going to spend a hard two hours working, that was time to do it.

Q : Would you trade preopen, would you watch the activity preopen?

A : I pretty much just walked in, had my coffee, the bell rang, and I'd start to work. I really didn't do any, pre- or postmarket analysis. At that point I was trading as a scalper. I didn't care about much outside of Level 2.

Q : So you really learned how to read Level 2?

A : Right. My style is momentum based. I never really tried to fight the overall market either.

Q : If it was screaming up, did you buy the offers?

A : If I thought I was early enough—those days with fractions you could—there could be a quarter- or half-point spread in some of these things. If you entered 1,000 shares you're down $250 out of the gate. But sometimes you just get the feel for the way the markets and these stocks were moving. It was only by trading four or five stocks that I developed a feel and was in-sync with how they move.

Q : But generally you try to always buy the bid, sell the offer?

A : When I could, but when stuff started moving, I realized it cost you more if you didn't go in and get it early versus watching it run a point or two.

Q : Right. And then you would try to offer out, right? You would at least try to make half of the spread by just trying to get yourself lifted on the offer?

A : Yes, I'd always try and get out and make the spread. I would refrain from exiting to bid or offer. But on the flipside, when things turn, they would turn fast. So it was a quick decision, whether I want to try to make an extra dime or quarter—or if I should just get out and lock in a winner.

Q : Now most of this kind of trading was really not software driven. What we mean by that is when you get into a trade, you didn't have a predefined stop-loss automatically in your software. You would have to physically take yourself out of the trade, right?

A : Right.

Q : So a huge amount of this was very reactive. You had to make lightening-fast decisions based upon the movement in Level 2?

A : Right. As fast as our software would let us [laughter], which at times, was brutal.

Q : Sometimes you would just get stuck in queue and the whole thing would spin forever, and you wouldn't know if you got out of position or not, right?

A : Oh, it was horrible.

Q : What do you think made you different, made you success-ful in this kind of very instinctive, seat-of-the-pants type trading that most people absolutely fail at miserably because the speed, the pressure and the ability to quickly make decisions is just over-whelming?

A : I think it's the same reason that I'm still around today. I just got done saying I was pretty undisciplined and could have done things a lot better back then. But I was still, I think, above the rest of the guys in the room in terms of self-discipline and patience. Additionally, I moved to a better software platform.

Q : In other words, you would be selective about your trades and you would be disciplined about getting out of the trades?

A : Right. Taking winners was part of it. You know there were plenty of trades where, if held them a little bit longer, I would have made more. But there are plenty of trades where, if they did the same thing and I just waited another minute to exit because I thought it might go in my favor, I would have lost a lot more. So I came to understand that you can't pick the top and the bottoms of your trades. You have to be willing to take money while it's still in your favor and cut your losers small. It sounds simple, but most can't do that.

Q : Right.

A : Lock in your winners and keep losers small. But that was so hard for some guys to do. They were just losing, bleeding thousands and thousands around me. It was really sad to see.

Q : We can imagine.

A : Some of these guys were good friends.

Q : That was the one thing that really kept you in the game—just protecting your capital?

A : Yeah. I found a system that worked consistently. So, pretty much day in and day out, I was making money.

Q : Is this the core of a system you still use today?

A : Exactly. And it's changed a lot because of the markets. The stocks and prices have changed. It's been a game of adaptation ever since, but the core remains the same.

Q : Without revealing the key algorithms behind your system, what's the cornerstone of it? Can you share some of the broader philosophical principals behind it?

A : I would say it's still momentum based. I still follow the market. I don't try and fight it.

There are great traders out there that fade stocks. The market is screaming up. They're getting short and waiting for that rollover when it happens. They bank sometimes really well. But I tried to fade stuff and [laughter] you can start fading way too early and build up a sizeable loser. I'd rather wait for a reversal and join.

Q : The other thing we want to ask you is just on a mechanical basis. Are you a single-entry, single-exit type of a trader? Or do you scale out?

A : I would say I try and scale most of the time. But then there are times it's clear that I'm going to lose or need to bail quickly. I don't really scale out when I'm losing. I just bang out.

Q : So you don't average down? You just take your loss and go, right?

A : Right.

Q : But if you're in the money, you give up maybe half the position to bank some profit and then try to milk the rest?

A : Yeah. Over the years I've been able to enter and sometimes add to the winners.

Q : Really?

A : Before, when I held a position and it was going my way, I always used to lock it in, bid out, offer out. Now if it's early enough, and I think I'm really right and see something shaping up, I will add to it early on.

Q : When you add, do you typically add same amount of size, half the size, or do you have any kind of parameters as to what size you would add on when scaling up?

A : The smaller stuff, anywhere from half to doubling my position. The higher price stuff, half at most.

Q : So this way if it comes in, if it starts to go back against you, you can at least get out or break even, right?

A : Right. I mean, obviously, there are cases where breakeven doesn't appear [laughter].

Q : Right. You never want to turn a winner into a loser. How often does that happen? When you add up to the position, it's always the danger point of that kind of strategy. But how often does that happen where you know you're right, you think it's going to go, you add, and then it just viciously turns and the winner becomes a loser?

A : On occasion. The key is being disciplined to scratch it or take a small loser. All losers start small.

Q : So you basically never let it go below breakeven on average-up trade, right?

A : Try not to, unless there's something really big telling me to hold it, maybe a nickel, 10 cents below my entry.

Q : But really, no more than dime below your entry, that's your uncle point?

A : Trust me, it happens, I try and keep that as my goal, breakeven to a dime and you're not going to get cut up too badly.

Q : What is your day like now?

A : It's changed a lot, and it keeps changing as the years go on because I do something different outside the market. Where I used to trade from 8:30 A.M. and turn it off at 3 and it was great. It was a good lifestyle. But I'm just trying to do more stuff now.

Q : Do you do some mentoring?

A : Yes, I got into consulting over two years ago. Now, every other month, I go overseas to China and trade/train for a week. Currently, I have 85 traders now under my mentorship.

Q : That must be an experience.

A : Yes [laughter]. If two years ago you said I was even going to China, much less trading over there, I would be surprised. It's quite an experience.

Q : Do you find the same flaws and phobias of human nature there or do you find the Chinese to be more disciplined in their approach?

A : After my first trip I saw some of the traders and met some people, and I thought, wow, what an opportunity, because I thought these people are the hardest workers, They're supposed be smarter and more disciplined. You think of all that. You're like wow, what a great resource, what a perfect person to turn into a disciplined trader. After about six months, I realized they are no better than any average American kid whom I used to trade with.

Q : Human nature is universal.

A : Yeah [laughter].

Q : Now some of them I had to teach capitalism. I have a lot of drive and passion, and I think you really just had to instill that in them. Some of them don't take to it well. The ones that do, and run with it become good traders. There are some kids over there who produce right along with me and some out produce me. So I'm thrilled.

Q : That's great. In China do they trade their own stock market or do they trade Nasdaq with you?

A : No, all the U.S. equities.

Q : You trade Nasdaq basically from there?

A : Yeah, I do the exact same thing I would do if I was sitting in my office.

Q : The only difference is do you trade overnight there? What time does the market open there?

A : Yes. It's the inverse of New York, so it's 9:30 P.M. to 4 A.M.

Q : But stepping back to Chicago, when you have your own business, how is the day? Is it still basically 8:30 you're on the desk? Do you trade from home? Do you trade from prop?

A : Well, over a year ago I left the office and set up at home just because I moved out to the suburbs from the city and the commute was just killing me. I hated it. I thought I would try it and see if it was possible. I never thought you could trade from home unless you actually ordered up a T1 and spent the money to do it right. Which I was willing to do, but I thought I would go ahead and try it because I noticed my Internet at home—DSL—was getting a lot faster. So I set up at home and was shocked that it was actually better than being at the office because you weren't connected through the office servers. I was piping directly into New York versus going through all the servers that serviced 100 or so of our traders in the office. Less issues, less problems, fast, if not faster. So I run cable and DSL from home.

Q : For redundancy?

A : Yes, exactly.

Q : What kind of a setup do you have? How many screens are you looking at?

A : Three CPUs. I have six screens—but one is just for instant messaging other trading buddies. Also one is just a full page of the live briefing news, and another just for e-mailing. I trade using two or three.

Q : So how many stocks do you watch on a day-to-day basis? Are you back to four or five core stocks, or are you watching more?

A : No. Over the years, since the market changed, I find I rely mostly on filtering. So now I have about eight filters running. I'll try anywhere from 20 to 40 stocks in a day.

Q : And these are filters where you are looking at volatility, volume, things that could give you a clue that there's momentum in the stock?

A : Exactly. I am looking at volume, specific chart patterns, and momentum plays.

Q : At the core of it, you're still ultimately a momentum trader. That is still what you like to do best, which is follow the flow, right?

A : Right, I never really tried to predict. I just tried to react to what was going on.

Q : Now you said you have a news screen. Before, in 2002 to 2005, did you know the fundamental story behind the stocks you were trading or were you really not interested?

A : No, I didn't care.

Q : You just watched price action, right?

A : Right. That and the overall market, which way it was going.

Q : When you are doing all these filters, let's say there's a stock that you're just not familiar with, do you need to know what the story is behind the stock?

A : No, I don't have to know anything. I don't think it helps for what I do, which is momentum. If the Level 2 looks right, the chart lines up and it's going the right direction, I'll get onboard.

Q : So you really think that fundamental news is a detriment because it kind of biases your reaction time?

A : Oh, I won't say it's bad; I just don't have the time typically. I'm basing my entry off the way the filters are set up, and my trading style. I really don't care about anything else besides that. But on the flipside, I run full briefing news now and another audio news service. I'll jump on a news trade here and there.

Q : Using sort of fundamental, momentum play, where there's news on the stock that's going to materially impact it. You want to be the first guy to the ball?

A : Exactly. And I won't play too many of them—probably one or two a day. I'll jump on, and if I'm 50 percent successful I'm pretty happy. This week we caught a couple of nice ones. For example, say an FDA approval is announced, first on the squawk, then briefing, and everybody's buying, then it comes across CNBC a couple minutes later.

Q : You can sell it to those guys, right?

A : That's right. I'm not going to hold it for long. Sell it to the late buyers . . . [laughter].

Q : These days, what would you say is your average holding time in a position?

A : Good question. It differs. If I take the average, I would probably say seven minutes now.

Q : How many filters do you have running?

A : Eight.

Q : Are these filters a result of your experience? How did you come to designing these filters?

A : Experience is some of it, and the other is just tweaking them, a lot of trial and error. You can get pretty advanced now.

Q : And you use all those tools? You will use chart ideas, volume ideas and other tools in your filters?

A : Right. I'm not a real technician; I'm more of a momentum trader.

Q : When did you start to move to more of a filter-based trading?

A : Probably 2004, definitely all of 2005. I pretty much don't have any staple stocks I go to, like I used to.

Q : So you don't have emotional attachment to any of these positions. It might as well be an A-B-C-X-Y-Z symbol in many ways?

A : Right.

Q : During the day, are you trading intensely every hour from 8:30 A.M. to 3 P.M.?

A : Yes, as long as the market is active. I think to me, or at least for what I'm doing, it's getting harder the longer I'm in the business. So I'm actually working harder. I'll probably start now at about 7 or 7:30 A.M., and I'll even trade after hours now when the earnings are released. I don't get out much. My wife brings me a bowl of cereal at noon and that's about it [laughter]. I just lock myself downstairs and trade.

Q : How do you maintain your focus for seven, eight hours a day like that?

A : Well, the market hours are only six-and-half hours long. I always thought if you can't work six-and-half hours you're in big trouble. It's a heck of a job and lifestyle, and I enjoy the freedom to sacrifice six-and-half hours versus going out and working 8 to 12 for somebody else—that scares me worse. So I have no problem sitting here.

Q : Trading these days obviously costs so much less. You went from a penny and a half now to basically about a half a penny per share. Also leverage is quite different these days. Can you talk a little about how your account is structured now? Do you maintain as much capital as you used to or do you maintain only a sliver of equity in your account and keep most of the money elsewhere?

A : Yeah, the model really changed. It went from 2-to-1 buying power to 4-to-1, so that helps. The LLC model is popular, very similar to that of a prop model. They pool the buying power and require a reasonable amount of risk capital.

Q : And then every month you sweep your profits out of the account and maintain a certain amount?

A : Every month they send me a wire from my account for what I'm up that month, and they retain an agreed amount of risk capital.

Q : Do you have a core group of buddies or students whom you trade with during the day, whom you communicate with on IM?

A : I would say three—and those are all guys in the U.S.—and then I have multiple IMs up in China. But it's more for management. I don't try and interact too much with their trading when I'm not there. I'm not calling out trades to them.

Q : Do you find that actually to be a major distraction to call out trades?

A : Sometimes. That's one of the benefits of being with just two or three guys on a daily basis.

Q : What is the conversation between those three guys and you usually about?

A : It's typically typing a stock symbol and a question mark. An opinion or two about the potential trade might be exchanged. If we both enter, we might discuss exit points or point out something we like or dislike about the trade.

Q : So you sort of communicate in shorthand with your close friends?

A : Yes, just a couple guys I have been trading with in an office. Actually, one amazingly since I started trading in '99, and one guy that I've been trading with since '03 to '04. I trust the way they trade and visa versa. We are very similar.

Q : So you guys sort of electronically point out certain interesting things that you are seeing and sharing, sometimes pooling your ideas.

A : Exactly. Sometimes trades happen so quickly that I can't type, "Hey, join me." Or maybe the stock is too thin, but maybe after the fact I'll say, "I caught this one for 30 to 40 cents. It looks like a good one to watch for the rest of the day." Just alerting one another to stocks that are good to put on a watch list for later.

Q : Once you find a mover in your filters, something that's really going strong, will you go back to it the next day and the next day to see if there is more juice to be squeezed from the fruit?

A : Yes. If they're really good ones, we'll keep them on our "in-play list." Last week there was an IPO, and we've been on it every day. Until it runs dry, we'll keep hitting it.

Q : So you close shop essentially three, maybe four o'clock—do you then do some after-hours trading, some news trading if there are earning releases, or things like that?

A : Yeah. Then my second job starts, till five or six.

Q : Your mentorship job that you do with China?

A : Yes. It's a lot of e-mails, looking at reports, doing some analysis either on traders or their trades. I'm working with another guy now on some automated trading programs as well.

Q : There's a lot of projects on your plate. This year, since you pretty much go flat every single day, how many winning days—no let's ask the question differently—how many *losing* days have you had out of about the 200 trading days that we've had so far this year?

A : Since I started trading I average around 80 percent winning days. I've probably had around 50 down days in 2006.

Q : How do you handle that? Are there months where, let's say, you have eight bad days? That means almost half your trading month is negative. Which means it's probably going to be a pretty flat month, how do you mentally handle that kind of situation?

A : I think, the first thing I do is I check around me, check with my trading partners, not specifically dollar-wise, but to get a feel about how their month is going. I definitely have China as a good gauge; I've got 80-plus people doing what I'm doing. How are they doing? Are their numbers going way down this month? If I'm in check with them, no alarms go off. But if everybody else is doing well around me and I'm just sitting idle or going the other way, then I know it's something with me.

Q : Do you set a hard money target for yourself every day?

A : Yes, I change it from month to month depending on what the market is doing. But yeah, I'll typically go in and say, at minimum, I want to make 500 bucks a day. And that way, when the markets moving decently and things are going my way, I will definitely target $1,000 to $1,200 plus a day. This way you are working towards something every day. I am a big fan of goal-setting.

Q : Say you reach $1,200 by 10 o'clock your time. What happens then? Do you keep on trading, do you stop?

A : No, I don't stop, I just keep going. When you try to average $1,000 a day and have to average in flat or a few down days, you really have to strive to get some nice days in. I will put a stop to the downside as well. If I'm up $1,200, I want to guarantee that I walk out with $900 or $1,000. I'll keep trying to drive forward and I've seen those 1,200-dollar days have the possibility to turn into three- or four-grand days.

Q : On the other hand, let's say you start slipping. Your $1,200 slips back to $900, do just watch stocks for the rest of the day, or do you physically turn off the screen and walk out of office?

A : I'll sit tight. I just call it sitting on my hands. I'll still go through the motions. I pull up stocks with my filters, but I won't get in unless I'm at least 90 to 95 percent certain. That keeps me pretty much at bay for the rest of the day. Walk out and leave? Never! [laughter.] I probably should at times.

Q : Is it the excitement? Is it the game that keeps you in front of the screen so much? The love of the action?

A : Yes, I really enjoy it. I will say I enjoyed it a lot more in previous years because it has become so much harder I think. But, yes, I enjoy it and again it's only six-and-half hours. If I lose that discipline, I would hate to see the other side. I love the daily competition and strive to improve every day.

Q : Has it gotten harder because volatility has compressed? Or has everybody become sort of sharper and better in markets, less of an edge there?

A : I would say volatility has a lot to do with it—the automation and all of these computer programs in the market. I heard that they now trade upwards to 70 percent of all the volume—which is fine if you can figure out the program and you use them to your advantage, but I think they're getting better.

Q : They've gotten a lot sharper in their algorithms.

A : Oh, yeah very much.

Q : Are you still doing maybe 50 to 60 trades per day? Or are you doing a little bit less now?

A : At least. I'm trading over a 100,000 shares a day, every day. Typically I trade 2 to 3 million shares per month now.

Q : Just a couple of last questions. What's your number one rule for trading?

A : Don't hold losers. Others: Keep a positive mindset. Think like a winner. Go to the market every day and take out some money. Be patient, be disciplined, be passionate.

Q : Best trade ever?

A : Ever? It wasn't the biggest profit trade, but it was the biggest point gainer. And I can't remember what year it was—'01 or '02—somebody had put something on the Internet about a stock called Emulex.

Q : Yeah, Emulex.

A : So it just started tanking. I watched it and I watched it and this is one thing I typically don't do—fade stocks—but I just thought this is crazy spike down [laughter]. I bought 100 shares and I swear 10 seconds later it was halted. "Oh brother, what have I done? I'm so stupid." I thought. After it was unhalted, I think I made close to 60 points on it. That wasn't my biggest P&L trade, but I would say my most memorable was the fact it was so fast.

Q : The Emulex saga was a very famous story of the Internet age, when a fake press release caused the stock to plummet and then bounce back hundreds of points in one day. Worst trade ever that you can remember?

A : Oh boy. It would have to be probably some of the overnight bleeders that I held back in the day. Some of these stocks don't trade anymore. I do recall one that we traded a lot before it got bought out. It was a stock that traded over $400 and we would typically try and make the spread on it because it would carry a 10- to 20-point spread at times. We might flip 100 or 200 shares and, if we made the spread, it was a nice little winner. Actually it traded north of $600.

Q : So these were very big stocks?

A : Yeah, in the Nasdaq. We thought we could play the bid-offer game on some thin pricey stocks. The bad trade I was shorting, and I actually got too many on, can't remember—at least 400 or 500 shares—and the news came out: A buyout. I got steamrolled probably for like $20K.

Q : Ouch. Was the stock halted?

A : Yeah, it halted, came unhalted, and I just got rolled. It was such a thin stock and, of course, any volume at that point was just volume coming in to buy it.

Q : So you are short the stock. It gets halted—takeover news—what's going on in your mind at that point? What did you decide to do the moment you heard all that news?

A : Pucker up, it's going hurt. Nothing good was going to come out of it. So I just had to get out.

Q : And getting out meant you were taking any offer that was going to be out there. You didn't try to get cute, go to the bid?

A : I tried a combination because the spread was so wide. But yeah, I was taking offers that were way out there. Then I proceeded to trade it the whole following week and half and made it all back.

Q : You did? Was that revenge trading?

A : Maybe a small inkling of it was [laughter]. But I knew over the past couple years of trading that I did very well trading it.

Q : So you had a good feel for the stock?

A : Yes. After the initial craziness was over, it was good actually because it had more volume after the buyout. So it was trading more actively.

Q : So you could make more bid/ask?

A : Right. I was now flipping 200 to 300 shares because the volume was there.

Q : Yeah, you did what you had to do. Final questions. What do you find to be the most interesting part of this job?

A : The competition. The constant strive to become a better trader and learn new things. Every day is a new game and usually differs from the previous day.

Q : Competition with yourself or the competition against others?

A : Both. I strive to be better and go to market and take money out of it every day.

Q : Are you sports fan?

A : Yes, I am. Ideally, if could do something outside of trading, I'd be a professional athlete. But my abilities just don't allow for it, [laughter] or my size. I'm not a sports fanatic, but I love watching football. I even watch golf now, which I never used to do. I found that sports and competition is a real common thread of good traders.

Q : Yes, we find that to be a very common personality trait, particularly of equity day traders. Traders in other markets differ somewhat, but equity day traders tend to be very athletically minded.

A : Right. On a China trip, I think it was over a year ago, I said let's go play some basketball in the morning after work. I just announced whoever wants to play, show up. We met up at the university gym and I noticed 95 percent of the 15 guys who showed up were the top traders out of the 200 traders plus.

Q : Very interesting.

A : Yeah [laughter]. I think there's some correlation to trading/competitiveness. And, you know, it all makes sense. But it was just neat to see, so far from home, guys who aren't athletes but competitive. It was the most unorganized, horrible game of basketball ever played [laughter].

Q : It was the spirit of the thing that mattered.

A : Yeah, they were hacking every chance they got. It was fun though. The best part was I was the tallest guy! Rare chance for me to dominate on the court!

Q: Lastly, what's the most difficult part of this job?

A: I would say just the thought that—or maybe it's just an inherent fear—that someday I won't be able to adjust or they're going to change rules in the marketplace. I hope it never happens, and I've been able to adjust for seven years now. But you never know.

LESSONS FROM TYRONE BALL

Focus on Only a Few Stocks to Develop a Feel

Tyrone's message is similar to Steve Ickow's: If you chose to be a jack-of-all-trades, you will be master of none. In order to succeed in trading, you need to establish an expertise in a particular domain. As in all professions, specialization pays. For equity day traders such as Tyrone, specialization means focusing on only a select group of stocks and watching their price action intently. This is the only way to learn the particular quirks of the stock and to discover who the dominant players are in that particular instrument. In the parlance of the game, it is very important to know who is the *axe* in the stock. The "axe" is simply a term used for the dominant market maker who can literally make or break the price of the stock. Knowing this information can help the trader to stay on the right side of the trade.

Being Just a Little More Disciplined Than the Average Guys Can Give You an Edge

The house edge in roulette is only 5.26 percent. That means that on any spin of the wheel, the casino stands to win approximately 53 percent of the time while the player wins approximately 48 percent of the time. This illustration is not intended to compare trading to gambling, but rather to demonstrate that it takes a very small skew in the odds to create a very profitable enterprise. Casinos bank billions of dollars of profit per year on what, at first glance, may appear to be only a small advantage. Similarly, Tyrone's most interesting point is that one does not have be perfect, just a little more disciplined than the next guy, to survive and prosper in the game. The most common reason that most traders fail is because they refuse to properly respect and contain risk. One stubborn bad trade is all it takes to wipe out years of gains. Tyrone's insight is that by simply never putting oneself in that position, the trader already stands a better chance of success than the rest of the crowd. Just to underscore this point, he talks about his experience with Chinese traders, which presumably given the strong cultural emphasis on hard work are far more disciplined than their American counterparts. Yet, in the end, he states that the Chinese are just as susceptible to the exact same flaws in risk control as their American counterparts. Human nature is universal and discipline is the common thread that unites all great traders across the world.

Constantly Learn and Adapt

Finally, as we mentioned in the chapter introduction, what makes Tyrone such a successful trader is his ability to constantly learn and adapt. As you follow the course of his career, you see that he learned how to scalp the open after the glory days of buy'em-and-hold -'em bull market of the 1990s disappeared. Then, when decimalization made mincemeat of most momentum traders, he learned how to use a variety of filters to look for better setups. Finally, as a trader who simply traded price action and technical indicators for most of his career, Tyrone then learned to effectively trade the news by exploiting his old momentum trading skills. The key takeaway point from Tyrone's experience is that there is no "one way" to trading success. The path to profitability requires constant willingness to try new setups. Just like the markets, trading is not a static discipline, and Tyrone's career is a testament to the need for flexibility and adaptability.

CHAPTER 10

SURFING FOR PROFITS

ASHKAN BOLOUR

With an unusual combination of strong quantitative skills and a deep background in psychology, Ashkan Bolour provides unique insights into the art and science of trading. One of the earliest entrants into the retail Forex market, Ashkan has achieved tremendous success matching wits against some of the most sophisticated players in the biggest financial market in the world. An avid surfer, Ashkan compares trading to the ocean—calm one day, turbulent the next—and counsels traders to take it all in stride. Although he uses a variety of complex quantitative algorithms, Ashkan never loses sight of the mental aspect of the business and often practices meditation to enhance his focus and place him in sync with the overall market. We chatted with Ashkan from his California home as trading in the U.S. session was coming to an end.

■ ■ ■

Q : How did you start in trading? What was your first market?

A : Basically I started in equities. My background was in mathematics. So it was easy for me—to understand the quantitative nature of the markets. I would just get daily graphs and go through the numbers and look at the market in a quantitative way.

Q : What was your profession when you started to get involved in the stock market? Were you an engineer by trade?

A : No, actually, when I started trading I was still in high school. My mom opened an account with my money and threw in a little of her own. Then I started to trade. I was always good at mathematics; I was basically just good at making money.

Q : You started making money right away?

A : Yes, in a sense, I used William O'Neal's strategy of picking stocks. I would pick a company where I would buy 300 to 400 shares. I would stick with them for several months and that just seemed to work. I would find a company with expanding earnings and go from there. They were small-cap stocks. You know $5, $6, $7 stock, always under 10. Then they'd go up to like $14 or $15 over several months. That type of trading just went on for several years. Basically that's how I got started, but my background is not engineering, I studied psychology and in psychology I was enrolled in an experimental quantitative program that had a lot of statistics. We did a lot of analysis with multiple-regression equations, time-series analysis, factor analysis, and things like that. So I just applied that to the stock market. I obviously studied charting and technical analysis. I really got in-depth, trying to understand all aspects of the market and I actually went and worked for an investment bank that took a couple of companies public. Then I went to work for another firm, in Beverly Hills that had high-net worth clients that day traded big blocks.

Q : When you were in Beverly Hills and were working for this firm that had high-net-worth individuals, were you doing block trading for them or were you a sales trader?

A : No, actually I came in there just as a broker. I had 7 and 63 license, and I basically came with a couple of clients that traded big blocks. We would do all kinds of research together and find stocks. We'd try to find out good ideas on a daily basis. I started learning how to trade options. There was another guy that traded options. He had expertise in that area, so just being around different traders at that time, I picked up a lot of different things.

Q : What year was that when you were brokering this kind of stuff? Was it in the late '90s?

A : Yeah, it was in the late '90s. I think I got my license in around '95. I was younger then, so I kind of hopped around to try and figure out just what it was I really wanted to do, and being with the investment bank I knew that I really didn't want to do that. Also I liked trading, but I knew I didn't want to be scalping a couple thousand shares for a quarter or half a point. So I went and worked for some firms and then eventually a friend of mine wanted me to come down to his office to look at something called *foreign exchange*. That was seven years ago, and so I kind of just fell into that. I looked at the markets and with my technical analysis background, my eyes and my mind just matched with the market.

Q : At that time foreign exchange trading was just starting to become available to the retail clients. The Internet made it possible for these retail brokers to go out and offer FX to the public.

A : Yes. It's funny you say that because back then the first place I traded at they didn't even take trades over the Internet. They had a little window in the office where we placed our order ticket and then the lady would stamp it. It would be attached to an account

281

at HSBC, and you would ask for a quote on a pair. The lady in the "cage" would call a hotline and ask for a quote and you'd say, okay buy x amount at that price. Now you can just log onto the internet and trade instantly, but I am actually glad I got in at the beginning. It's nice to see the FX market grow and flourish over the past several years.

Q : One of the things that differentiates the FX market from every other electronic market out there is that it's a spread-based market. It doesn't have commission, but on the flipside you are not allowed to buy on the bid or sell at the offer. You have to pay the bid offer spread. At that time the bid offer spreads must have been considerably larger than they are now right?

A : Yes. I'm pretty sure, from what I remember when they'd give us the quote, it was ten pips. So you had to be patient and be a good trader, look at it from a longer perspective because if you took the offer, for example, you had to make 15 pips just to be up 5 pips wide. So, yeah, it was like that back then and I've seen those spreads steadily come down and at some places its now just two or three pips wide on majors. It is just so much more liquid now.

Q : As a matter of fact there was a recent article in *Financial Times* saying that next year the foreign exchange market is going to do 3.6 trillion per day.

A : Wow.

Q : The growth of it is just massive. And they are actually attributing quite a lot of it to the advent of retail traders coming into the market, which was absolutely nonexistent at that time. If you were trading at a 10-point spread, your typical holding period must have been longer. It sounds like it was more position type of trading, right?

A : Yes, it definitely was. You had to trade the daily charts and you'd come in maybe towards the top of a daily bar. You were not trading the one minute bars for example. So we would just trade on the longer-term timeframes. It was a lot more difficult. I think right now my trading activity is a hundred times greater. Back then I would place maybe two to three trades a week and now I do that intraday.

Q : Back in those days you probably tried to shoot for 50 to maybe 75 points per trade. Now you're able to trade for 15 to 20 points?

A : Exactly. Basically you know you could scalp the market more. If the market back then was moving in a 20-point range, back and forth, back then you wouldn't be able to get out of the position, but now that the spreads are tighter in that 20-point range you can get 10 pips out of that trade.

There is money to be taken off the table every day in foreign exchange just because of the volatility in the markets. I think the foreign exchange markets really lends itself to that. It's a great place to be for volatility, for liquidity. So I think it's a good market.

Q : Do you have several strategies? Let's say x amount of your capital—how much percentage-wise do you allocate to intraday trading and how much of your positions are longer-term daily, perhaps, even sometimes weekly type of trades?

A : Yeah, I would say usually I'll take a position every day based on a certain standard amount of money that I'm willing to risk. So that's 20 times a month basically, Monday through Friday, and then through that month if I see a trend, if I've identified what looks to be a several-day trade, then I am willing to ride that. I'll take one position of that same amount and then, if it's going in my direction. I'll add to that position. So, basically, I like to keep things standard in that manner.

Q : Will you initiate a trade, let's say based upon your short-term bias? But then if that trade becomes profitable, will you simply hold on to part of that trade and then even add to it and turn it into a longer-term trade?

A : No, I wouldn't change it into to a long-term trade. If I was trading a short-term trend and I felt that it was over, I would take all my profits. Hopefully, I'm also in that trend with a long position. I'm riding that long position in a sense already. A good trader never changes the timeframe that they initiated their trade in, only bad traders do this when their trades are going against them. They will usually change a short timeframe to a long one when in a bad position.

Q : So on occasion you will have essentially two of the same position? One position will have a short-term target and the other one may have a longer-term perspective—is that correct?

A : Yeah, I'll do that, definitely.

Q : So they may be at the same price essentially, or relatively close, but it's literally two separate positions in the same direction?

A : Right, exactly.

Q : Let's go back to your start in the business. You were brokering. You were trading. You were getting exposed a little to options. Did you trade options actively, or was that more on the side while you were brokering?

A : We did trade options actively, and I learned to trade in my own account. Basically I had some clients who were very active. So it evolved from me brokering with them and then again having a mathematical mind and wanting to try new things. Having higher leverage with options, I traded it for those reasons to familiarize myself with the different product that I've never traded.

Q : Were you trading options essentially as proxies for stocks? In other words were you basically trading delta or were trading volatility as well? [*Authors' note:* delta in options is typically defined as the amount of percent an option will move in relation to $1 move in the underlying. For example, at-the-money call options usually have a delta of .5, meaning they will increase by 50 cents if the stock rises by $1.] Were you doing any kind of complex option strategies or primarily just using them as directional tools?

A : No, it was basically in one direction. Sometimes we tried to acquire some stocks and we would sell puts to get into them. If they didn't get them, that was fine because they would make money off selling the put. When you got them, they become stock. So those were kind of unique things I saw that seemed to work. [*Authors' note:* Ashkan refers to an option strategy called put selling. The seller of the put collects the premium if the stock remains at the same price or rises. However, if the stock falls sharply, he is obligated to purchase it at the agreed upon strike price, which can sometimes be far higher than the actual market price.]

Q : That strategy works great in a bull market—until it doesn't.

A : Exactly. That was when the market was really running in the one direction. So it worked in any form, but I personally never really got into it. I never really made money the way I did trading stocks. So, even though I like options, it never really caught on with me.

Q : It's interesting because the progression was from stocks to options to foreign exchange, and one of the things that we see is that there is an enormous amount of similarity between options and foreign exchange if you just simply trade them on a directional basis. Foreign exchange in many ways contains the same type of properties as options—highly directional, highly leveraged. Is that what appealed to you?

A : Yeah. I mean it was that and it was also the fundamental reasons of what a currency stands for when you look at a currency pair—which led to my understanding of the currency markets better than the options markets. Foreign exchange is definitely similar to options in terms of leverage and the way it was very technical. All those things made me want to trade it. I'm glad that I went from equities to options to foreign exchange because I think it was a natural progression. It seemed to work well for me.

Q : What specifically about the FX market made you realize that it was different?

A : Well, say the pound/dollar or euro/yen or whatever you're looking at—there's always going to be both sides to the price. You compare that to equity, and equity has underlying value. You can always buy it for a certain concrete amount. You would take the number of shares and the stock price and you would know what the company was worth. Currency is more of a conceptual idea of prices, and currencies never, in a sense, go to zero. Sure, it can devalue in a huge manner or the price can appreciate greatly. But the fact that value was conceptual appealed to me. Plus the fact that currencies trade so technically and trend well all really appealed to me.

Q : You were saying that the FX market is a bounded market, meaning that it doesn't go to zero and it doesn't go to a million like the stock market could. Can you give us an idea how FX lends itself to technical analysis?

A : Well, basically I think if you have a certain fundamental understanding of the markets and you understand what direction the market is moving in, then you choose an area based on

technical analysis to get into the markets. There are many different techniques—from candlesticks to moving averages—but if you
stick with one technique that you've identified and use it over and
over with proper risk management, I think you can definitely make
money in this market.

Q : It's quite interesting because what you're saying though is
that you really create a directional bias based upon fundamental
analysis, and then you enter the market based upon technical analysis. So you get an idea of where you think the trade is going to go
and then you use technical analysis to time your entry?

A : Yeah, I think that's accurate.

Q : What are the key factors in FX that you feel drive directionality?

A : If you look at a certain country, there are certain fundamentals—facts that support the strength of that country. For example, is the economy booming? Are they in a recession? Is job
growth strong? What are interest rates like? Things like that. So
essentially you need to know those factors to get a pulse of the
country and compare that to the pulse of another country.

I try to make sure I understand everything regarding each
country of the pair that I'm looking at. If you have all the information, you should be able to make a decision. If that decision looks
good and matches with positive technical areas in the market, then
you can make a trade.

Q : In FX there are basically two types of trades, there is the
prodollar and the antidollar trade, where you're trading the U.S.
dollar against an array of world currencies: the euro, the yen, the
pound, the Australian dollar, and the other commodity currencies.
Then there are the cross-trades, where you're trading countries
outside of the U.S. against each other. Do you concentrate on one

or the other? Do you do both? Do you have a preference for either one?

A : No, I usually kind of just stick with the U.S. dollar versus the majors and the Australian and Canadian dollars. There is enough volatility and enough information to be analyzed with those currencies.

Q : And then what catches your eye? There are about seven primary dollar pairs on any given day. What makes you decide which side of the trade you want to be on and which pair you want to choose?

A : Coming into the day, I already have an idea based on the last few days of the week what's kind of happening. Then I see what news has come out, since that's what drives the market. I look at all the economic releases, all the numbers that have been released to see if the market has to adjust itself. If the market had a certain consensus and it was wrong, then everyone is basically wrong and then the market moves. And so you have to come in, assess all that information, add that to the equation of what has happened over the last several days, and then formulate a decision and see if it's viable to make a trade.

Q : Generally there are two type of traders. There are the traders who are continuation traders and there are traders who are reversal traders. Looking at the model you've described, well let's just say for argument sake right now, we have generally dollar-positive information, right?

A : Correct.

Q : So continuation traders would pretty much always try to get long the dollar given the fundamental background that we currently find ourselves in. Reversal traders will clearly look for

points of exhaustion where the information flow is going to start to
turn and go the other way. How would you classify yourself?

A : Basically I am a continuation trader. When the trends are
going in that direction, I don't see any point in trying to find the
turn. It will tell you when it's reversed.

Q : How would you know that it had reversed? What kind of
technical telltale signs would tell that the trend has stopped?

A : It's got to come to some area where it's reversed before. That's
number one. Then, even though it may reverse, it always takes at
least a day or so for that happen. If you look at any chart pattern
where the market's reversed, you'll see a daily reversal. Reversal
only happens once, but the continuation's happening all the time
until the moment the reversal is hit.

Q : Given that kind of layout, since you obviously look at previous support and resistance levels, how would you approach a trade
where—and again let's use the dollar—we have a slew of positive
data, a good fundamental background, the U.S. dollar strengthening over the last several days, but approaching critical prior
resistance levels. At that level, even though the fundamental news
continues to be supportive, do you become more cautious because
of the technical barriers in front of you or do you simply stay in
there until proven otherwise?

A : Yeah, definitely I do become more cautious. I'm just a trader.
At the end of the day I just try to make money for myself. If
it gets to a critical technical area and I've made enough money,
maybe I'll stay out of the market for a while or lower my leverage.
I say to myself, I'm not sure here, I'm going to wait. I've already
made money coming into this. So let me just assess my personal
situation or my relevant situation around me and see what's going
on. I may do something like that, which has nothing to do with
trading, but has to do with being and living as a trader. Let's say
it's Christmas time or Thanksgiving or something like that. You're

planning a trip, for the last five weeks you've made money, and it's around this resistance level. So you just close the trade, get on an airplane, and take a week or two off. That's the great thing about being a trader. You can do things like that. So that's how I'll manage it.

Q : How about your short-term trades? Are they triggered off of news events or are they triggered off of technical considerations? What we mean by that is, you clearly monitor the news. You probably have a news feed. If news comes out that's dollar favorable, do you simply jump on the bandwagon right away and try to see if you could get a continuation move for 10 to 15 points off of that? Or do you simply have your own technical triggers—when your moving averages cross or whatever algorithm you're using—concur with your bias and then you take the trade?

A : Yes, I'll trade off these numbers. For example, I'll look for some type of news that adds to dollar strength. I may not trade if the news is negative for the dollar for example. On the other hand, if I come into the day and all the numbers have come out at 8:30 in the morning, and there's nothing else the rest of the day, you have to adjust your game. Then I just look for technical areas where the market kind of bounced back and forth. Then I'll try and go into the direction of where I think the market's going and I'll just be patient.

Q : Interesting. So, in an environment where all news is already been presented and the market retreats into more of technical trading environment, you will then refocus your energies on technicals and look for opportune points of entry that are in sync with your overall fundamental bias. In other words, if market bounces but then starts to weaken again in a direction of your long-term bias, that's when you will use technical algorithms and you'll come into the market, right?

A : Yeah, that's correct. Once the news comes out, everyone should have adjusted their books to the current news. So new bids and offers and new support and resistance have been set by those prices. Having that type of conceptual framework, you can then trade technically. You have to look at the market every day as a different thing. You have to adjust your game plan every day. You know, sometimes you do a trade and its really easy and sometimes it's very difficult. Like you go to the ocean, one day it's calm and beautiful. It has five-foot waves and you're just surfing. The next day it's 20-feet high and disorganized and you can't even go out. Then the next day it's calm again. That's kind of the way I see the markets. You really have to just make yourself knowledgeable about all aspects of it. Then come in and look at what's going on and you can formulate an idea based on that and with that idea you can make your money. In the end we're here just to make money for ourselves. That's why we trade.

Q : Let's talk about the day-to-day basics. FX is a 24-hour day market. It has three primary sessions, the Tokyo session, which begins around 7 P.M. East Coast time, the London session, which starts around 3 A.M. East Coast time, and the New York session, which basically starts around 7:30 A.M., maybe 8:00 A.M. East Coast time. How do you manage your trades and what is your typical day like?

A : I try to trade in the mornings, I'm on the West coast, so I look at the night before. I look at what's going to happen tomorrow based on what numbers are going to be released. It allows me to gauge when I might want to trade and allows me to pick one point where I can feel comfortable.

Q : Because you're on the West Coast and because, obviously, you trade the primary currency pairs against the dollar, sometimes there is very important news in the Asia-Pacific currencies which are the yen and the Australian dollar and the New Zealand dollar. Sometimes the news can be extremely important on the European side, and almost always there's important news on the U.S. side.

So do you occasionally trade the Asian session and sometimes the U.S. session?

A : Actually, I trade mainly the U.S. session and the European session. I usually won't trade the Asian session because that's the time of day I would already be done with trading. If I've traded the morning session, I should be done by then and just be living my life in a sense. I don't want to be trading all day, 24 hours a day.

Q : It's an occupational hazard in FX.

A : Yes, it is. I think you have to define yourself in this market. If you don't, you could lose yourself over the 144 hours that the market's open during the week. I know this because I think everyone who trades FX has been through it. There are the nights you're up all night. I learned that I don't want to do this.

Generally I'll be up at 3:30 A.M. or 4:00 A.M. West Coast time and I'll start my day then, at 4:30. Say I want to trade that 5:30 number, I'll make sure I'm awake an hour ahead to have everything up and running and watch the news, absorb everything that's happened for an hour before that number comes out, and then when it comes out, I'm ready to go and I've already got a game plan.

Q : If you're starting at around 3 or 4 or 5 o'clock West Coast time, when will you finish trading? What time do you knock off for the day?

A : I'll have a goal in mind of what I want to accomplish moneywise or tradewise for that day. I'll know what that is. Maybe because of something that's going to happen—I think the market is going to be very volatile—I'll say, okay, I think because of the volatility I'll get two good trades off it and accomplish that for my day. I'll stay however long it takes me—maybe it takes me a couple of hours. I've traded—honestly—for 20 minutes, placed a trade and then 20 minutes later I've closed it and it's been up 30 pips. So you have those days. I wish they were all like that. But then there are days you try to trade for three or four hours, maybe, because the market's not as volatile but there's still activity. It just takes a little longer, It will take me several hours for those trades. But it's basically goal oriented. Say the market only moved 50 or 60 pips overnight or over a day, and to me that's not enough volatility to want to get in the market so I won't trade. I'll just watch the market. There are those days, too.

Q: Do you set a particular point goal or a dollar amount goal that you want to reach? Also, if you can talk a bit about the amount of risk. You said there's a certain amount of risk you're willing to take during the day, and it's a dollar amount of risk. But is it also a point amount of risk? Do you say to yourself, "If I'm 50 points out of the money on this trade that's my stop limit"?

A: I always have a hard stop because you never know what's going to happen. I try to keep it pretty tight. I don't really like things to get away by more than 40 pips or so. I think I'm a good trader. So if something gets 15 to 20 pips away from me, I've got to just close it. I know I'll make it back on the next trade or the next several trades.

Q: A very interesting point you just made. You said, "I think I'm a good trader and that's why I keep my stops small." You're assuming that if it has moved 20 points against you, then the trade you initially analyzed is just wrong and you need to get out of it.

A: Right, exactly. I've analyzed my trading and the analysis shows if I am down 15 pips or so, I'm saying, "Okay, I just made the wrong decision here." So that's why once it goes to 20, I just click and close it out or at least close half the position.

Q : We think we've come to very similar conclusion in our trading. Basically you're either right or you should be out.

A : Exactly. You said it perfectly. You're either right or you should be out. Then you have to gauge how good of a trader you are, and for me it's around that 15 pips. If I didn't find that 15-pip top or bottom and the currency keeps going, I may have come in too early. But then, you know, I'm not scared to come back in that same direction a little higher. So once that happens then, you know, hopefully I've done some right risk management. Maybe I haven't used all my leverage. Say I've only come in with $300,000 on the first trade and it's gone 15 pips against me, then I'll close it. Then I see that it starts to exhaust again. I come in with a million. So hopefully the $300,000 that I lost 15 on becomes negated in just 5 or 6 pips of the new larger trade and then I'm in the right direction at the right time.

Q : Just to clarify, because essentially you're talking about exhaustion levels and trying to come in at the right time. You're basically looking to come in at weak points but in the direction of the overall strength. So if, the dollar is strong on a long-term trend, what you want to be looking at is for the euro to rally a little bit. But once the euro/dollar rally reaches its point of exhaustion, that's when you want to short it. Is that what you mean by picking those spots?

A : Yes, that's correct. I look to do that. If I picked the right direction, and again I'm assuming I know the overall direction, I am going to be confident in the trade.

Q : Talk to us about leverage. Leverage in the FX market is enormous. It can be as large as 200 to 1, meaning that you could control 10,000 units with as little as $50 worth of equity.

A : Right.

Q : What kind of leverage do you think is prudent and what kind of leverage do you yourself use?

A : I don't think there's any point to using anything more than maybe 5 to 10 times, something like that. But I would keep it low. If you're trading, try it to keep it five times.

Q : Is that the general level you're comfortable with, do you usually use between 5 or 10 times leverage for your positions?

A : Yes. The key is you should use the lowest amount of leverage you can. That's what I always tell people because you want to spend time in this market. That's how you're going to get better and that's how you're going to be a better trader if you can stay around. I remember I think I had a mini-account that was maybe $1,000 way back when. I loaded up on something at 100 or 200 times leverage and so my thousand bucks ended up making $4,000. Then I loaded up again. But this time I was wrong and my account went back to a thousand. I could have lost it all, But if you keep your leverage low, if you lose, your $1,000 will turn into $900 instead of nothing. I think leverage is a good and a bad thing. It's a good thing if you're a good trader and that's about it [laughter].

Q : Can you talk about your desk setup? What do you look at? What tools do you use?

A : I have several different packages that I use. I have a couple of algorithms I've developed myself and have written with several guys. So those programs are on a [three screen]three-by-three screen computer that runs charts. Then I have another computer that has three screens attached to it also. That is my order entry and news feeds. That is what I have as a setup. Then I have TVs in my trading room, and basically that's it. I will come in the morning and turn everything on. I have a bunch of different news sources that are linked, and I will try to get caught up with what happened in the market from the day before. From there I apply all my knowledge. I start to make decisions based on my model on my plans. So that's really my setup.

Q : What particular research do you like to read?

A : I have a list of different banks and one of them is UBS. I like to see what they're looking at. I just look at what everyone's doing. Honestly I don't like to base my decision on what they are doing because I like to have my own perspective. Even if I'm wrong with my perspective, that's fine with me. I have a game plan for how to deal with my mistake: Always have a plan on each side of your trade. You always have to know what's going on and reading what other people are up to and what people are thinking helps you to be on the leading edge of what's happening out there. You need to know what changes are going to be made in the FX market so that you are always up to date with the market.

Q : Back to risk control. When you said there's a certain amount of money that you are willing to risk per day, is that a percent of equity? Is it a hard money stop? What kind of a risk limit do you put on yourself per day?

A : It's one of each of those. I'll have a hard stop. But when I get into the market, I'll have that hard stop and like I said it's basically 25 pips at the most. Usually if it gets around 15, I'll make a decision—okay, do I start getting out? But then if you are asking if I'm down an x amount during the day, will I stop? Yeah, if I'm down a certain dollar amount. There's a hard stop for that also. I feel if I made two trades in a row in the wrong direction, then I'm missing something and there's just no point to trade again. I have faith in myself that I'll make money many more times than I'll lose it, so I'll step away from the market.

Q : Have you had a situation where you've been wrong for two, three, four, five days in a row? Have you had a bad run in your career and how do you handle that?

A : You know, I have. Basically what I try to do is focus on the big picture. For example, I had a bad week last week. I made money the first day and part of the second day. Then I came in again later in the week. Over those three sessions I didn't make money, just spun my wheels. That was really frustrating for me. So, in those cases, I'll focus on the times that I was right 2 months in row or 5 months in row or 12 months in a row. I just go back in my mind and then I just try to rest. We are an organism. If I was a computer program that would be great. But I am not. I have step away from the market. The market is going to be there for the next 50 years. It's going to be there tomorrow.

Q : Do you sometimes just go away for two or three days to clear your mind, go to the beach?

A : Yes. Yes. Actually I surf, and after trading, after I printed my screens, looked at the trades, logged all my stuff, I try to go the beach and go surfing because that clears your mind. It gives you opportunity for your mind not to think about technical analysis, it allows you to rest. So when you come to the market again you're fresh. You need to do that as a living, breathing human organism. You need to take care of your mind and your body. Trading is very demanding. It will take a physical toll on you. What I like to do is trade for a couple weeks, make a good amount of money, and then just go on a trip. My girlfriend and I will go to Hawaii for a week. We go there, just hop on plane and go. We have friends we stay with, or we'll go to Mexico for four or five days. Maybe I'll trade for three weeks in row and then I'll take a trip for a week. Again, I'm a trader. I chose to be a trader in order to have this type of freedom and live this lifestyle. So I definitely take advantage of it in a very big way. I'm not scared to be away from the market for a week or two weeks. It doesn't matter.

Q : When you're away from the market for two weeks and you come back to screens, do you ever get rusty? Or does it just come back like riding a bicycle?

A : It's kind of like riding a bike I would say. Although when I'm not trading I like to watch the news and kind of absorb it. We went on a trip to Brazil last year, and during the time I was there, for about one month, I didn't trade. But I watched the news and I'd get the quotes, every day, throughout the day, just watching Bloomberg at the hotel. Although I didn't actually trade, I was watching the news and position trading in my head. I would say, based on all this, I would be buying dollars and then I'd wake up the next day, was I right, yeah, the dollar got strong by a penny. So I mentally keep myself in the game, keep a pulse on what's going on. Then when you come back, you do have to do some extra work, be a little more cautious in the beginning. I always suggest you come in with a lighter leverage at the beginning. Just knock off a couple trades and get comfortable again and then you can start stepping it up and hopefully you're on another two-week, three-week run of making money.

Q : While you are physically away, you're never really mentally away from the market—that's how you stay sharp?

A : Right, exactly. And during those times I try to get caught up on my reading. I'll study some more technical analysis or I'll read a book about trading. Even though you're away from the market, there are always things to do that can help you become a better trader. I get caught up on my candlestick reading.

Q : Are candlesticks your primary technical tool?

A : I use them to find tops/bottoms and reversals, but I use different algorithms and different functions that are written by me and my associates.

Q : You don't rely on the standard technical indicators, oscillators, moving averages? You have your own proprietary indicators that you developed?

A : Yes. Several of my good friends are mathematicians and we put them together.

Q : How many years did it take you to feel competent in this game?

A : In FX, you know, it took me a while even though I was a good trader before that. It took me a while before my mind realized I could make money trading FX.

Q : Without giving away your secrets, what are the key things in your mathematical algorithms that you find tend to prove themselves in the market? Is there an underlying mathematical truth to the markets?

A : I think there is.

Q : Much of academic research talks about the fact that there's an enormous amount of randomness, that there's very little stationarity in the data. [*Authors' note:* Most academic studies show that past price behavior has absolutely no predictive value to future price behavior.]

A : Right, right. I don't know [laughter]. That's about a theory and I've heard all the theories myself, too. I think it's all going to be theory. It's whether you can make money on it or not. I believe that there's a point where there's a guy who has a huge bid and then a guy who has a huge offer that no one can get through—and there's no randomness to that. So if you can understand what I mean when I say that, conceptually there is a kind of formula for the market. But then there's also going to be a time when people are going to hit that offer so many times that guy's not going to be there anymore and the market's going to a new place.

So if you look at the market in that respect, I don't think there's randomness. I think the randomness that's in the market comes from not knowing when the big guy with, say $10 billion, will sell. Is he going to sell it right now? Or will he sell it in 10 minutes, or is he going to sell in 20 minutes? Maybe right now the market's going up 10 pips and he's selling and it's not doing anything. But maybe if he sells in 15 minutes, when the market is going down, and at that point he just adds and accelerates the market downward at that moment. So there is some randomness—but there is also order.

Q : How do you differentiate between the two?

A : Well it's an art. That's why you have to define yourself. If you define yourself you know where you are coming from.

Q : So clarity really doesn't come from the market but from yourself?

A : Yeah, exactly [laughter]. Spoken like a true Zen master [laughter]. But it really does. I think you know because again, like today, the market went up 40 pips for a few seconds after the 5:30 A.M. announcement. Then it went down 100 pips after that. So you could have made money long or short it—just depends when and where you were at those 20 seconds. That's what I mean—you have to define yourself.

Q : What's your number one rule for trading? If you were to distill it to one key issue, what would you say it would be?

A : One key thing? Wow, that's very broad. As a trader I think I'm going to take that question abstractly. One key thing is if you're going to do this, be very serious about it and work at it. Make yourself be that trader to the nth degree, to the infinite degree because I think if you do that that's where you're going to find success.

Q : So if you're going to do it, take it seriously, is that your one piece of advice?

A : Yeah, take it very seriously because, if you do, that's when you'll reap the benefits, I think. But if you don't, you'll always see the potential, but you'll never reach it. I think a lot of people see the potential but they never take it to that next level. Then, if you're going to trade, if there's one thing I'm going to tell you, is keep your leverage low. Low, low, low. That's the key thing, especially since that will keep you in the game. If you stay in the game and keep playing the game, what will happen is you'll gain experience and eventually you'll figure out the one thing that works. Then just stick to that one thing and it will make you money.

Q : Could you replay your best trade ever?

A : You know, that's funny. My best trade ever was a combination of a lot of things. What happened was several years ago I was trading the pound with a group of traders. A couple of the guys had been up all night waiting for this number to come out, but I actually went home, slept, came back in the morning, got set up in like five minutes, and then the market started moving before the numbers had come out. I can't remember which numbers, I think it was an unemployment number or something. But for some reason I decided my game plan was to go short. I had my whole game plan that I was supposed to wait for the number. But I decided to place my trade before the number, which you shouldn't do. I ended up getting into position right before the number and the number came out and the market moved about 200 pips.

Q : It was waterfall.

A : Yeah, it was just amazing. And literally in that second, when I closed the trade, I started laughing. There was a little luck obviously, and the whole point was it happened so fast everyone missed it, There were some guys who had been waiting around for like

301

six, seven hours for this to happen. So it was a burn on everyone. I kind of walked in five minutes before, made 200 pips. I was done. We went and had breakfast and just had fun the rest of the day. I was in New York when that happened, so it was kind of cool. That was the most memorable trade. But really, the best trades for me are when I just do everything right for the day. Whether I made 15 pips, 12 pips, 8 pips that day, 20 pips everything works the way it was supposed to. Even if I'm down one day, but I took my stops, I know that was a good, day, too. The best days are when everything goes well according to your plan.

Q : The question everybody hates but everybody must answer—the worse trade you've ever been in?

A : The worst trade I remember, too. I was long the dollar and the euro/dollar was strengthening. I couldn't close the position out. At one time it was only down 22 pips, which for me is nothing. You close and you trade the next day you make that back. But I couldn't close it, it was just mental block and it ended up going higher. I had to close it at minus another 100 pips. It was just a weird thing when I was a younger trader, I just couldn't get out of this one position. It haunts me in a good way to this day because now when I think of that 22 pips—maybe that's why I get nervous when it gets around 20 pips—I just close the trade.

Q : It created a sensory memory in your brain. Final question: You bring a couple of very interesting attributes to the game. You clearly have a highly quantitative mind and a very, very rigorous mathematical education. But also an education in psychology, and many people will argue that markets are not logical, they're psychological. So we are wondering if your education and background in psychology had any value, if it offered you any additional insights that you may want to share with us about the market?

A : It has I think because I understand how the mind works and the way it processes information. Then I could use that information to adjust and adapt myself as a trader.

Q : How does the mind work? What does the mind do that helps you make yourself a better trader?

A : Well, I think always having a plan and being organized produces discipline. If you're able to do the same thing over repetitively, I think that helps. Also, there are different ways of processing information by remembering the good moments and forgetting the bad moments, as well as having clarity of mind to know when to be more alert or when to pull back. As a person, if you're getting nervous about a position what should you do in that moment? There is a psychology to that. You need to do something because once you start getting nervous you stop thinking clearly, so maybe your cognitive action is to close half you position. That's what psychology has been able to teach me—to be able to manage myself. Like when you said, what do you do when you have several down days in row? Well, my psychology has taught me that I don't reflect on that. I look at the situation with the logic of what's happened over the last several years. Namely, that I am successful more times than I am not. I focus on that rather than letting my mind go astray.

LESSONS FROM ASHKAN BALOUR

Trend Is Continuous but Turn Happens Only Once

Sometimes someone makes an observation that seems so obvious that you have a "V-8" moment, slapping yourself on the head to say, "Why didn't I think of that?" Ashkan's view that it is far easier to trade with a trend—because a trend is essentially continuous while turns are rare and difficult to time—is one such kernel of wisdom we picked up in our interview with him. Although in principle, the majority of novice traders agree that trading with the trend is the way to go, in reality most of traders are inveterate top and bottom pickers. Too many times we have seen traders get seduced with the notion that they are smarter than the market as they try to fade every rally and buy every dip. Few, like Chuck Hays, are excellent contrarians and can execute this strategy well. Most wind up simply getting stopped out or worse—margined out of their positions. Ashkan's point, that it is far easier to go in the direction of price flow rather than against it, is something that most traders would be well advised to remember.

Two Losses in a Row and You Should Stop

There are only two reasons why trades get stopped out—either the trader is not in sync with the market or the market environment has changed so dramatically that the traders' analysis is simply wrong. In either case, taking a break from the market at that point is usually the best course of action. Ashkan's rule of turning off the computer after taking two stops in a row on any given day would probably save countless dollars of lost capital if most traders followed it. Typically, the greatest point of vulnerability for any trader is right after a losing trade. The need to "get it back" is one of the strongest and most destructive impulses of human nature. Study the history of any blowup from that of the tiniest of retail speculators to the phenomenal flame outs of massive hedge funds such as Long Term Capital Management and you will see that the ruin is always triggered by the desire to recover losses quickly. This impulse typically devolves into random, seat of the pants decision making and ultimately utter destruction of capital. A physical pause in activity is one of the best ways to avoid the very unpleasant consequences of "revenge" trading.

Take It Seriously

Often success does not belong to those with biggest talent but rather to those with the greatest persistence. As with all other endeavors in life, talent can only take you so far. In the end skill is a function of effort and experience. Ashkan's suggestion to take trading seriously speaks directly to that idea. Many novices regard trading as either an electronic version of a slot machine looking to hit a quick and easy payout or some form of passive income stream like a vending route or a McDonald's franchise. The reality, of course, couldn't be more different. Would any rational person expect to become an expert in surgery, law, or molecular physics after only six months of training in the subject matter? Hardly. We accept the fact that those professions require years, sometimes decades, of intense training, but somehow scoff at the notion that trading could demand the same amount of dedication. As Ashkan says, "If you don't [take it seriously], you'll always see the potential but you'll never reach it. I think a lot of people see the potential but they never take it to that next level."

CHAPTER 11

THE ALL-AMERICAN TRADER

PAUL WILLETTE

If there was ever a trader to epitomize the classic all-American values of dedication, hard work, and discipline, it would be Paul Willette. Self-taught, Paul started day trading stocks using a dial-up connection and a single, old laptop. But despite these humble beginnings, within two years he was able to parlay his success into a mid-six-figure account. Next, Paul moved into the toughest trading arena of all—the electronic e-mini stock index futures market—where high leverage and whipsaw volatility destroy even the most seasoned traders. Again, he succeeded where so many others have failed by practicing the simplest yet the most elusive rule of the game: cutting your losses short and letting your profits run. A very competitive, highly disciplined trader, Paul leaves little to chance, approaching trading with the intensity and focus of a world-class athlete. We had the pleasure to interview him from his Midwest home, which he shares with his wife and three children.

■ ■ ■

Q : How did you come to trading futures?

A : Here's my story. I graduated from college in 1992 and from there I became a stockbroker. I actually saw the movie *Wall Street* in 1988, which kind of tipped me off that this is what I wanted to do for the rest of the life.

Q : Who is your hero in *Wall Street*, Gecko or Bud Fox?
A : Bud Fox.

Q : You saw yourself as Bud?
A : I saw myself as Bud.

Q : Unfortunately, many of us saw that movie, and many of us went to Wall Street for that same reason.
A : Yes [laughter]. So I was a stockbroker until February of 1998.

Q : Were you working for a regional brokerage house or big wire house?
A : I was working for a company called R.J. Steichen & Co. here in Minnesota, and then a company called Josephthal.

Q : How did you build your book as a broker?
A : I built my book by doing well for clients—doing my own niche, working on little Minnesota-based companies. They were growing. They were kind of undiscovered by Wall Street.

Q : Would you do your own research and meet with management?

A : Yes, I did my own. I think personally, just my opinion, for what it's worth, analysts don't know much. I mean a perfect example was when I worked at R.J. Steichen & Co. and they were telling us to sell this company called Insignia Systems and we could deal it out with a dollar in it. I think it was about a $4 stock as I remember. Then about two weeks later they came out with bad numbers and I have come to find out in my schooling that it was just the big guys at our firm. They just needed liquidity in the markets. They were just selling it to us. So they wouldn't screw up the market.

Q : There was no liquidity, so they're selling it back to you.

A : They were selling to us, so then we'd sell it back to all of our clients. I said enough of this and went on my own. That way I could blame no one but myself.

Q : Was that the straw that broke the camel's back? Was that when you had enough of being a broker?

A : That was one of them, and I also just thought that I could trade these stocks in my own account.

Q : At that point you were already in the business for about six years, right?

A : Yes.

Q : You built a book, what kind of tricks of trade did you pick up in your six years as a broker? What was your methodology like then?

A : It's more fine-tuned today but it was just technical analysis, big fat technical analysis. I didn't care what the company did.

Q : Earlier you said you were doing a lot of smaller Minnesota undiscovered companies?

A : Right.

Q : Which would require a lot of fundamental analysis because you would talk to management, then find out what they were doing.

A : Right. Then after being bagged in a couple of deals with management telling me one thing, the stock acting another way, I got more involved with the technical side of it, which really propelled my whole trading and career.

Q : Was there any particular book that you read at that time that had a very strong impact on you?

A : No, as a matter of fact I didn't read many books. I was kind of self-taught.

Q : How did you discover the basic concepts of technical analysis?

A : There was a friend of my dad who's a stockbroker. I interned with him before I became a broker in 1992. He taught me. He gave me the backdrop of moving averages and different formations, head and shoulders, double tops, etc.

Q : Was this your primary method of analysis when you were doing stocks, you started to become a pattern reader?

A : Right. Then I got big into candlesticks, too.

Q : When did you get into candlesticks? Was that before you went to trade on your own or while you were still a broker?

A : While I still was a broker.

Q : Were you applying these technical analysis concepts mainly to smaller, less-liquid stocks, looking for big break outs?

A : Exactly. You know the long base and then the big break out. The longer the base, I found that the higher it would go.

Q : You were a classic break-out trader where you wouldn't buy until it made a new swing high?

A : Yes. That's right.

Q : And that worked well for you?

A : Yes.

Q : Especially in 1998, if there was ever a time to be a breakout trader that was then.

A : That was then. Yes. When I went on my own, I mean everyone was golden back then, it was easy.

Q : So let's go to that time you went on your own. You've been a broker for six years. You probably accumulated a little bit of trade capital at that point?

A : Yes.

Q : What was going through your head? What made you say, "I'm going to pull the trigger and go trade stocks on the screen"?

A : I had $85,000. The reason I decided to trade for myself was because I had all these stupid rules that I couldn't basically do all this stuff for my clients and trade the stocks for myself.

Q : Did you have a 30-day holding rule? Some brokers won't let you trade in and out of a position for shorter than 30 days.

A : Yes, it was crazy. I mean I was being audited by the compliance officer every other day for the stuff I was doing. All of it was legal. But there were so many rules and so many sheets, that I had to sign. I said enough of this. I figured I could do it on my own.

Q : Were you married at the time?

A : Nope. I was not married at the time.

Q : So no responsibilities. You had money. You had capital. How much time did you give yourself to be a success? Six months? Three months?

A : You know I didn't really put a time on it. I just kind of went with it. Just took the risk. I figured I didn't have any kids. I wasn't married. I had a house, but that was about it.

Q : What was your first experience? Which kind of a shop did you go with?

A : I called over a phone line using E*TRADE.

Q : So you were trading on a dial-up connection?

A : Yes.

Q : Using E*TRADE?

A : With one screen—it was a laptop as a matter of fact.

Q : [Laughter] What was your holding time at that point? How were you trading then?

A : I was kind of a swing trader, and held things for five or six days.

Q : Were you trading a thousand shares for three or four or five points?

A : Exactly. And then I'd sell half and then just move my stop up.

Q : And then just milk the rest?

A : At that time, I mean those things just went to Pluto. You know every stock, no matter which one really.

Q : You happen to remember any of the early big winners at that time?

A : The big hits?

Q : Yes.

A : Oh, one was Qualcomm.

Q : Oh wow. You must have been in Qualcomm at around 50 or 80 right?

A : Yes, that's exactly right.

Q : That's the stock that went to the 600?

A : Six-hundred and split, yes. It was crazy.

Q : You took it for the ride because you basically went to break even on the stop and just held on and held on?

A : Held on, yes, pretty much. Then I sold a quarter, sold another quarter, then sold another quarter, you know I just kept riding it up.

Q : Most traders have a problem with holding on to their winners and yet you tend to naturally do that. What do you think makes you different from everybody else? Why is it easy for you to hold to winning positions and not want to cash them in?

A : Just learning from my past mistakes.

Q : So you also have an inclination to ring the cash register, but you've learned how to control it?

A : Exactly. I mean being around other traders and other stock-brokers and they would always seem to add to losers. They'd double down. They'd sell their XYZ stock that went from 5 to 10 because they doubled their money. But they'd buy the one that went 20 to 5 because it was so-called cheap. As I learned from my mistakes, that's not the right way to do it. If anything, you want to add to your winners and get rid of your losers.

Q : So that kind of methodology, where you have a single entry, single stop, no doubling down, no averaging down, stayed with you? Do you still follow that methodology?

A : Absolutely. I do. To a T.

Q : So you're trading E*TRADE. How long did that go on for on your dial-up connection with a single laptop screen?

A : [Laughter.] I know you laugh about that. I do too. I can't believe what I did on that dial-up. I'd get kicked off and have problems getting through on execution. It's crazy but I did it until May 2000.

Q : So that was about two-years' worth, and how much did you run up the account at that point?

A : Let's see I started at 85 and took it to 490.

Q : So you quintupled you account.

A : Yes.

Q : Now comes the year 2000. This is pre-Nasdaq crash, right?

A : Yes, pre-Nasdaq crash. I pretty much got stopped out of everything and was at all cash.

Q : How were you managing your stops at that point? How were you trailing them up?

A : Candlesticks. Just a little bit below the last candlestick, like if it was a green. Obviously there were green candlesticks back then. I put the stop just below that day's low.

Q : So it was just prior day's low, not even two days' low, just prior day's low?

A : Yes, prior day's low, and depending upon how strong the stock was or what kind of move it made I might do it on a weekly basis or whatever.

Q : It's 2000, still precrash, what happens then?

A : The market dried out and some of these techniques that I was using started to not work. I didn't know a lot about shorting a stock and that's what the market did.

Q : How did they not work? You would buy a breakout and then the next day you would be stopped out because it would reverse and take out the low of the candle?

A : Right, exactly.

Q : So you started getting stopped out a lot?

A : Started getting stopped out a lot, yes, and so then I had to go get a real job.

Q : What was that job?

A : That was selling photocopiers, and I hated it.

Q : I can't imagine a bigger change of work from trading Nasdaq stocks in the go-go years to selling photocopiers.

A : I absolutely hated it. I mean, my passion was always the stock market and along the way I still followed the stock market during those times.

Q: Would you still trade smaller, swing size there?

A: Very small. Yes, very small. The liquidity and the volume in the stuff just wasn't there like it was.

Q: When you started getting stopped out, how much of a draw-down did you incur? Did you give up a third or half?

A: I gave up about almost $100,000.

Q: So about a little bit less than a third.

A: Yes.

Q: You started selling copiers, and then what happened?

A: I met a girl, we got married. Like I said, I still did my job, but at least she got her MBA down at Duke.

Q: So you met a smart girl.

A: Yes, I met a very smart girl. Kind of told her that my passion was the stock market and I wanted to get back to doing something with the stock market. She said, "Well, I'll tell you what, I'll get a job and I'll support us and I'm going to trust you on this."

Q: That's a very unusual story.

A: She paid all the bills for about three-and-half years.

Q : Do you know how lucky you are?

A : Hey, I mean, I married a gem. I had three-and-half years, and I quit selling copiers about a year and half into it and went back to doing stocks but this time on broadband using a cable modem. I got the stuff and got it all hooked up but then I started to learn that E*TRADE was brutal.

Q : They are intermediaries. They weren't direct access, execution brokers.

A : No, they were horrible. They were eating up my profits. I put the order in and it didn't get filled for a minute, Then you come back and it's already gone up a half point. At that time I was more of a quick in and out guy. So that wasn't working. Then in November 2004, I went to my cousin Andrea's wedding and I met a guy by the name of Chuck Hays. She married his son and I was picking up chairs on the beach and Chuck's wife asked me what I did. I said I trade stocks. She said, "Well, you should talk to my husband, Chuck, he trades futures." All I knew about futures was that they were very hard to trade and, like in options, you could lose all your money quickly. That's basically all I knew about it. So I went up there, and he said, you know, I have a chat room, and he told Andrea to give me the password at the end of weekend. I got in there and asked Chuck more and he told me you've got to open up account and you've got to do this and that. That's kind of where it was born. He was hooked up with a guy who knew all about computers. So I set up five screens in front me. I'll never forget that first day when I looked at this ER2 thing. I just couldn't believe it. I'm like, "How in hell are these guys trading this thing? It's impossible. There's no way." My analogy was like being a high school quarterback going to the pros and just the game being lightning fast. It started to slow down after a while and I started to do paper trades. Then I went and did the simulator mold and, in January 2005, I did my first trade and I made .70.

Q : Which translates to 70 dollars on one contract.

A : You got it! Minus $5.40 commission [laughter].

Q : So you were paper trading and simulator trading for how long approximately?

A : Three months.

Q : While you were paper trading, were you keeping a diary and analyzing your style?

A : Yes. On paper. I really didn't have a style yet. I was kind of doing scalps. I was very jittery. As soon as it got up, I'd sell it. I was overtrading. You know I traded probably 20 times during the day.

Q : But this was all on simulator, you had a lot of data.

A : Yes.

Q : Then what happens, how do you get a little more comfortable with the instrument?

A : Then I added a couple little things to my work and my candlesticks and slowly but surely developed a style. There was a guy by name of Daniel in our room, a.k.a. "Jazz." I was very impressed with how he would get these plus fives and plus fours. I was more Chuck's style—the quick scalp. So I really developed a system that was a little of Chuck's style and a little of Jazz's style, which holds longer for bigger trades. Using moving averages and candlesticks, I started trading in parts, selling a third of a position at .6, selling a little more, and then just keep lowering my stop by using the candlesticks.

Q : You mean selling a little bit at the beginning just to bank some profit?

A : Right. Lowering my stop and letting the profits run a little bit. The mentality I learned back in my stock days.

Q : Is your methodology that if the first target is hit, you go to breakeven on the stop?

A : No, not necessarily. Again I use candlesticks, and I put the stop right above that. I basically trade off the five minute. I mean I've got 15-minute and 60-minute charts that I blink on and off, but the five-minute is what I use.

Q : In other words if it takes out the five-minute high or low, you are out. It's interesting that you were obviously a pure long trader in 1998 and forward and now you say you're always thinking on the short side. Can you explain a little about that? Why do you primarily trade from short side now?

A : I hear from other traders that they go down a lot faster than they go up. So I've done all my statistical analysis looking back on my stats. I make way more money at picking tops than bottoms for some reason, and it's hard to get that thing out of my head. But that's just the way it is. I'm a better short trader than long trader.

Q : You say you're better at picking tops yet you are using moving averages and candlesticks, which are primarily long only type of tools. What do you do to figure out when momentum is waning?

A : I use moving averages, MACD, and candlestick.

Q : So MACD is your momentum indicator, if you start to see divergence that's going to be your clue to a turn in the price action?

A : Exactly.

Q : Do you wait for a red candlestick to develop before you initiate a short?

A : Yes. I not only do that, but I don't try to pick exact tops and I don't try to pick exact bottoms. I don't really care if the thing is trading at 770 at the top and I get short only at 765 because I know it's going to 762. I've gotten burned way too many times trying to pick tops and bottoms. I'd rather know where it's going. All I care about is where it's going.

Q : What gives you confidence in knowing where it's going?

A : The candles, the volume.

Q : In candles what you are looking for?

A : I'm looking for a medium-size candle with a small wick on both sides. Those are golden.

Q : Okay.

A : I'm looking for the big fight, like just a small wick on top and bottom. Then I will get inside that candle, inside that fight and I will put my orders inside that candle and usually put my stop three to five ticks above the body of the candle.

Q : So not even above the top of the candle?

A : No. No the true fight, where the fighting is going on that's the body. Not the wicks, the wicks are worthless.

Q : Really? You don't even use the candle high/low as your reference points? It's only the body of the candle that you're interested in?

A : The body, I use the bodies. I love the bodies.

Q : In that kind of a scenario, generally how frequently do you get stopped out versus you being right?

A : Rarely. I think it's about an 88 percent of the time, I'm right.

Q : Because you know a three-to-five-tick stop is a sneeze in the ER. [*Authors' note:* The ER or Russell 2000 index can move 200 ticks on average day.]

A : This seems to work. The markets change. You have to go with what works right now. It might not work six months from now, but right now it works. I don't believe in adding. If I've got my position in there and it starts going against me I'm not going average down. I'd rather have it go down and add more.

Q : How many times a day do you trade? How many round turns?

A : Depending upon the market, but usually I look back and it's about one to five trades a day. Today I had four and I was done. Once I get to a certain number, I usually quit unless the market's really, really good. I mean, once that volume tapers off, I don't like to trade.

Q : So generally you trade the open?

A : First two hours.

Q : What about the last hour of the market?

A : It depends if I've got a hunch, or just how I'm trading that day. It just depends on circumstances. But the first two hours is really my bread and butter.

Q : What do you do after 11 o'clock East Coast time? Once you've done your trades, do you watch the markets?

A : I watch, yes. I watch. I do a lot of homework at night. I go back and look and I spend about two hours every night and look and see why I did something wrong, what happened. I don't like to lose—*period*—in anything. I like to win in everything that I do. I get frustrated even if I have one small loser. I don't want that. So I go back and do homework.

Q : Do you always enter every trade with a stop?

A : Most of the time, but not always. I have a mental stop in my head.

Q : If you're trading with such tight stops, let's say three to five ticks, which is nothing in ER—where is your mental stop? Do you say, "I'm never going to give up more than a point"?

A : Yes, 1.2, 1.3, I think. If it goes beyond that, I think the market is telling you that you are wrong.

Q : Did you ever have a hard time bailing out of position?

A : Admitting I'm wrong?

Q : Yes.

A : The biggest loss I've ever taken in the ER was two points.

Q : What is your typical day is like? How early do you get to the screen before the market starts to trade?

A : About 8 o'clock. I've got three kids, a two-and-a-half-year-old and two twins, so they get up about 7:30. Then I come on down here to trade, setting up shop at about eight o'clock.

Q : What do you look at? What is your routine in the morning?

A : Well, pretty much I've done my homework from the night before. I like to have a plan. For the next day, I write down my bias, where the market went at the end of day to give me some flavor. I try to think like the guys on the floor, meaning, if I were a rookie, where would I put my stop? I try to figure out where they are going to run their stops. I really try to get into their melons because they usually run these things just above their resistance or just below support.

Q : Right. Is that your bread and butter routine—try to figure out where they are going run the stops that day?

A : Yes, that's kind of one of them.

Q : Let's say you have a general game plan of where the points of vulnerability are, where the stop runs are going to happen. Once that happens, what do you do? Do you wait to see if it bounces back or clears those stops and starts to have more momentum? Is that when you start to develop your directional bias?

A : Yes. Exactly.

Q: That's when you start to formulate a trade?

A: Right.

Q: Instead of just having a bias?

A: Right.

Q: Do you read the news at all?

A: No, I don't really care about it. It's not necessarily what the news is, it's how the market reacts to the news.

Q: Do you watch CNBC?

A: Yes, CNBC. I've got it on right now. I turn the volume down, way down.

Q: But you are aware basically of what economic indicators came out that day?

A: Oh yeah.

Q: And how the game is going to be played?

A: Yes, for FOMC. I play that. [*Authors' note:* FOMC stands for the Federal Open Market Committee of the New York Fed. It meets 10 times a year to set short-term interest rates and its policies can have huge impact on the financial markets.] I didn't do anything in the morning and I just waited for the FOMC.

Q : Right, run us through your FOMC game plan yesterday because FOMC is always one of the more interesting days in the futures markets.

A : What I do is I usually watch whatever the initial reaction is. I'm not a big fader, but I will fade that.

Q : How do you fade it? Do you wait for the candles to turn around?

A : When the announcement comes out and they yank it up, I'll fade that. Or vice versa if it also comes up and they yank it down, I'll buy.

Q : At what point do you start? Yesterday they yanked it up first, then they brought it down, and then they brought it back up. On that first initial thrust forward, did you get short?

A : I shorted it, yes. It hit a moving average that I watch right on the noggin.

Q : At that point you weren't waiting for any weakness in the price action, you just got short on the move?

A : Right.

Q : What would you have done if it continued to move forward? How much of a rubber band were you willing to give yourself at that point, on that trade?

A : I let that go about 1.6 to 1.8 against me. However, I have a few spots. I won't put all my stuff in at one spot—so that I get a nice average—and it really doesn't go above that. Like I said, if it does . . . *hasta la vista*. Yesterday I played it to a T. I shorted from my moving average, and then I caught most of that bottom.

Q : Once it fell into the support level, did you turn it back around and go long?

A : No.

Q : You were done. What makes you stop? Is it a money target for the day?

A : It's kind of a money target. I don't like giving it back to them. I've done that too many times where I overtrade and start giving money back. I had my plans for the day and that was to trade the FOMC and fade it. It worked accordingly and then I didn't really have a plan after that. That was it, bears make money, bulls make money, and pigs get slaughtered.

Q : So it was almost like a one shot, one kill, kind of a deal.

A : Yes. And that's kind of what I did this morning. The big move. My honest opinion is there's really only two good moves during the day. Why does a guy need more than that? One to five trades a day to make some bread and you are done.

Q : What's your general target for the day? Do you set a morning target for yourself?

A : Yes, 3,500.

Q : And generally are you trading 10 lots? How much leverage do you allow yourself to trade?

A : Oh, I'm trading anywhere from 2 to about 25 depending upon what the move looks like or what my plan is—what I saw the night before I decided how many I'm going to trade. I traded that FOMC with 24 contracts.

Q : That was basically in multiple entries. You started out with five and then you added five more, right?

A : Yes, but I won't be afraid. If it's going one way or the other, I will not be a afraid to hit bids. I'll go market, I'll just bank it.

Q : You mean get into the trade with market orders instead of limit orders if you feel that it's the right trade?

A : Absolutely.

Q : Is that because you'd rather be in a trade than miss it?

A : Yes.

Q : Given your capital base, how much leverage do you allow yourself?

A : I don't go crazy. I have a $350,000 account. I take a draw out of there at about $15,000 a month.

Q : Basically it's no more than four-to-1 leverage, so it is not exorbitant.

A : Yes, I use one contract per $10,000.

Q : That's your rule of thumb?

A : Yes, in my head. Like if I had $20,000 account, I would trade two at most. I mean, I started this thing two years ago with 30 grand.

Q : How many contracts were you trading when you had 30 grand in the account?

A : One to three. I followed Chuck's rules to a T and that's the way I'm going to continue to do it. I'm not sure if I'll ever trade or need to trade 50 to 100 or 200. I might.

Q : At this point obviously liquidity is not an issue for you because basically ER2 is 10 to 20 up on every price level. [*Authors' note:* The ER contract usually displays a minimum of 20 contracts on the bid and the offers at the inside price.] Therefore, even when you get stopped slippage is not bad.

A : Exactly.

Q : Was there a period of time when you had days or weeks where you were just missing your trades? And if you did, how did you deal with that kind of pressure?

A : The whole time I've been in this, I've never had a losing week. This month of October here I've had two losing days, one was October 3 for about $800 and the other one was October 24 for 575 bucks.

Q : Did you get upset both of those days?

A : Oh hell yeah. Absolutely. Like I said, I don't like to lose anything. I mean playing cards with my wife, just playing, I don't like to lose. Hate it. Can't stand losing. Can't stand it! Drives me crazy. I'm very, very competitive.

Q : Did you play sports when you were younger?

A : Yes. I played them all and I expect to win. I have high expectations of myself. I do get bummed out when I lose.

Q : Yet losing is such a fundamental part of this game.

A : Right. To relieve stress, I go golfing a lot. I really like to leave the whole thing at work and just be done with it. It's just money. It can be made back. I've learned that there's more important things than money. I've got three healthy kids. I've got a great wife. I've a great family that I'm married into and a great family myself with three brothers. I think having three brothers is where a lot of competitiveness came from.

Q : What order were you in the brotherhood?

A : I was oldest and a couple of my younger brothers are competitive, too. I have one that challenges me constantly in golf.

Q : It that your off-the-field competition?

A : Yes. Absolutely—and my stress reliever, too. A lot of times after wrap-up here in Minnesota, I'll just play golf by myself. I like to go by myself, do thinking, and just kind of relax.

Q : You play 18 holes by yourself or just drive and putt?

A : 18 holes by myself.

Q : So, as time has gone by, you learned to walk away from the losing days? Just closed off the screen and said, "Hey, tomorrow's another day, tomorrow's another trade"?

A : Yes.

Q : Obviously your wife is very supportive, so that is a huge positive.

A : Huge! It's come back to reward her because she hated work, hated the 9 to 5. We have three kids and she wanted to spend more time with the kids. This has given her the ability to do that. So she was able to quit her job and she found out by being home she didn't want to be a housewife per say. So she started her own little gig and works 15 hours consulting. This whole thing has helped us to just be able to do what we love to do and spend a lot of time with our family. That's why I wanted to do this because I hate working for someone else. I love my own hours. I love my own stuff and family time is a big thing to me. I've been able to do that, spend a lot of time with my kids. Back in my day, the thing I regretted most is my dad and mom had to work three jobs and I didn't get to spend a lot of time with both of my parents when I was growing up. That was one the thing I was hoping I would be able to do.

Q : And now you get a chance to do that. That's very nice.

A : Yes.

Q : Aside from Chuck, did you have mentors in the business?

A : There was a stockbroker friend of mine. He is the guy who taught me technical analysis early on when I was an intern.

Q : How about now, do you mentor other traders? We know you're in Chuck's room. Is there any other community that you participate in or are you pretty much on your own?

A : Pretty much on my own. That's about it. You know every once in while Chuck will get a new guy and we'll work with him for a while and then he'll come here and watch me. I've actually done that recently with a guy who has passion for the stock markets. He's actually starting to get it quick. He didn't do well in stocks. But he is starting to get it in the futures.

Q : Have you traded any other futures instrument besides ER2?

A : Yes, I traded the ES [the e-mini S&P 500] a few times. I found it was pretty boring though.

Q : It moves in quarters instead of dimes.

A : And it takes forever to move a quarter sometimes.

Q : It's much harder to make bid/ask on ES, almost impossible. [*Authors' note:* Trader slang for being able to buy on the bid and sell on the ask.]

A : Right. No, I love helping people because it also helps me. I learn from it and maybe someone who I'm helping out knows something that I don't. I want to learn, I'm a sponge. I don't claim to be great, because I think you can always be greater and I strive to be. I want to win 100 percent. I know that's impossible, but I strive to just get better and better.

Q : Would you say most of your own learning is derived from your own experience rather than from any academic environment?

A : Absolutely.

Q : You basically study yourself, refine yourself, continuously?

A : Yes. There's no book. There's no class that can teach you any of this. My opinion again. My own experiences have helped me become what I am today and the key is to learn from what you did wrong and use discipline.

Q : Speaking of discipline, would you say that trading is really about entries or exits? Clearly it's both, we all know that. But does the edge lie in the entries or does the edge lie in the exits?

A : Exits.

Q : It's how you manage your exits that ultimately turn you into a winner or a loser.

A : That's right.

Q : Any particular insights as to how people should manage their exits that you might care to share?

A : Do not let it get way out of control. It's easier said than done but you can always reenter.

Q : But you can never get back that one catastrophic loss.

A : That's right [laughter].

Q : Final questions that we ask everybody. Your number one rule for trading, if you were to boil it down to one thing?

A : Discipline. I don't know how many times and how many guys I've worked with that hang onto their losers and they get into this hope mode. They think it's got to come back. But no it doesn't have to come back. Discipline. I've got discipline posted in big black letters, right here on my desk, *discipline*.

Q : Even though you hate to lose, are you perfectly willing to cut your losses when it's necessary?

A : Right. I'm a gracious loser. I mean if someone beats me on the course, I'll shake their hand. But I'm mad that I lost and I want to understand why I lost because it's all in your head.

Q : So you believe that most of the time you lose it's not because of your physical handicaps, but because of some mental mistake?

A : Yes. There are so many guys that are better than me in golf, but I can beat them every time because I can get in their head.

Q : And would you say that's probably your biggest skill that you try to refine every day?

A : Absolutely.

Q : Because moving averages, candlesticks, all of those things are just supporting indicators?

A : That's right. It's a big psychological game. If I had a fight with my wife or something like that I might not even trade, if I'm in the wrong state of mind.

Q : You wake up you have a cold, you're feeling sore, you're tired, you're hung over, whatever, you're just not on top your game physically, will you pull back sometimes?

A : Absolutely.

Q : So before you read the market you read yourself first and foremost, right?

A : Yes.

Q : What about the best trade ever?

A : The best trade ever was in January of this year, or February, I can't remember. There was also another one in May. I made

$12,000. What can I say? It wasn't anything that I did in particular. I just followed my rules. Everyone in the room said it's got to turn, it's got to turn. But I just kept lowering my stop, lowering my stop, and it became a huge winner.

Q : You were lowering your stop by candlesticks?

A : Yes.

Q : So basically your rule is I'm not going to get out of it until the market takes me out of it?

A : You got it. Yes, the market will tell me when to get out of it. It's gone against me too. But my big huge days have been letting the market tell me where the bottom is.

Q : How often during 20 trading days of the month does that kind of dynamic develop where it's just a one-way, you catch it and it's the grand slam?

A : For me grand slam is taking three pointers here and there and I probably get those, oh two to three times a week.

Q : I'm talking about where it goes four or five continuous points without really retracing a lot?

A : The four and fivers? Actually two or three times a month.

Q : That's quite a lot actually.

A : I got a couple 10 pointers. I think I had an 18 pointer [an $1,800 gain on single futures contract] once.

Q : Really?

A : Yes.

Q : When you have those kind of very, very long trades are you scaling out? You obviously take one third off on an initial move just to bank some profit?

A : Yes. Exactly.

Q : What kind of proportionality do you typically use?

A : What I like to do if, let's say, I have 24 on, is to take five off right away, then another five at 1.1 points, and then I'll another five at 1.9 points, and then I'll start breaking it down into twos and threes.

Q : Twos and threes. So basically the last third of the trade you'll just kind of let it float out there for a while?

A : Yes.

Q : And what happens is that even though you're left with maybe 10 to 15 percent of the initial position, you may still be able to ride the move.

A : Yes.

Q : That 10 or 15 percent has such a massive gain that it contributes disproportionately to the overall profit, right?

A : Yes, exactly.

Q : What about the worst trade ever?

A : Worse trade ever was that one where I thought I was right and then lost the two points. Then I added to it too, to boot. That was when I tried to get a top. I tried to pick a top and I shorted the top and it just kept going. Lo and behold, it was good. I took the loss because it ended up going to the moon.

Q : After you did your post-market analysis, did that have a very strong impact on you? You never did that again. You never tried to pick a top the way you did in that particular trade?

A : Oh, absolutely. That's another one of my big things—don't try to pick tops and bottoms. No reason.

Q : What's the most interesting part of this job?

A : Most interesting part is the high I get when I'm right. It's the flexibility. It's the ability to spend large amount of time with my family.

Q : Anything that's boring about this job?

A : Well, it's tedious. Every day you start with zero again and there's no paycheck coming in if I don't work, if I don't do well. It's all on me. You make a few bad moves and then things could get a little tricky.

Q : How do you deal with that type of daily pressure? Golf?

A : Golf. Yeah. Golf and I just try not to think about it, I really do. I don't think about it. I focus on the trade, I come up with plan and that's it.

Q : You could say that you focus on doing the trade rather than worrying about the trade.

A : That's right.

LESSONS FROM PAUL WILLETTE
Support from Loved Ones Is Key

One of the least appreciated aspects of trading is that it requires an enormous amount of emotional support and understanding from family members. Because the game is so fundamentally psychological in nature, criticisms from loved ones will exacerbate tenfold the normal doubts and pressures of the job. Every successful trader who we interviewed was either completely and totally autonomous or enjoyed the strong support from his family and spouse. No one exemplifies this dictum more than Paul Willette, whose wife essentially put him through trading school by going to work while he stayed at home and refined his day-trading skills. Willette's story is extremely unusual. Few spouses would be willing to back someone in such a high-risk venture. But fortunately for both of them, it resulted in a very successful career for Paul that provides security and freedom for their whole family. Yet even Paul is the first to admit the fragile nature of the job. He will often pass up on trading if he has had an argument with his wife the night before. Just like athletes or actors, traders need complete peace of mind in order to perform well. The game requires not only concentration but more importantly, emotional equanimity. While support from your loved ones certainly doesn't guarantee success, hostility from those closest to you will almost always result in failure.

Do the Small Things Well

Paul Willette's trading strategy is fairly straightforward. No fancy customized indicators. No complex statistical algorithms. He trades what he calls "the meat of the candle," ignoring the wicks on either side and while his entry criteria are proprietary, his exit rules are crystal clear. Paul maintains at least a partial position in the trade until there is a reversal in the trend. Plainly put, if he is short, he will only get out of the trade if the prior candle's high is broken. If he is long, he will only exit if the prior candle's low is broken. Note that Paul follows the classic definition of trend with an uptrend defined by higher *lows* while a downtrend is defined by lower *highs*. This is a very simple, disciplined approach that keeps Paul in position for those few long-trending trades that can account for the disproportionate amount of profits. Although Paul's approach is exceedingly simple, by executing every detail of his trading plan with discipline and precision, he has become very successful.

Don't Overtrade

One of the most common mistakes traders make, especially when they are trading on a shorter-term basis, is to transact too much. Almost every trader is guilty of overtrading, and the consequences of this practice can be quite costly, especially in commission-based markets such as electronic futures. Take, for example, a typical $10,000 account that trades electronic e-mini futures. Trading just one contract 20 times per day at very low $5 per round trip commission rates would debit the account $100/day even if the trader managed to break even on all of his trades. After only 20 days the account would lose 20 percent of its value just through the bleed of commissions. One of Paul strongest attributes as a trader is that he remains disciplined and very selective in his setups. As he says, there are only two to three good moves in the market on any given day. By not overtrading, Paul puts himself only into the highest-probability setups and at the same time keeps his transaction costs to a minimum.

CHAPTER 12

FX FAMILY VALUES
MARCELINO LIVIAN

When we asked Marcelino, Livian—who simply goes by his last name—how he approaches FX trading. His response was, "I never lose." Most of us would like to approach the market with the same attitude and results. With a return of 80 percent over the past four years, Livian seems to have come very close to his mark. Having traded the Forex markets since the early 1990s, almost a decade before it went electronic, he can tell you all about the headaches of exchanging one currency for another physically and opening up a local bank account to earn the interest. Nowadays, he has gone fully electronic and has still managed to maintain an average return of 20 percent a year. However, the most interesting aspect of his story is not his trading, but how trading has improved the bond within his family. He has been married to his wife for 29 years, with whom he has three beautiful children. This couple looks far younger than their years. Livian has used finance to teach his now grown children the importance of making their money work for them rather than sit idle in a bank account. Now, trading currencies not only has become the talk of the dinner table, it has also been the source of multiple calls from his children on a weekly basis. His success in the

FX market has enriched his bank account, but, more importantly, it has enhanced his relationship with his family.

Timing really helped us on this interview as we were able to invite Livian and his wife, who live in Spain, into our offices for an afternoon chat during their vacation in New York.

■ ■ ■

Q : Livian, can you tell us a little bit about yourself?

A : I have been a businessman and an entrepreneur since I was 19 years old. My business only requires me to work about 10 to 12 hours a week. To that effect, I trade the Forex markets about four hours a day. Over the course of the week, I'll spend about 25 hours dabbling in the financial markets. Forex has become a very big part of my life and my family's life as well. In fact, I have had such great success in trading currencies that I had a talk with my wife and children to encourage them to open up their own FX trading accounts while, of course, making sure that they maintain their day jobs.

Q : What kind of business do you do regularly that gives you such good hours?

A : My main business has been public relations and helping my wife manage our own chain of beauty salons, 35 to be exact. We also do importing from China of such things as hairdryers and products for the bathroom. The reason why I am very interested in trading is because I feel that with trading, instead of just letting your savings sit there in a bank account, you can put it to work and hopefully multiply the fruits of your labor.

Q : So what was your first foray into trading? How did you become interested in it?

A : Fifteen years ago, in Spain, there was no one who was really doing Forex or currency trading. We didn't even have the euro at that point. But I started becoming interested in the fluctuations of exchange rates and began to change one currency to another in a very informal way and essentially try to speculate on how I think currencies will move.

Q: So were currencies the first product that you tried trading?

A: No, I began with commodities trading in Chicago—coffee and sugar—and then started trading the stock markets before I moved onto currency trading.

Q: How long ago did you start trading commodities, and why did you decide to pick that market?

A: I started approximately 16 or 17 years ago. I began out of eagerness or the desire to get something started because I didn't have an academic background. I was really looking to start with something. I began paying attention to the price of coffee and at the time Brazil, which exports and produces 50 percent of the world's coffee, had a very bad crop. So I knew that prices were going to rise. I chose to take advantage of that, and that was when I started to trade.

Q: What made you eager to trade something? Has anyone in your family ever traded before?

A: No, there was no precedence in my family. My family is very humble. No one has previously traded. But it was really just something instinctual for me. I'm not a good basketball player. There are people who are good at basketball. But instinctually, I felt that this was something I could be good at.

Q: So when you first started trading coffee, how much did you start with?

A: Approximately $8,000.

Q : Was this from your savings or did you borrow money to do it?

A : It was from my savings.

Q : Were you married at the time?

A : Yes.

Q : So how did your wife feel about your plan to trade?

A : She felt very good about it. Like me, she liked the idea of making money electronically. You see, it took a tremendous amount of effort to really get her salon business off the ground and then to make the money from it. So when we learned about the opportunity to make money by trading and not having to be on top of it all the time, it sounded ideal for us.

Q : Did you stop trading commodities and then trade stocks or did you do both at the same time?

A : I stopped trading commodities when I started trading stocks because it was more interesting for us given our infrastructure. But then I moved to trading currencies predominately because I feel that in Forex, I have more direct access to the market. I can enter in my trade station and place a trade immediately as opposed to doing stocks, where I have to call my broker and wait for him to enter into trades and then wait for him to give me back a fill price.

Q : When did you get started in the FX market?

A : It has been about 14 or 15 years, which means that I started in approximately 1992 or 1993.

Q : So back in '89 or '90, when you were trading it, you were mostly doing it by shifting around money between your bank accounts and not trading electronically, right?

A : Yes, it was very simple. It was something where at any given moment I could say that I wanted to hold a certain amount in, let's say, the Spanish currency, the French, or, you know, if the timing was right, the Japanese currency. At the time there was no leverage, it was just a matter of exchanging one currency for the other in the bank account.

Q : What kind of returns were you looking for at the time?

A : I never had any set goals at the time because I was in it for the long haul and simply because the Forex market interested me.

Q : What were the spreads like when you were doing that?

A : At the time it was about 18 to 22 pips. The Japanese yen was the least expensive to trade at the time. The Deutsche mark and the British pound were a lot more.

Q : When did you start trading electronically?

A : I started trading electronically about eight years ago, but not on my own computer. I had a bank that had a direct-order line. So I'd call in my orders and they would trade for me. I did not trade electronically for myself until two years ago.

Q : So how do decide what currencies to get into?

A : I look at the context of the general economy, political events, geopolitical risks and things of that nature.

Q : It sounds like you are more of a fundamental trader then, right?

A : Yes.

Q : How long would you usually hold your positions for?

A : That is a very interesting question because it's really been changing. At the very beginning I'd hold positions for a long time, but things in Forex change so in reality I don't set trades with specific time limits in mind or timeframes in mind. Instead, I simply just look to make money on the trades.

Q : If you don't have a time, do you have like a weekly or monthly dollar profit target that you're looking for?

A : Yes, I do have a goal when I trade Forex. I look to make 20 percent on returns. But I do it in such a manner that the risk is minimized—so 20 percent, but with low risk. I don't gamble. I don't play the lottery. I come to Forex to make money and don't look at it like a bet.

Q : What is your general risk or loss limit?

A : I don't lose. In terms of stocks, you know you exit positions because there's a risk of loss, but in the Forex markets I don't lose. If one is attentive and very balanced, you can expect returns. I'm not interested in what I can make in a day or if I make explosive profits in a very short amount of time, that's not enough. It has to be consistent profitability over the long run or the course of the year that I make my profits. I have a strategy that I look to make 20 percent per year with very little risk. Once I have made that 20, that's what I take out. The only real time that I get out of my trade is when there's a factor, a variable in the market or something changes according to my perception of the market such that I feel like I should get out of the trade. Otherwise, sometimes I'll be in a position and I feel like I can get a better price for it so you know I'll get out but with intention of getting back in. Or there's sometimes when, let's say, I'm losing in a position, but I'm still making money on the interest rate, so I'll get out.

Q : How do you determine very little risk?

A : Well, I really define it in terms of where the exchange rate has been in the past. I look to buy cheap, like multiyear lows or sell at multiyear highs. For instance, I will look at the U.S. dollar/yen and if it's currently trading at 110, I may look at historical data and see that there is very little risk that it go to 100 by next year. So I will set a band that I am willing to trade in—meaning that I am only willing to add to my position, regardless of whether it goes up or down within those bands. If it breaks those bands, I am out of the trade. Also, interest is very important to me because I am holding very long-term positions. If I am long the U.S. dollar/ Japanese yen at 110 and I earn interest on the position, the interest income may eventually lower my entry price to 107 to 108, for example. For my style of trading, I need to take active measures to lower my entry price such that eventually I only need a very small move to push me back into profits.

Q : Do you look at charts to figure out the zones?

A : Yes, while I'm studying price activity, I go back in the charts about 25 years and I just keep on zooming in and zooming in to see if there is any previous market activity that reflects the current market activity—basically how the currency has behaved in the past and how that relates to the future. It really helps a lot when I take a look at the charts and zoom out to see the long-term trend, go back in, zoom out, go back in, and after doing this I sit and think about the price action.

Q : So how do you enter into trade? Do you open the entire position at once or do you enter in increments?

A : I enter little by little.

Q : Do you go in the direction of profits or do you average down?

A : I'll buy below because I'll have a goal where, let's say, in the next four years I want to buy with an average of a 110.

Q : Your strategy sounds very much like the Martingale strategy. How long do you end up holding these positions for?

A : Just the timeframe in which I'm able to make my 20 percent goal. That can be six months or it can be one year. I don't care.

Q : Let's say that you want to buy the U.S. dollar/Japanese yen at 110, and you initiate your first position at that price level. Instead of moving lower, the currency goes to 111 and it just keeps on going up, and you're in a small position that is making money. Do you then add to it or just stay with the small position?

A : Yes. If they continue to make money, I will also add to a winning trade. Even if it moves to 115, I will continue to average up because remember, with the interest rate differential, my true entry one or two years later will be lower.

Q : Do you ever go into positions where you have to pay interest?

A : I always look for favorable interest rate differentials, such that I'm not looking for short U.S. dollar/Japanese yen positions, instead I'm looking to long U.S. dollar/Japanese yen and I'm not looking for long euro/U.S. dollar positions. I am looking to short the euro/U.S. dollar. I don't enter into these trades to lose, I know no one does. But for me, this is an investment and not speculation. Therefore, it is important for me to find ways to optimize the probability of this trade winning, and one of the ways is to follow the interest. Following this strategy, I have had cumulative returns of 80 percent across the past four years.

Q : When did you decide to trade like this, averaging up and averaging down? Did someone teach you this?

A : Well, it was really at the point where I saw that when you're losing, especially when you're losing on negative interest rate differential position. The interest rate doesn't help at all it actually hurts you. So it's at that point I realized that I only wanted to enter positions that I received interest on. Not only that, I also don't want to enter positions into currency pairs that have very high volatility, for instance, the British pound/Japanese yen. Even though it has a very favorable interest rate differential, the trading range is so high that the risk may be huge.

Q : Which currency pairs do you like to trade?

A : The U.S. dollar/Japanese yen all the way and, to a lesser extent, the euro/U.S. dollar—but not as much the euro/U.S. dollar in recent months because I feel the interest rate spread is going to narrow. So presently, it's definitely with the U.S. dollar/Japanese yen.

Q : What do you *not* trade?

A : I'll never trade something with an unfavorable interest rate differential. I can't keep track of all currency pairs so there are a lot that I don't trade because I just simply can't keep track of everything. Occasionally I will trade the British pound/U.S. dollar, but not often. As for the commodity currencies [the Australian dollar (AUD), the New Zealand dollar (NZD) and Canadian dollar (CAD)], there are too many factors that impact them, especially New Zealand, which has a very tiny population. This can make the economy very volatile.

Q : Do you have only one position on at a time, or will you trade euro/U.S. dollar and U.S. dollar/Japanese yen or just U.S. dollar/ Japanese yen by itself, one at a time?

A : I will trade more than one currency pair at a time.

Q : What is the longest timeframe you've held a trade?

A : Eight months.

Q : Shortest?

A : Two or three minutes.

Q : How often do you check the price of the currency when you are in a position?

A : It really depends on the day, because there are certain days that I don't look at the computer or price action whatsoever and those are the best days. But then there are other days where I'll look at the computer and markets four to six times a day. I can be at my computer for two hours straight or for five minutes, it really depends. On average though, like I mentioned earlier, I spend four hours per day from Monday through Friday looking and checking the markets and its more pleasure than work for me because I really like the Forex market.

Q : Can you tell us about what you do in those four hours since you are really in it for the long haul?

A : Well, I'll never sit at a computer for four hours, that's way too boring. Instead maybe one day I'll get up, I'll have breakfast, I'll take a look the charts, to see what happened overnight, then maybe later on I'll do some analysis on price action, look at charts for a certain amount of time, zoom out, zoom in. Otherwise I just read the news for any given day from international news wires, the *New York Times*, *Le Monde* from France, the Spanish press, things like this.

Q : How complicated is your trading setup?

A : Very simple. I have one computer, one screen, and nothing else.

Q : What is the best and most memorable trade that you have made?

A : Well, in terms of one big trade, I never really had one big trade because I'll enter a position and I'll hold multiple positions and it's really in terms of how I'm doing per day. Or, let's say, in recent memory we had a very good March, but it's never really that one big trade that is very memorable. I mean in terms of long-term memory, I remember buying the U.S. dollar/Japanese yen (dollar/yen) at 92 and then later selling it 112.

Q : How long did you hold that for?

A : Eleven months.

Q : That is a very long time for most people, so how often do you end up adjusting your trades?

A : I never really change trades because I'll have a trade and I'll be in that trade as long as it takes to achieve a certain goal or position. I never trade to make myself rich over night, for instance, because one day that may work, but the next day it won't. I really look at my yearly performance to see exactly how I'm doing.

Q : What was your worst trade ever?

A : My worst trade was with the euro/U.S. dollar sometime ago. I was trading the euro/U.S. dollar and U.S. dollar/Japanese yen and I was making some very good trades. I had it with this bank that then decided there was too much risk exposure in my account and started arbitrarily closing positions such that I ended up losing about $700,000 because the bank took it upon itself to close out these positions. Meanwhile, had those positions been left open, I would have made money in three or four months' time. But in the end I had two options. I could have gone to the courts or I could have just gone on my way and learned from this. I'm a person who avoids conflict so I really decided just to leave it be.

Q : $700,000 in losses, that's a lot of money. What kind of leverage do you use?

A : Two percent, or 50 to 1.

Q : Can you tell us a little bit about how trading has impacted your family?

A : I am a big believer of teaching my children the value of letting your money work for you instead of sitting dormant in the bank. In fact, I remember when my children were little and Christmas time came around, I would actually give them shares in companies. This was very unique because there's very little finance culture in Spain, and this was seen as strange in my family. At the time, I would buy five or seven shares of a specific company, like Microsoft, and tell them this was a company in the United States. The total value of the shares were no more than $100.

Q: How many children do you have?

A: Three. Two boys and one girl.

Q: How did they feel when you gave them shares? Were they upset or were they happy?

A: Well, I told them these were shares in American companies and they were part owners of this American company and they just viewed the American technological sector with wonderment.

Q: How old were they when you started giving them these shares?

A: Well, the smallest child was 6 years old, the other ones were 9 years old and 12 years old.

Q: Did you give them any toys as well?

A: [Laughter.] Yes, toys and a couple of shares.

This has gone very well for them because now they're in their twenties and it's really helped boost their savings. More recently though, they've become so interested in Forex that they've sold all their previous holdings in stocks and really dedicated more time to the Forex market.

Q : Does your wife trade as well?

A : She has mini-account. She's seen me doing this for years and decided to trade for herself. But she trades a bit differently. She'll open and close positions throughout the day and trade little by little. She does it to make some extra spending cash. She's actually been doing quite well, such that she's taken out an average of about $2,000 a month, and she's very happy with that. The best thing about her trading is the fact that we have something else to talk about. We can talk about our children, the weather—and how we think the Forex market is moving. It creates a much more interesting dialogue, fosters a lot more cooperation. Basically, it helps to improve our marriage.

Q : Do you ever take opposite trades?

A : No. That never happens, we have a system such that if she's trading the British pounds/Japanese yen, then I'll be trading the U.S. dollar/Japanese yen.

Q : Do you extract your profits on a regular basis like she does?

A : Well, we don't necessarily take money out of the account, and when we do it's not because we need it, we'll occasionally just take money out of the account and buy something for ourselves. More generally, we'll aim to take about 12 percent of our total profits out of our trading accounts, and we take money out one to two times a year.

Q : Does your wife also follow your rules of trading, such as only trading positive carry?

A : Yes, she trades in a similar style that I do.

Q: What about your children, how did you teach them to trade?

A: Well, they've actually been even more prepared than we have because they've done the business track at university. But even so, they'll concede that a lot of success really comes with experience. Like my wife, my children and I will trade ideas back and forth. We'll call each other and say I think this is happening, I think that is happening, and really try to come to a consensus. That way it's really within the family. Swapping trade ideas also helps to keep our family very close. For example, my oldest son will call me on a given day and say, "Hey, I did really well today." And I may say, "No, we did really well today, we made this much." It's a bit competitive, but we also spend a lot of time sharing information. My wife and I have been married for 29 years, and we have set in stone since the beginning that our primary business is our family.

Q: Have your children adopted their own trading style, or do they trade similar to you?

A: Their personalities will push them to do something different, but they have taken the base from me and use it as a starting point.

Q: When you were teaching your kids to trade, was there any time where you said, okay, if you made a certain amount that's what you could you spend it on? Did you encourage them to trade in order to buy things, or was it just to build their saving?

A: In the beginning we would establish smaller trading accounts if they said they wanted to learn how to trade. I would teach them to keep risk low, but it was really up to them to make the money. My only real guidance to them was to trade well, but to never guide themselves solely by money or greed.

Q: How old were they when you gave them their FX accounts?

A: It's been about a year and half.

Q : When they lost money, what would you say them?

A : Well, we would tell them that if a person is intelligent, they could actually learn more when they lose than when they make money. Also, we were worried that if they became successful too young, they would never want to get a real job. If they made in a day in the Forex market what they can at a regular job in 15 days, then they may not be motivated. We wanted to instill a very powerful work ethic and not instill the notion that money is easy to come by. So I would talk to my children and say that you can take your savings and really put them to work by putting them in trading. But first and foremost you really have to become a useful member of society. You have to look at trading as this other resource that puts your savings to work.

Q : In terms of your own trading, what is the number one lesson that you've learned from your mistakes?

A : Well, the very first thing I have learned is that the only way to make money is to actually open a position. Once you open that position, the second big rule is that you need to have enough funds behind your position such that if it drops one or two cents, you are not completely out of the position. Although I am very successful, my strategy does require a large amount of capital. In addition, the most important thing that I want to impart on new traders is to tell them not to expect to achieve riches overnight, especially with a very small amount of money. You want to make sure that you have a consistently profitable strategy, not one that makes money one day but does not work weeks or even months down the road. You have to trade in a balanced way such that not only do you have a good strategy, but also that you control your risk. You never want it to turn into something that you beat yourself up about. Even if you make money, it's only going to hurt you in the long run because you are so unsettled about the excessive risk that you are taking. The purpose of trading is to add to your quality of life, not take away from it. You want to makes sure that you are actually doing things properly, that you live well, sleep well, knowing that your strategy is working the way it should.

LESSONS FROM MARCELINO LIVIAN

Make Sure You Have Enough Funds to Sustain Your Position

Livian is the epitome of a long-term trader. With positions open for as long as a year, he aims for big movements. Although this style of trading comes in contrast to many of the shorter-term traders in our book who look to make as little as 10 pips a day or 50 pips a week, Livian's 80 percent return over the past four years rivals that of most hedge funds. However, in order to trade the way Livian does, you need to have deep pockets. The core of his strategy involves identifying a trading zone and then scaling into a trade little by little toward the bottom or top of that zone. By doing this, Livian ends up building a large position that has a low average entry price. However as you build your large position to the point where only an incremental movement is needed to bring you into a profit, any small move against you also becomes more damaging. So it is extremely important to ensure that you have enough funds to maintain that position.

This idea is important even if you do not trade the way Livian does. If you hold too large a position and end up not having enough capital to sustain regular fluctuations, then you can easily get stopped out by short-term market movements.

Get Paid While You Wait

One of the Livian's primary trading rules is to always be on the side of carry, which is another word for positive interest. In currency trading, you are buying and selling countries. In every currency transaction, you are long one currency and short another. On currencies that you are long, you have the potential to earn the interest. On the currency that you are short, you have to pay interest. The difference in the spread of the interest rates between the two countries is the net amount that you can earn or pay. Being on the side of positive interest is extremely important to Livian because in long-term trades, a negative carry position would actually reduce profits or exacerbate losses in the account. When you are taking a position where you have to pay interest, this payment needs to be made every day, so it becomes an added trading cost. In contrast, being on the side of carry or holding a position where you can earn interest actually helps to improve performance. Every day an interest payment is deposited in your account which increases account equity and helps to reduce losses. In other words, it lowers your entry price. On a long-term trade, this can offer a very significant advantage. If you are holding a position for one year, the interest income can really add up. For example, a currency like the New Zealand dollar/Japanese yen could pay $10 in interest every single day, which represents one pip or point on a standard contract. If you held the position for 100 days, that equates to 100 pips. Therefore if you were long New Zealand dollar/yen, your entry price would be reduced by approximately 100 pips after 100 days, which is quite significant.

Share Trading with Your Family

Livian's final piece of advice is to share trading with your family. Not only has it helped to bring his family closer through for friendly competition, but he has also used it to teach his children to be financially savvy at a very early age. The key, of course, is to ingrain the discipline of risk control rather than a betting mentality. Trading should be perceived as a way of making your money work for you rather than letting it sit idle at the bank.

CHAPTER 13

MAN VERSUS MACHINE

STEVEN ICKOW

As computerized "black box" trading has proliferated across equity markets, sometimes accounting for as much 70 percent of the daily volume on NYSE and Nasdaq, traders have bemoaned the fact that machines have made trading impossible. Yet Steven Ickow is one guy who is testament to human ingenuity and resourcefulness. Not only has he been able to adapt to the new "black box" regime of the machines, but he has prospered by taking advantage of the software robots. A highly disciplined trader, Ickow lives an almost ascetic existence, locked in his home office for six and half hours each day without any interruptions from the outside world. This sense of focus and discipline has made him one of the most consistent traders in the game, registering only 4 losing days out of the last 180. From his home in suburban Chicago, Steve sat with us one day after the close, to chat about his approach to the markets and to share some of the tricks of the trade.

■ ■ ■

Q : One of the things we found interesting with many of our interviews is that most people developed an interest in trading from high school or earlier. Was that the case with you?

A : I always had an outside interest in stocks. But I was a premed major so I came into it a little later in life. My dad was always into it, but not into trading, more like retirement stuff.

Q : Was he a casual investor?

A : Yeah, my mom too. But we always had—I don't want to say a gambling background—but an interest in gambling.

My mom especially. She liked blackjack. Games of chance like that. My brother too. He is professional poker player now. We had a heavy sports background in our house, watching sports, playing sports, and so on.

Q : And handicapping sports too?

A : Yeah, handicapping sports too.

Q : Did you do any trading while in college?

A : No, not really. I got into it later when I got a job as clerk at the Merc. [*Author's note:* The *Merc* is the Chicago Mercantile Exchange. A *clerk* is the go-between for the customers of big wire houses and the pit. He or she updates the market for the customers and helps facilitate trades for those customers in the pit.] I was in the Nikkei pits, Nasdaq pits, and the SP pits. This was during the Internet stock craze. So I decided to try it out. I had a friend who was successful trader, so he backed me.

Q : Did you go off the floor when he first staked you?

A : Yes, I traded stocks off the floor.

Q : What was the reason to try a clerkship at the Merc?

A : I got my degree in biology, but I decided I wasn't going to go into that. I did various other things and then I had friend who had a friend who had a friend down at the Merc and he said he was doing well, so I decided to give it a try.

Q : How long did you clerk for?

A : About three years.

Q : Do you think most of the trading skill that you use now was learned on the floor? Or is a lot of it inapplicable to what you do now?

A : No, it was definitely applicable. The way I trade now I learned from the Nikkei pit. It was smaller pit with less going on. And the stocks I trade now are slower with less going on. You can watch what's going on, who is doing what. That's kind of how I trade—the way people do in a smaller pit where you can see who is buying, who is selling, trying to get in between the players, buying in front of them, selling in front of them. So the Nikkei is what molded my style. When I first started trading, I was trading thicker stocks like Microsoft. But I couldn't get an edge, so I went to thinner stocks, which are less crowded and easier to identify the players.

Q : Is most of your trading done on Nasdaq?

A : 100 percent Nasdaq.

Q : Is that because you need that open book on the Level 2 entry? [*Authors' note:* In the Nasdaq market unlike at the NYSE all bids and offers are displayed on the single Level 2 screen providing the trader with much better transparency than the specialist book on the NYSE which only shows the topmost bids and offers.]

A : Yes, Level 2 entry. Most important is immediate fills. You are not giving your order to a specialist. Everything is done right away. Watch the book, watch where all the bids and offer are on Level 2. On the NYSE it's not easy to do that. There is less transparency.

Q : Is mostly what you do these days tape watching, or are you a chart reader as well?

A : No. I watch charts too, but I would say Level 2 is primary. Charts are for confirmation. If the chart looks good, but Level 2 isn't there, I won't trade. But if Level 2 looks good, but chart is shaky, then sometimes I will trade even if the chart is not good.

Q : What timeframe charts do you look at?

A : My screen. What I am looking at right now is Level 2. One that I trade off of and seven others that I am watching. The Level 2 that I trade off of is linked to two charts: a five-minute chart and a daily chart. I also have five-minute charts of S&P, Nasdaq, and E-mini Russell futures, and I have daily charts of indexes. But what I am really watching is five-minute charts, and I also have the S&P squawk box just for the general tone of the market.

Q : Can you give an idea of the type of stocks you are trading?

A : I am trading stocks priced between $30 to $70 with average daily volume of 300,000 to 1 million shares.

Q : So these are intermediate stocks—not extraordinarily liquid, but liquid enough. How large a size will you go into stock that trades 300K a day?

A : My size can vary from 100 to 5,000. But usually it goes between 100 to 2,000 shares. It depends on the day and what is going on in the stock. If it is a slow day, and I am just trading back and forth, I will trade small size. If I see there is a buyer, I will put on size. But I will never put on a huge position because I never want to have a single trade that will put me out of business.

Q : When you go large size, do you average up?

A : No, not necessarily. Usually, when I put size on, it is because I have an edge where I see someone pegged to the bid or offer and I know there is a buyer or seller. Market makers and hedge funds have a lot of positions to watch. They often have a big order to work. So they are not micromanaging the order. They may have 100,000 shares to fill. So they put them on the computer, which puts them on the bid. So, if the bid moves, they move. If it goes down, they go down. They just want to get their stock filled. But usually they have some sort of limit. So me, I am watching fewer stocks. I see more of what's going on. I bid up, and he comes up. I bid up to a certain amount, and he won't go any further. Anyway, I can usually tell where he can go to. So I will try to buy up all the offers, bid up to the point where he won't go any further, and then sell the position to him.

For example, if I know the buyer will go up to 80, and I see 60 bid by 65, I watch the 65 offers and I buy those. I buy 70 offers, I bid 70. I bid 75. I bid 80 on one ECN. I see him bidding 80 on another ECN. I sell to him. I do it again and again. That is just one thing. What I am trying to tell you is that these guys are watching 20 stocks. They don't have to worry about micromanaging the position. They have a lot stock to do. They get filled and that's all they care about. Once in a while the guy leaves and you get stuck. But you have to know your size and limits and know from experience how to do this. When a market maker has to fill a big order, they can't really hide from someone who is watching the stock very closely. If the fund is buying 100K shares of stock and they are going to hold it for a year, what do they care if they buy it at 65.60 cents or 65.90 cents? But me, if I can make a dime on 10,000 shares, that's $1,000.

Q : Do those seven or eight stocks change frequently? Or do you sit with the same portfolio for a month or more?

A : No, they don't change that often. As long as the stock is good, I am making money in the stock. I don't look at anything else. The only time it changes is if the stock goes bad. Let's say it has really bad news. Then I take it off my list and look for another stock. When things are good, I don't change at all. I am very focused on what I am watching. I don't watch anything else, and that's why I trade now, basically, from an office by myself. I used to trade from a big office, where you hear other things and sometimes it's hard not to pay attention. I am in the room by myself now where I don't hear anything. I just know what the overall markets are doing and what my stocks are doing, and that's all I care about.

Q : Do you watch CNBC at all?

A : I have it up in the background just for noise. Sometimes someone may be talking about one of my stocks on there. So I will know why it is going crazy. I do have a news service which tells me the numbers when numbers come out and if something is mentioned about my stocks. Then I will probably just get out and watch, because I don't like it when there is too much news on my stock and I don't know about it. I know I am not going to get the news first. I don't trade on news.

Q : Do you know the story behind each stock quite well?

A : Yes, I do know the story behind each stock. I know when they have their earnings because a lot of times they will trade a certain way around earnings.

Q : Does that have to do with institutional order flow? Since institutional buyers are going to be positioning themselves before news event, do you try to capitalize on that?

A : You should know when earnings are going to be because a lot of times there will be position squaring and things going on that are out of the ordinary.

Q : Could you give an example of what kind of price action would make you think something might happen? If you see buying ahead of the earnings, does that suggest there could be positive news?

A : For example, if there are big buyers into the earnings and the company reports better than expected, then it will usually gap up and it's a good place to get short. But if the stock is weak into the earnings, then they beat the estimate. Then even if it gaps up, it's still good to get long after the earnings because there are still a lot of people who were wrong. So a lot of is just watching. If I see who the buyers were before and the news is good, then I see them getting out of positions.

Q : So you could divine a lot of market-making strategy just by watching the tape very carefully day in and day out—even with the fact that everybody tries to hide their identity?

A : Yes, it changes all the time. But a high percentage of Nasdaq volume is now composed of black box trading. So a lot of times I will test price just to see where the market is. Let's say I am long and I start bidding up and bids come with me, then I know I am good. Let's say I offer and now no one joins me, no one is an aggressive seller. That's how I get information on the stock by constantly bidding and offering.

Q : Let's zero in on this. Would say that by doing this kind of probative touch-and-feel action you, you are actually testing the machines, not the human beings? By doing this you are actually able to understand the programming behind those machines so you can trade off of it?

A : Right, exactly. Here is another example. If you know some of the big market makers in the stock you can sometimes see what he does. It used to be that you could see on Island [*Authors' note*: Island was a very popular Electronic Communication Network on which traders could make bids and offers for stocks.] who sold or bought from you. I remember one time Goldman was on the offer, and I would offer Island, and he would buy from me, so you knew he was faking his offer in order to make sure that the stock wouldn't get away from him. By becoming familiar with the stock and knowing who the big players are, you could tell who is faking or not. If the market is 79 by 80, and I buy all the 80 offers, then the market maker gets pissed off. But if I join him and buy the 79s with him, and as long as you are buying with them and not taking all of their 80s, then they'll take you up for the ride. In that case the market maker is really a buyer at 79 and he doesn't want to sell at 80. There are a lot of fake bids and offers in the Nasdaq, and if you are able to identify what they are, then you can use it as a clue for information as to what is going on. So by watching I get my edge. If you don't have an edge, you don't have anything. An up market means nothing. Every day you can have the Dow be up, but you will have 100 stocks up and 100 stocks down.

Q : This brings us to the next question. Precisely because these are not Dow or the SP 500 or the Nasdaq 100 stocks, they are less subject to broader market swings. Are they less vulnerable to market sweeps by the stock index futures as well?

A : Sometimes they are, sometimes not. But you will know. Here is an example. The market is going down. It is going down hard. But you see there is one guy buying, staying on the bid. You identify who he is and then you want to buy with him. But if he leaves you, get out. I don't like to buy highs and sell lows. I like to buy pullbacks. Or I'll take a shot at buying a low or selling a high if I see a seller and go with him.

Q : You day trade, meaning that you don't hold anything overnight. Were you always this way? Did that just develop over time? And if it did, can you tell us why you adopted that style?

A : I like to micromanage everything. So I don't have control after the market closes. I don't want to think about it. I like to go home every day and think about other things, forget about the market for a little bit. I like to be flat every day because anything can happen overnight.

Q : How much of a risk do you typically allow yourself on a trade? 10 cents ? 15 cents?

A : It depends, but usually not much at all. I am typically getting long on the bid with someone and if the guy leaves, I am out. Now there are times when the guy bails and there is nothing I can do. But usually my risk is 5 cents or less.

Q : Pretty much always?

A : Usually. The only time when I deviate from that rule is when there is no one there and I can't get out.

Q : So what happens in that case?

A : Well, it's a percentage game. Most of the time you can get out—9 times out of 10 you can get out.

Q : When you get trapped, how badly have you been stung? Has it been as much as a dollar?

A : No, never. Maybe in the old days when stocks were $300. But now I would say 20 cents is the worst that I get hit. I am always watching my stock.

Q : You have seven Level 2 screens that you are watching, but you are actually trading only one stock at a time, correct?

A : I may be in two or three. I won't be in more than that. But I want to be watching everything. I was in a stock today. It sat in a range of 15 cents for four hours. But I just traded it back and forth, back and forth.

Q : Now that you are trading for such small spreads, how is your cost structure?

A : Prices have come down a lot. When I first started trading it was 3 cents a share. So $30 for a thousand shares. Then it came down to a penny a share or $10 a thousand. Now it's 0.4 or 0.5 cents a share. So, basically, when I trade in and out on a stock I can scratch the trade on just 1 cent gain, which is nice because I can trade bigger size.

Q : A nickel is about as much as you are willing to sacrifice on each trade. But on average, and of course each trade is different, how much do you try to profit from each trade?

A : I don't set hard targets. If I am in a stock and the buyer comes up, I will stay in it and I can make a dollar sometimes. I can make 75 cents. Whatever the market gives me depends on where I got in. If I got in at the bottom and the market turned and there is no reason to get out, no one is offering, and the bids are holding up, I will stay in it.

Q : That brings up an interesting question. No financial instrument goes up vertically. There are always retraces along the way. So even if you have a 50 cents move up, there is at least a 10 cent retracement somewhere along the way. What gives you the confidence to hold through those retracements?

A : That's the hardest part of trading, and to tell you the truth, I am not as good of a holder as I could be. I get out of my losers right away, but I don't hold winners as long as I could. A lot times if I am in a stock and it starts to retrace I will try to get out.

Q : Since you don't average down into your losers, do you scale out of your winners? Or are you doing a single-entry, single-exit type of strategy?

A : I will definitely scale out of my winner. I'll offer out some—not all—of my position if starts moving my way.

Q : Let's step back from trading. Could you run through your daily routine? What is an average day in your life like?

A : I've always worked out. I was a competitive weight lifter. I have always been into sports. So, every morning, I will get up at 5:30 and check what the markets did overnight. Then I will go to the gym 6:30–7:30 Chicago time. Shower, hang out with the family a little, then get into the office by 8:05, check the news. I will trade until 3 o'clock. Then I will usually go pick up my son from school, and if the weather is nice, we'll hang out. We'll go to the pool or the park. Then I'll do half an hour of work at night and hang out with my wife. I am in bed by 10 o'clock.

Q : When you are trading all day, do you go out for lunch? Do you have any interruptions?

A : No, I don't eat much. I will have a little coffee, a little oatmeal, go to the bathroom, and trade all day because I don't want to miss anything. It is a relatively short day.

Q : But at the same time it's enormously intense. You are not just sitting. Every single moment you are focusing on the screen. Having done this, we know how draining this can be. How do you relieve the pressure and maintain the focus for six straight hours?

A : I just do it. I just concentrate and focus, wait and watch, and then attack. You are up in a tree like a hunter waiting for prey. If the opportunity comes you, got to be there. If you are in the bathroom or walking around, you miss it.

Q : Yes. But often in the market, sometimes for an hour, nothing happens. If you ask a normal human being to stare at the screen for even 10 minutes—when there is no action—most people can't do it. Do you use any meditation or mental tricks to help you?

A : No. No, mental tricks. I am always watching, and something is always happening. Whether it's something big or something small. Yes, sometimes I do get bored. Sometimes I do something I shouldn't do. But generally I try to stay disciplined and wait for the opportunity to happen.

Q : Do you ever dream about the day's trading?

A : Yes, sometimes that will happen. I will see the Level 2 in my head. It hasn't happened recently. As I traded more I have been able to relax more. Now, when I come home, I am not as happy after my big days, and I am not as upset after my bad days. The highs are not as big and the lows are not as low. I come home every day and try to do it again the next day.

Q : When you first started out, the pressure of being profitable—where you had to make money or you didn't eat in a sense—how did you deal with that?

A : Yeah, that was terrible. My first day, when I started, I made $1,500. After the first week I was down $5,000 because I had no idea what I was doing. I thought I knew, but I didn't, and I didn't approach breakeven for about five months where every day I would come home depressed. I'd lay on the couch and think, "I can't figure this out." After five months I was down $20,000. And then in the sixth month, I made $20,000 and that was it. At the beginning it was very hard because I couldn't figure it out. You'd feel a sense of failure, why can't I figure it out? And then it just clicked. I tell people that after six months you either get it or you won't. Most people don't get it. If you don't get it after six months, it's time to do something else.

Q : What skills would you say a person needs in order to do the kind of trading you do?

A : I would say someone who is disciplined, someone who can follow a plan, someone who is risk averse, but not so risk averse that they are afraid to trade. I've had people whom I've trained who would make or lose $50 every day for a year. They were just afraid to trade. As soon as they got a winner they would try to get out.

Q : In general, I would say, someone doesn't have to be book smart, but someone who is a good poker player, a chess player, somebody who understands how to read a situation. Someone like a quarterback who comes up to the line of scrimmage and looks at the defense and knows probability-wise what will work with this formation. Just like I look at Level 2 and I put on a trade and, sure, it may not work all of the time, but it will work 8 out of 10 times based on what I've seen before. So, in short, the ability to read a situation and process that information as things are going on at a fast pace and stay cool under pressure. I always thought that guys who were good quarterbacks in the NFL would make good day traders.

Q : How many people have you trained?

A : About 20.

Q : Of the 20, how many are still in the business?

A : None. I've been able to help people who were already successful traders in futures or other instruments and show them my methodology. But someone who was not a successful trader already I was not able to train. They can understand what I am doing, but they just can't follow through.

For example, I had a guy. I'd tell him we are buying evens—buying stock at the round figure like 101.00 or 102.00—we are buying evens with the bid. The market is going down. The futures are going down. It looked bad, but I tell him, "Don't get out unless the evens leave." Well, the guy panics. He sees the market going down. There is nothing below evens and he gets out. The market turns. All the 01 offers get lifted, but the trader is not in the stock. I am in the stock, but he is not because all he could think about was if the evens leave he can lose money. So we put on the exact same trade. But he couldn't hold the position. So I can tell people exactly what to do. But their emotions get the better of them. But I have trained people who were good traders to become better traders.

Q : What do you do specifically for those good traders to make them better traders?

A : Mainly I showed them things about Level 2. Maybe they were overall market traders or chart traders, and I got them to pay more attention to price action—more micro stuff rather than the macro. I showed them how market makers and funds work their orders and how to capitalize on that.

Q : You've trained people. But was someone a mentor to you?

A : The guy who got me started, who was a very successful futures trader, taught me more about how to handle myself, than actually giving me an idea on how to trade.

Q : Would you say that it is much more important to learn that aspect—the ability not to sabotage yourself—rather than any specific methodology of trading?

A : I would say they are equal. If you don't have a methodology you won't make any money anyway. But if you do have a methodology, and you know how to control yourself, that makes you a better trader. But without the methodology, you have noting.

Q : True. There are million ways of making money in the market. Every one of them will also lose you money because every methodology ultimately fails, and the problem is that most people don't have the self-control to abandon the methodology when it's not working.

A : That's definitely true. You have to know when things change and you have to change with them. It's survival of the fittest. If you don't change, you are done. But at the same time, you have to have the discipline to follow your methodology.

Q : During the day do you IM anybody? Is there a support group you hang with?

A : No, I do it all myself.

Q : What about once a month, are there meetings you attend?

A : No, I talk to a few of my buddies, but the stocks I am in, there is only so much to go around and you really don't want to give them out. That's one of the things I like better than trading in big office. Then you may have a few traders in the same stock and then you have the problem of who goes first. I'd rather just not know. That's what's so good about electronic markets instead of the pit. You hit the button. Whoever is first is first. Generally, I prefer to be left alone. My wife doesn't even call when I am in the office unless it is an emergency.

Q : Speaking of that, does your wife work? Does she have a source of income?

A : No, she is a stay-at-home mom. She used to be a teacher before our sons were born.

Q : So the period when it was kind of hard—the first six months—was your wife supportive? Was it difficult for you guys? How did you handle that?

A : We had some savings, I didn't have any bills, and she was very supportive.

Q : That must have been important.

A : Yes, definitely.

Q : Some operational details. Do you trade one account or do you trade multiple accounts?

A : I trade one account.

Q : You run a self-proprietorship. You pay all your expenses, medical bills. It's as though you are running a hardware store. You had the same set of possibilities and problems.

A : Exactly.

Q : Do you target income for yourself? Do you say I want to make $1,000 per day or $20K a month? Or do you not believe in targets?

A : Yes, I do have targets for myself. But if I don't get them, I don't get them. It not like I say to myself, oh, I made x amount today. I am going to stop trading. I never stop trading until the close.

Q : Even if you had a $5K by 11 A.M. you wouldn't stop?

A : No, never because if there is opportunity to make more, that's what I am there for.

Q : Have you ever had a situation where you were up by $5K at 11 A.M. and back to $0K at 3 P.M., where you gave it all back?

A : No. Not after my learning phase. Usually I will trade more conservatively if I am up. I will try to trade only much higher percentage setups, smaller share size. Just trying to pad what I already have.

Q : What do you consider to be a great day to make money? High volatility? Big ranges?

A : It depends. Sometime the stock will move but I can't figure it out. I have no edge. I don't know who is buying and I really don't know what going on. But if the stock moves and the clues are there, I see bids, and they cancel offers. A lot of times what will happen is that the market maker will come in and will hold the price up even if the market is going down. And he will do it for a couple of days. When I see that, I buy them with him on every pullback. He may do that for three or four days in a row. If I can identify that early I can get with him and make money.

Sometimes guys will hold the stock in very small range on the bid and the offer and I can't make any money, but a lot of times there may be a buyer at 15 and a seller at 70, and I'll try to trade that in between all day long. As long as I can identify who the buyers and sellers are, I can make money. But if the stock goes straight up and the market is flying, it doesn't necessarily mean I can make money because I have no clue what's going on.

Q : You may actually stand down then, even if there is movement just because you don't understand the reason behind the directionality?

A : Exactly. Let's say they took out a big level. Say they took out all the evens. But if I don't know who the buyer is, I don't necessarily want to buy the 01s or the 02s. I need to know where I am out if I am wrong. On every trade I always answer these two questions. Number one: Why am I getting into this trade? And number two: Where am I getting out if I am wrong? If I can't answer those two questions, then I can't get into the trade no matter what the stock is doing.

Another thing other traders always ask me is, why don't I watch more stocks? So I can have more opportunities on, say, days that my stocks are not moving. My response is that I need to watch my stocks—in case they do move, I want to be the first one to know it. I try to know everything about these stocks, and I watch enough stocks such that there is always something to do. Sometimes I may trade less shares, sometimes more. But I have this little niche. There are people who make a lot more money than me. But I am one of the most consistent traders.

Q: Speaking of that, and again obviously on average—wins versus losses—what's the ratio like?

A: So far this year I have traded every single day. So we've had approximately 180 days so far and I have had four losing days. And three of those days were $100.

Q: On average, how many trades do you do? 150?

A: More than that.

Q: Really? So let's for argument's sake say it's 250 round turns per day. That means at six and half hours worth of trading it's almost a trade every two minutes or so.

A: Right. I would say that's correct. It's nonstop.

Q: So that makes no single trade meaningful. You take losses quickly and move on to the next one?

A: Right. I just move on to the next one.

Q : Out of that basket of 250 trades, how many winners, how many losers?

A : I would say more than half are winners and my winners are always bigger than my losers. I scratch a lot of trades just trying to figure out what is going on. For example, if the stock is 50 bid 51 offer. I may try the 51 offers because in stocks you can show anything you want on the size. You may have a million, but only show 100, and then just refresh all day long. If you show a million, you have to do a million unless you quickly cancel. So I'll buy an offer or hit a bid just to see if the buyer or seller is real.

Sometimes I want to see if the bid will come up so I will buy the 51 offer, lift him, and then go 51 bid just to see if the 50 bid will come up and join me.

Q : Some final questions. What's your number one rule for trading if you were to boil it down to one idea?

A : Number one rule of trading is risk aversion. To make sure that no matter what happens, no one trade can put you out of business.

Q : What was your worst trade ever?

A : The only thing I can tell you is once I was in a stock and the stock got halted. There was nothing you can do. I was long the stock. It got halted and it was bad news. It was a biotech stock. It opened a dollar and half lower and I had 1,000 shares. So I got hit.

Q : So you never had a 10-point gap against you.

A : No, because I don't hold stuff overnight and the only thing that can happen to me is the stock gets halted.

Q : What about one of your better trades?

A : I made good money on Imclone [IMCL] when there was congressional investigation. I got short and the stock went down a good amount. Sometimes it takes a few minutes for news to disseminate and this was one of those times.

Q : What was the most humbling experience for you?

A : My first six months I could not figure out how to make any money. I was just humbled. I was saying to myself: Wow, this is not as easy as I thought. Trading is not easy and not for everyone. If it was, everybody would do it.

Q : What is the most interesting part of this job?

A : It's just like sports. You come in. You play every day and there is a scorecard at the end of the day. I liken trading to baseball. There is a game every day. Some days you play well and some days you play badly. But you play every day. When the game is over, you do it again the next day.

Q : Do you gamble at all?

A : No, if I go to Vegas I don't gamble because there is no edge. The house has the edge. If I know I can make money 9 out of 10 time trading, then why would I gamble when someone else has the edge? I have no interest in it.

LESSONS FROM STEVEN ICKOW

Make Your Stand in the Right Domain

Success in trading is as a much a function of finding the right instrument to trade as it is a matter of using the correct strategy. Building on his experience from trading on the floor of the Chicago

Mercantile Exchange, where he found the smaller, slower Nikkei pit provided him with a much better edge than the more crowded S&P pit, Steven Ickow took the same philosophy to the screen and decided to specialize only in medium-cap stocks that trade an average of 1 million shares per day. Those types of stocks attract less attention from the day-trading crowd and allow Ickow, who is a master of observation, to better handicap the price action, quickly picking up on the nuances of the move. This idea can be extended even further for most traders. We, for example, have never been comfortable day trading the stock index futures, which tend to move in very herky-jerky fashion quite often in direct opposition to the news. On the other hand, we took to the currency market like fish to water, instantly making the connection between macroeconomics, geopolitical events, and price flow. Therefore, struggling traders should examine their market of choice before examining their methodology.

Use Reconnaissance Orders

A big part of Steven's day is spent breaking even. Of the more than 200 trades that he puts on every day, a significant proportion ends up in scratch because he is using the small orders to probe the market. By watching how the market reacts to his moves, Steven often gleans very valuable information about the intent of the players in the stock. He can then exploit this information for profitable setups. This use of "reconnaissance" orders is a technique employed not only by him but by some of the biggest and most famous traders in the world. George Soros was well known to put out orders in the opposite direction of his true view just to see how well the markets absorbed the order flow. If his "opposite" trade became profitable, he would revaluate his thesis and would on occasion hold off on trading his real intentions until market conditions became more favorable.

Focus, Focus, Focus!

Speculation is observation. In order to observe carefully a trader needs total concentration and complete focus. Steven Ickow does not do lunch. He does not putter about in his backyard during market hours. He does not surf the net looking for gadgets to buy. During every second of market hours Steven stares intently at the screens carefully assessing the price action. He eats lightly, takes no personal phone calls unless there is some sort of emergency from his wife, and even tries to keep his bathroom breaks to a minimum. It may seem like a monastic existence, but this is the price of success. Just like any other endeavor worth doing well, trading requires total dedication and complete commitment. The hours may be short but they are intense.

Know the Reason to Get into the Trade and the Reason to Get Out

Perhaps no other lesson is as valuable as this rule from Steven Ickow. The biggest difference between professional and novice traders is that professionals do not make random trades. They don't just go into a position because it "looks good" or "looks bad" or because it "feels" cheap or dear. Winning traders always have a crisp, clear and logical foundation for their trade. The reason may be technical or fundamental in nature or it may rely on their ability to read price flow on the tape. But they always know exactly why they are in the trade and much more importantly at what point (both profit and loss) they will get out. Trade your plan and plan your trades may be an overused maxim in trading, but it is the underlying truth of the game.

CHAPTER 14

GETTING STARTED IN TRADING

1. BE WELL CAPITALIZED

Why do most businesses fail? Is it lack of desire on the part of their owners? Is it inferior intelligence or the absence of people skills necessary to succeed? Although many failed entrepreneurs believe that these are the causes of their demise, the truth is often far more mundane. The majority of businesses fail simply because they do not have enough money to survive the inevitable mistakes that befall all startups. Often the difference between eventual profit and dead certain loss is the amount of money at the disposal of the business owner. Money buys time and time turns into experience, which is the necessary ingredient to master any skill. Therefore, the need to be well capitalized is one of the key rules for starting a career in trading.

Does that mean that a trader needs to have hundreds of thousands of dollars at his disposal in order to enter the trading business? Not at all. Many of our interviewees started with very modest amounts. However, none of the traders who started small relied on trading as their sole source of income during their initial learning stages. Several like Paul Willette and Hoosain Harneker had their spouses support them while they learned. Others such as Chuck Hays, Steve Ickow, and Tyrone Ball set aside savings and lived quite frugally as they studied the art of the trade. Finally, some like Indi Jones simply learned on the job while their employer paid them a nominal salary. The critical point we are trying to make is that if you do not have any other source of income while you focus on learning how to trade, be sure to have enough capital set aside to meet your daily needs for at least six months to a year.

Failure to properly capitalize yourself also applies to your trading capital. Many novice traders, especially in markets with astronomical leverage such as futures or foreign exchange, will abuse the liberal margin requirements and quickly rack up massive capital losses. Chuck Hays's advice to use $10,000 of capital per one standard futures contract is a good rule of thumb to use. Typically one standard contract in futures or foreign exchange equals to approximately $100,000 of underlying, which in turn implies that traders should never exceed more than 10-to-1 leverage factor. Of course, it is very important to research the actual value of the instrument as there is wide room for error. One contract of Great Britain pounds for example is worth nearly $200,000, while one futures contract of Dow Jones stock index is worth only $63,000 at current market prices. Traders should make adjustments accordingly, but keep in mind the need to have ample capital to live on and keep the leverage limit on the trading account at no more than 10 times the equity. This will go a long way in helping you properly set up your business.

2. EXPECT TO LOSE FOR AT LEAST SIX MONTHS

Learning how to trade is like learning how to do many things in life such as riding a bike, driving, or even cooking. None of us were successful at these activities from the start. We are sure everyone has fallen off a bike once or twice, stopped short too abruptly when driving for the first time, and may have even added sugar instead of salt while following that new recipe. The same is true with trading. Don't expect to be successful from the start. You will make mistakes and probably blow up your first trading account.

But you are not alone since this has happened to every one of our star traders. Chuck Hays, for example, lost $50,000 in his first year of trading. Steve Ickow made $1,500 his first day, but was down $5,000 in his first week—and after five months, had lost $20,000. Indi Jones lost $8,000 on his first trade, which included both his own money and money he borrowed from his father. The difference between most new traders and our pros is their perseverance. It is much easier to give up trading and move on with our lives than to have the dedication to learn from our mistakes and ensure that we don't repeat them. Discipline is always easy to say, but hard to do.

Not all of us can afford losing $20,000 or even $8,000. Therefore, we encourage you to demo or paper trade before you actually go live. Make sure you have a decent strategy, and then start trading small and work your way up. Log your trades and analyze them on a regular basis. Expect to lose, expect to make mistakes, it is all apart of learning to trade, but the difference between becoming a pro and being an amateur is the ability to improve.

3. TEST BEFORE YOU TRY

Testing before you trade live is so important for new traders that it deserves its own section. Trading is very exciting. It is tempting to jump into the markets and begin trading before you are even ready. However, if you are serious about trading, we encourage you to slow down, to test every strategy before you implement it. Hoosain Harneker imposed a very strict rule on himself when he decided that before putting his hard-earned money at risk, he would have to triple his demo account three times in a row. Certainly not an easy feat, this is also a huge barrier of entry. Yet in doing so, he forced himself to develop a disciplined trading style that he is able to replicate over and over again. At bare minimum, every new trader needs to prove to himself that he too can double his account three times in a row or triple his account two times in a row. Technological advances have allowed many brokerages to offer virtual trading accounts that duplicate real market activity. We urge you to use these tools to your advantage.

Along the same lines, trading strategies should also be tested. If you have a strategy that you think will work, review prior instances of this setup in your charts, look at what happens on multiple timeframes to make sure that the strategy creates more winning than losing trades. As you review your charts, you will also get a better understanding of how the assets trades. Then, test it live because quite often execution will alter your results, especially if it is a very short-term strategy or one that relies on breakouts. Only after you have achieved positive results on both back testing and live testing can you implement this strategy with larger or more meaningful trading sizes.

4. ALWAYS USE STOPS

The biggest prevailing theme in our book is that our traders protect their capital and protect their profits. Before putting on a trade, they always have a game plan and are conscious of how much they are willing to lose on the trade. Whether you are a new or seasoned trader, you need to do the same. Rob Booker said it best when he told us that he trades defensively. Indi Jones has a similar take when he said that in trading, your capital is everything because if your capital is gone, you will have no opportunity to recover. Most of our traders will risk no more than 5 percent of their account on a single trade. Although the majority of novice traders will agree that this is the proper maximum risk to take, few will do more than pay lip service to it. In order to truly appreciate the need to limit your risk per trade, all you have to consider is that if you lost 25 percent of your capital, in order to return to your original equity value, you would have to earn 33 percent. Alternatively, if you lost 75 percent of your capital, you would have to return a whopping 400 percent just to get to breakeven.

Protecting profits is just as important as protecting capital. Nearly all of the traders who we interviewed will scale out of their positions because they realize that the last 15 to 20 percent of your position can account for a significant portion of your total profits. Since most asset classes are trending, smart traders will realize that if they catch a breakout move, the move can last for a long time. The best way to take advantage of this dynamic is through the use of trailing stops that are either based upon key chart levels, equity, or volatility. This is the way that Paul Willette trades. He will harvest profits on a small portion of his position right away and move his stop to break even to make sure this trade remains profitable. Then he will continue to trail his stop to capture any further gains.

5. TRADE TO YOUR PERSONALITY

Do you like to fish in a secluded lake or ski down a black diamond slope? How you answer that question could determine the way you should trade. Fishing is a slow, solitary activity fraught with many unsuccessful attempts at snagging a catch. It requires discipline, patience, and the ability to remain focused on a single task for long periods of time. Downhill skiing, on the other hand, is a sport of speed and quick reactions. The ride down the mountain may be fast but it requires thousands of split-second decisions to navigate safely to the bottom without tumbling into a snow bank. In short, fishermen typically make good long-term traders as they patiently wait to squeeze every point out of the trend. Skiers, on the other hand, tend to be much better short-term traders who are good at scalping a few points at a time. Are there exceptions to the rule? Of course, there many trend trading skiers and scalping fishermen. Our point isn't really about skiing or fishing, but rather about knowing your strengths.

As adults, our personalities are essentially set in stone. The saying that you can't teach an old dog new tricks was practically invented for trading. It is very difficult to radically change your personality to accommodate a particular trading style.

As you have seen from reading the interviews in our book, you can be successful trading any product, timeframe, and methodology. We are all different, and the key to trading success does not depend on a particular timeframe or a specific indicator, but rather on making sure that the timeframe you pick is one that fits your personality. People who need instant gratification are probably not cut out for long-term trading and may find their best success focusing on shorter-term charts. People who are patient and willing to sit with a trade for days or weeks at a time are best suited for long-term trading. Hoosain Harneker is the epitome of a short-term trader. He goes for 10 points at a time, and his trading robot is in an out of positions within minutes. Marcelino Livian is the complete opposite. He takes a very relaxed approach to trading and has often held his positions for months at a time.

Each of our traders has different methodologies. Franki Law and Paul Willette go for big profits or, more specifically, a large number of points. Chuck Hays will trade a lot of contracts for very small profits over and over again throughout the course of the day. Steve Ickow places more than 200 trades a day, many of which ends up in scratch just to probe the sentiment of the market. He takes small risks, but when the trade moves in his direction, he aims for big profits. The key is to figure out what works for you and stick to that strategy.

Although it is important to know your strengths, successful traders also fully understand their weaknesses. Ashkan Bolour for example trades only the U.S. session in currencies, although the currency market trades 24 hours per day. Furthermore, he limits himself to only two trades per day. If he takes two consecutive losses, Ashkan will walk away from the screen, fully accepting the fact that he is out of sync with the market, but secure in knowledge that he will come back tomorrow to trade another day. Chuck Hays also makes it a habit to leave the screen during what he calls dead time—11 A.M. to 2 P.M. East Coast time—in the stock market because he knows that he will make many unnecessary mistakes if he trades during that time. In fact, the success of many of our interviewees depends on knowing when *not* to trade almost as much as it hinges on their ability to make timely entries into the market. As Chuck Hays, observes, "First you must learn not to lose money." That requires the knowledge of both your strengths and limitations.

Rob Booker said it best when he told us that after so many years of trading, no matter how hard he tries, he is only a 50- to 100-pip-a-week trader. Beyond that, he starts getting a bit crazy and a bit euphoric. Every one of us is similar to some degree, we just have to figure out our own capabilities and use them to our advantage.

6. TOOLS OF THE TRADE

Every craftsperson needs the right tools, and in trading they can be divided into two broad categories: mechanical and analytical.

Mechanical Tools

The mechanical part of trading is by far the most mundane aspect of the game, yet it is responsible for the overwhelming majority of woe and pain among trading novices. Imagine stepping on the gas pedal instead of the brake as your car careens toward the garage wall, and you can begin to appreciate the feeling of hitting the buy button when one meant to make a sale, or vice versa. In trading, mistakes have immediate negative consequences. Worse, because most of us naturally like to avoid pain, novice traders will often compound their mistakes by sitting on the trade instead of immediately closing out a wrong position.

To avoid this sequence of events as much as possible, traders should always practice on a demo platform for at least several weeks in order to fully familiarize themselves with their trading software. Almost every equity, futures, and FX broker dealer allows the trader to set up a practice account and learn to set entries exits and stops on the system.

Once the trader is comfortable with his (or her) software of choice, he should trade the account with real money but with nominal amount of size. In stocks that means 100-share lots, in futures and options one contract at a time and in FX that means one minilot sizes of 10,000 units of currency. Why such small amounts? This step allows the novice to experience the joys and tribulations of having actual money in the market without the consequence of assuming terminal risk.

Once the trader is comfortable with the process, what should his physical set-up be like? Although many of our traders differed greatly in their use of technology we've devised a generic list of components we believe are necessary for a serious, professional attempt at trading:

1. A good desktop computer with a minimum 2 GHz chip, 1 gigabyte of RAM, and 100-gig hard drive.
2. At least two 19-inch flat-panel monitors to view charts, price action, and various Web sites.
3. Preferably two broadband connections (i.e., both cable and DSL) to ensure redundancy. (Some traders even use wireless cellular modems on laptops as final form of back up.)
4. Speed-dial button on your phone to your broker in case all electronic systems go down and you need to liquidate your position manually. Make sure you get the direct phone number to dealing rather than sales, and have your account information memorized or stored safely near your trading desk.

That's it for the mechanics. Although the list may seem intimidating, technological advances have made most of the equipment quite affordable. In fact, there is almost no other business in the world with such low costs of entry.

Analytical Tools

Now for the analytics part. Some traders will choose to trade strictly off technicals and will require sophisticated charts with many technical studies. In some markets, such as foreign exchange, most of the software is available for free directly from the brokers. But for traders with more stringent requirements, top-line products typically do not cost more than several hundred dollars per month. Traders who will use fundamental information could choose from a variety of sources. The choice starts with a top-shelf solution of a Bloomberg-terminal, which costs approximately $1,500 per month and provides real-time economic data on virtually any financial instrument in the world, to much less expensive news feeds that cost no more than $50 month and provide real time reports on economic numbers, earnings, and other market information. Although many traders dismiss their content as entertainment fluff, Bloomberg and CNBC broadcast over satellite, cable, and the

Internet and provide good overviews of business headlines of the day and sometimes even cogent financial analysis. For specific stock ideas and economic analysis, the old media stalwarts of the *Wall Street Journal* and its weekend publication, *Barron's* remain the gold standard of information for equity and commodity traders. However, the Internet has spawned literally thousands of very unique financial analysis Web-sites, the vast majority of which are free. For the FX market, we like DailyFX.com, although you are unlikely to find specific trade ideas at most of these finance blogs, you will be able to garner very interesting and often opposing views regarding big macroeconomic issues, as well as specific industry sectors. For a source of community, many electronic traders head to www.elitetrader.com for endless conversations and arguments about every market and trading approach that we have covered in this book.

INDEX

INDEX

INDEX

INDEX